Part 2

hands-on mathematics
Grade 2
Revised Edition

Project Editor
Jennifer E. Lawson

Senior Author
Dianne Soltess

Mathematics Consultant
Meagan Mutchmor

Unit Writers
Joni Bowman
Gail Ruta Fontaine
Betty Johns
Kara Kolson
Suzanne Mole

Winnipeg • Manitoba • Canada

Contents

Note to Teachers

While using Part 2 of **Hands-On Mathematics, Grade 2**, you will occasionally need to refer to a page from Part 1. Please keep Part 1 close at hand for this purpose.

PART 2

Unit 5: Number Concepts   359

Books for Children   360

Introduction   362

1   Rote Counting   363

2   Counting Backward from 50   373

3   Skip-Counting by 2s   380

4   Skip-Counting by 5s, 10s, and 25s   384

5   Number Words to Twenty   398

6   Ordinal Numbers   410

7   Reading and Writing Numbers to 100   424

8   Number Lines   433

9   Sets of 100   437

10   Greater Than and Less Than   443

11   Equal and Not Equal   450

12   Even and Odd   454

13   Rounding Off to the Nearest Ten   460

14   Estimating   463

15   Zero as a Place Holder   471

16   Representing Numbers to 100   479

17   Fractions: Halves   484

18   Fractions: Fourths   491

19   Fractions: Thirds   496

20   More Fractions   500

21   Comparing Fractions   507

22   Using What We Know: Number of the Week   512

Problem-Solving Black Line Master: Number Concepts   514

References for Teachers   518

Unit 6: Number Operations   519

Books for Children   520

Introduction   521

1   Addition – Doubles   522

2   Addition – Near Doubles   526

3   Missing Addends   568

4   Think-Addition Strategy for Subtraction   572

5   Recalling Subtraction Facts   581

6   The Identity Property of Addition – Zero Facts   618

7   Commutative Property of Addition   622

8   Addition of a One-Digit Number to a Two-Digit Number   627

9   Addition and Subtraction of Tens   633

10   Addition of Two-Digit Numbers   646

11   Subtraction of One-Digit Numbers from Two-Digit Numbers   650

12   Subtraction with Two-Digit Numbers   655

13   Identifying and Counting Coins   663

14   Creating Equivalent Sets of Coins   680

15   Addition of Money   686

16   Subtraction of Money   696

17   Exploring Multiplication – Part One   703

18   Exploring Multiplication – Part Two   705

19   Exploring Multiplication – Part Three   707

20   Exploring Multiplication – Part Four   717

21   Exploring Division – Part One   719

22   Exploring Division – Part Two   721

23   Exploring Division – Part Three   722

Problem-Solving Black Line Master: Number Operations   729

References for Teachers   732

Unit 5
Number Concepts

Books for Children

Bader, Bonnie. *100 Monsters in My School*. New York: Grosset & Dunlap, 2002.

Cave, Kathryn. *Out for the Count: A Counting Adventure*. New York: Simon & Schuster Books for Young Readers, 1992.

Conran, Sebastion. *My First 1 2 3 Book*. New York: Aladdin Books, 1988.

Crews, Donald. *Ten Black Dots*. New York: Greenwillow Books, 1986.

Eichenberg, Fritz. *Dancing in the Moon: Counting Rhymes*. New York: Harcourt, Brace, Jovanovich, 1975.

Friedman, Aileen. *The King's Commissioners*. New York: Scholastic, 1994.

Geisert, Arthur. *Pigs from 1 to 10*. Boston: Houghton Mifflin, 1992.

Hamm, Diane Johnston. *How Many Feet in the Bed?* New York: Simon & Schuster Books for Young Readers, 1991.

Hoban, Tana. *Count and See*. New York: Macmillan, 1972.

Howard, Katherine. *I Can Count to One Hundred...Can You?* New York: Random House, 1979.

Kasza, Keiko. *The Wolf's Chicken Stew*. New York: Putnam, 1987.

Lottridge, Celia Barker. *One Watermelon Seed*. Toronto: Oxford University Press, 1986.

Manushkin, Fran. *Walt Disney's 101 Dalmatians: A Counting Book*. New York: Disney Press, 1991.

McMillan, Bruce. *Counting Wildflowers*. New York: Lothrop, Lee & Shepard Books, 1986.

Micklethwait, Lucy. *I Spy Two Eyes: Numbers in Art*. New York: Greenwillow Books, 1993.

Murphy, Stuart J. *Double the Ducks*. New York: HarperCollins, 2003.

_____. *Give Me Half!* New York: HarperCollins, 1996.

_____. *Missing Mittens*. New York: HarperCollins, 2001.

Nolan, Helen. *How Much, How Many, How Far, How Heavy, How Long, How Tall Is 1000?* Toronto: Kids Can Press, 1995.

Owens, Mary Beth. *Counting Cranes*. Boston: Little, Brown, 1993.

Pallotta, Jerry. *The Icky Bug Counting Book*. Watertown, MS: Charlesbridge, 1992.

_____. *One Hundred Ways to Get to 100*. Toronto: Scholastic, 2003.

Reid, Margarette S. *The Button Box*. New York: Dutton Children's Books, 1990.

Ryan, Pam Muñoz, and Jerry Pallotta. *The Crayon Counting Book*. Watertown, MA: Charlesbridge, 1996.

Schwartz, David M. *How Much Is a Million?* New York: Scholastic, 1995.

Slater, Teddy. *Ready or Not, Here I Come!* New York: Scholastic, 1999.

Thornhill, Jan. *The Wildlife 1 2 3: A Nature Counting Book*. New York: Simon & Schuster, 1989.

Tucker, Sian. *1 2 3 Count with Me*. New York: Little Simon, 1996.

Wood, Jakki. *One Tortoise, Ten Wallabies: A Wildlife Counting Book*. New York: Bradbury Press, 1994.

Introduction

This unit is designed to help students develop number sense and investigate number relationships. The lessons and activities in this unit provide students with hands-on materials to help them think creatively and logically, develop strategies, and solve problems. In this unit, students explore:

- counting
- greater than/less than
- equal/not equal
- rounding off
- estimation
- place value
- fractions

Several lessons in this unit include a section called "Next Step(s)," which guides teachers through a subsequent activity or sequence of activities to carry out with students, following developmentally from the preceding activity or activities. For example, in the main activities of lesson 3, students are introduced to skip-counting by 2s to 100. Once students master this, the next step is to move to skip-counting to 150, and so on to 200.

Mathematics Vocabulary

Throughout this unit, teachers should use, and encourage students to use, vocabulary such as: *backward, skip-counting, ordinal numbers to 31st, estimate, estimation, number words to twenty, hundred, tens, ones, ten frame, greater than, less than, equal, not equal, rounding off, odd, even, pair, pattern, half, third, fourth, equal parts, fair,* and *unfair.*

Continue to use your classroom Math Word Wall as a means of focusing on new vocabulary related to the unit.

1 Rote Counting

Background Information for Teachers

In this lesson, students count by 1s to 200, both orally and in writing, using random starting points. It is appropriate for students to practice rote counting to 200 even if their understanding of place value is not consolidated.

Note: The *Ontario Curriculum for Mathematics (2005)* identifies the expectation of students to count to 200. In this lesson, students begin by mastering counting to 100, then progress to whatever point the teacher deems appropriate. Keep the individual abilities of students in mind, and plan activities accordingly. Some students may need to focus on counting only to 100 while others may be challenged to progress as far as 200.

Encourage students to say numbers without saying the word *and*. For example: *one hundred eighty-seven*; not *one hundred* and *eighty seven*. In mathematics, the word *and* is used to indicate a decimal point and separate the whole number from the part of the number that is less than one.

Also, encourage students to practice using backward number sequences in conjunction with forward number sequences, to help them understand the relationship between the two number patterns.

It is important to note that when writing numbers that include three or more digits, it is inappropriate to use a comma to separate the thousands place from the hundreds place. The metric system (SI) uses a space before (to the left of) every third digit (1 000), although it is also common to express numbers without the space (1000). Once the number includes the ten thousands place (i.e., five-digit numbers), a space is required (10 000).

Materials

- chart paper
- 10 x 10 grid on chart graph paper (you will need ten 10 x 10 grids)
- calculators (one for each student)
- number cubes (one for each student. Ten-sided cubes are preferable but any number cubes will work.)
- pencils (one for each group of three students)
- number response cards (included. Photocopy three sets for each student. Cut out the cards, punch a hole at the top of each card, and collate them on binder rings. You may consider different coloured paper for the ones cards [first set], tens cards [second set], and hundreds cards [third set]. You can also attach the three sets of cards to a plastic 30-cm ruler with binder holes for each student (see diagram below). This allows students to keep the three sets of cards separate and yet in place to represent ones, tens, and hundreds.) (5.1.1)

Note: Begin by giving students only two place cards to create numbers to 99. As students progress, provide them with either "1" or "2" cards as well, to use in the hundreds place for building numbers to 200.

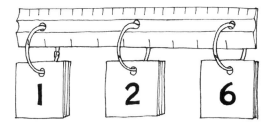

Unit 5 • Number Concepts

1

Activity: Part One

Write the numbers 1 to 100 on one of the chart-paper grids. Have students count aloud as you record the numbers 1 through 100. Then, have students read together several forward number sequences, using various random starting points on the grid. Also, have students read several backward number sequences, using random starting points.

Remove the grid, and encourage students to rote count without use of the chart.

Encourage students to look for patterns and discuss what happens when counting over decades (series of tens).

Next Step

Create a chart-paper grid from 101-200. Have students use the grid to practice forward and backward number-counting sequences.

Encourage students to look for patterns and discuss what happens when counting over decades and over hundreds. Have students count orally from random starting points. Encourage students to clap when the decade changes (149, 150) and stamp their feet when the century changes (199, 200).

* * *

The following activities can be completed throughout the year, using the numbers with which your class is comfortable. For example, if students have been rote counting to 200, all subsequent activities can be conducted with numbers to 200.

Activity: Part Two

Use a number line to demonstrate rote counting. Draw a horizontal line on chart paper. Record the numbers 0 through 20 on the number line while students count aloud.

Extend this activity by drawing a number line beginning with the number 45. Have students count aloud as you record the next 20 numbers. Then, encourage students to repeat the number sequence, both forward and backward.

Continue using number lines to have students rote count number sequences to 1000, both forward and backward.

Activity: Part Three

Distribute two sets of number response cards (5.1.1) to each student. As a class, select a random starting number between 1 and 99. Have students create that number with their cards. Then, have students count slowly by 1s, flipping their number response cards to show each number.

Tell students to stop just before they flip to a new decade (for example, 59). Ask:

- What do you think happens now? (the ones cards go back to 0 and the tens cards go up by 1)

Continue counting with students, and have them flip their number response cards to represent each number until you reach a new century (for example, 200). Ask students:

- What do you think happens now? (both the ones cards and the tens cards go back to 0, and the hundreds cards go up by one)

Have students use the number response cards to count backward as well. Select random starting points, and count aloud with students as they flip the cards to represent the numbers in the sequence.

Note: Using the number response cards throughout this unit will encourage students to create and visualize numbers and number sequences. This allows for each student to be fully engaged in all activities.

Activity: Part Four

Use a piece of scrap paper to screen (cover) one of the numbers on one of the chart paper number sequence grids. Have students use their number response cards to create the missing number.

101	102	103	104	105	106	107	108	109	110
111	112	113	114	115	116	117	118	119	120
121	122	123	124	125	126	127	128		130
131	132	133	134	135	136	137	138	139	140
141	142	143	144	145	146	147	148	149	150
151	152	153	154	155	156	157	158	159	160
161	162	163	164	165	166	167	168	169	170
171	172	273	274	175	176	177	178	179	180
181	182	183	184	185	186	187	188	189	190
191	192	193	194	195	196	197	198	199	200

Activity: Part Five

Note: In this lesson, students use the constant feature on their calculators. Different calculators activate this feature in different ways. On some, pressing "=" twice will engage the feature. On others, you must press "+, 1, =" and then continue to press the "=". On others still, you must press "1, +, +" and then continue to press the "=" sign. Before beginning this lesson, be sure to experiment with the calculators students will be using.

Show students how to use the constant feature on their calculators. Count slowly with students as they press the equal sign, stopping to draw their attention to number patterns. Ask students:

■ What number do you think will come after 49?

Have students enter 140 on their calculators, engage the constant feature, and then press the equal sign ten times. Ask:

■ What happened?
■ What changed?

Activity: Part Six

Distribute number cubes and copies of Activity Sheet A (5.1.2), and have students create two-digit numbers by rolling their number cubes two times. Ask students to count-on from their two-digit numbers, recording the next ten numbers they say. Then, have students make new numbers by rearranging the two digits they rolled earlier. Ask them to count-on from their new numbers, recording the next ten numbers they say. Finally, have students create three-digit numbers by rolling their number cubes two times, counting on from their three-digit numbers, and recording the numbers they say.

Note: Because there is already a 1 recorded in the first box, students need only roll their number cubes two more times in order to make three-digit numbers.

Activity Sheet A

Directions to students:

Roll the number cube. In the first box, record the number you rolled. Roll the number cube again, and record that number in the second box. Now, count-on from the two-digit number you created. Record the next ten numbers that you say.

Make a new two-digit number by mixing up the two numbers you rolled before. Write the new number in the boxes. Count-on from the new two-digit number you created. Record the next ten numbers that you say.

▶

Unit 5 • **Number Concepts**

Make a three-digit number by rolling your number cube two times and recording the numbers in the boxes, after the 1. Count-on from that number, and record the next ten numbers that you say (5.1.2).

Activity: Part Seven

Divide the class into groups of three to play "Pass the Pencil." Provide each group with a number cube, a pencil, and a copy of Activity Sheet B (5.1.3). Have the first player in each group roll the number cube twice, recording each number rolled on the first stepping stone to make a two-digit number. Have that player say the number aloud and then pass the pencil to the next player. Ask the second player to say the number that comes next, record it on the second stepping stone, and then pass the pencil to the third player. Have the third player say the next number, record it, and pass the pencil back to the first player. Play continues until students complete the activity sheet.

Activity Sheet B

Directions to students:

Have Player *A* roll the number cube twice and record each number rolled on the first stepping stone. Have this player say the recorded two-digit number aloud and then pass the pencil to Player *B*. Have Player *B* say the number that comes next, record it on the second stepping stone, and then pass the pencil to Player *C*. Have Player *C* say the next number, record it, and pass the pencil back to Player *A*. Continue in this way until you complete the activity sheet (5.1.3).

Next Step

Distribute Activity Sheet C (5.1.4), and have students continue the previous activity using numbers from 100 to 200.

Activity Sheet C

Directions to Students

Have player *A* roll the number cube twice and record each number on the first stepping stone. Have this player say the new three-digit number aloud and then pass the pencil to Player *B*. Continue the game in this way until you complete the activity sheet (5.1.4).

Problem Solving

Distribute the Problem-Solving activity sheet called "Number Line Train" (5.1.5), and have students record the numbers in sequence on the train.

Note: You can do this problem-solving activity together with the whole class by making an overhead transparency of the activity sheet. You can also modify and repeat the problem by using a different sequence of numbers.

Extensions

- Add the terms *forward, backward*, and *sequence* to your classroom Math Word Wall.

- Challenge students to use adding machine/ cash register tape on which to create a number line from 1 to 200. Display the number line on walls in the classroom so that students can see the number sequence grow.

- Alter commercial connect-the-dot activity sheets so that all numbers include a hundreds digit. For example, change 23, 24, 25 to 123, 124, 125 by adding the hundreds digit.

366   **Hands-On Mathematics • Grade 2**

1

Assessment Suggestion

In one-on-one meetings, assess each student's performance on the following tasks:

- Start at 95 and count as high as he/she can.
- Start at 145 and count until you say "stop." (Stop the student at 150, and note how easily he/she crossed the decade from 149 to 150.)

- Start at 195 and count until you say "stop." (Stop the student at 201, and note how easily he/she crossed the century from 199 to 200.)

Use the Individual Student Observations sheet, found on page 23, to record your results.

Number Response Cards

○	○	○
0	**1**	**2**
○	○	○
3	**4**	**5**
○	○	○
6	**7**	**8**
○		
9		

368 – 5.1.1   Portage & Main Press, 2006, Hands-On Mathematics, Level 2, ISBN: 978-1-55379-091-4

Date: _____   **Name:** _____

Counting-On

1A

Portage & Main Press, 2006, Hands-On Mathematics, Level 2, ISBN: 978-1-55379-091-4   5.1.2 – 369

Date: _____   Names: _____
_____
_____

Pass the Pencil

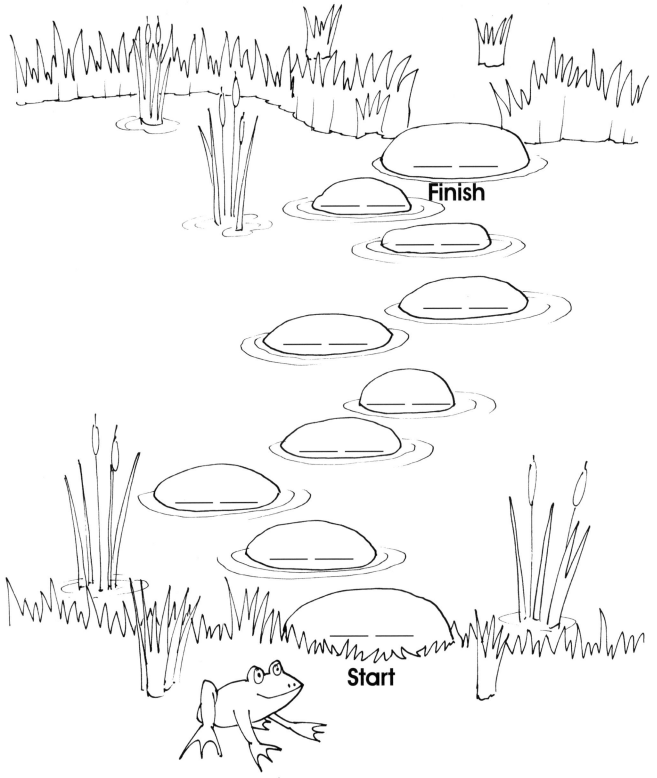

370 – 5.1.3   Portage & Main Press, 2006, Hands-On Mathematics, Level 2, ISBN: 978-1-55379-091-4   1B

Pass the Pencil – Again!

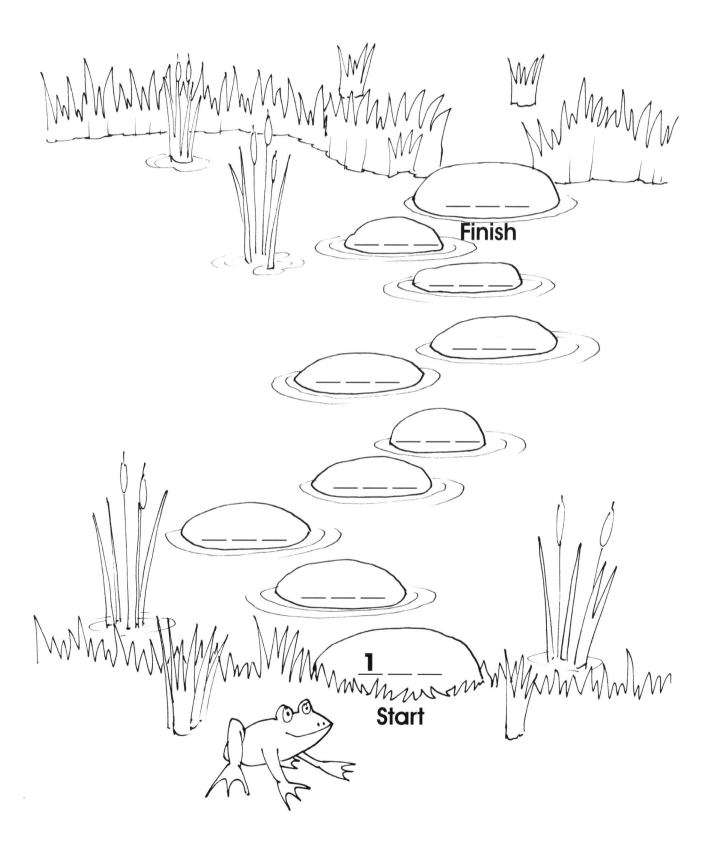

Number Line Train

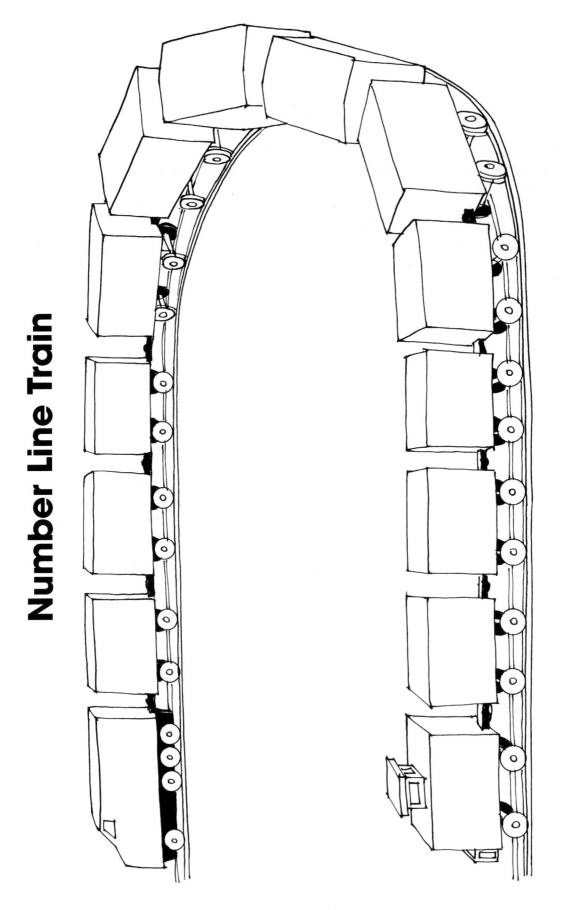

97, 100, 99, 105, 107, 106, 103, 110, 98, 102, 101, 108, 104, 109

2 Counting Backward from 50

Background Information for Teachers

This lesson offers ideas to help students master counting backward number sequences. As mentioned in the previous lesson, students should practice forward and backward counting simultaneously to help them understand the relationship between the number sequences.

Materials

- large, floor chart (Use an inexpensive vinyl tablecloth, or purchase some vinyl material from a fabric store. Use a permanent marker to create a 10 x 5 grid. Fill in the grid with the numbers 1 to 50.)
- numeral cards, 0-50 (included in unit 1, lesson 12. Copy cards onto sturdy tagboard, and laminate.) (1.12.1)
- small objects to use as counters (for example, dried beans, bingo chips, cubes, blocks)
- length of string to use as a clothesline
- clothespins
- backward-counting skipping rhymes from 20 and 50 (included. Make overhead transparencies or print each verse on chart paper.) (5.2.1, 5.2.2)
- overhead projector
- skipping ropes (one for each pair of students)
- "Drop of Doom" game boards (0-20 and 0-50) (included. You will need one game board for each pair of students.) (5.2.3, 5.2.4)
- number cubes (ten sided if possible. You will need one number cube for each pair of students.)
- scissors
- glue
- paper clips (one for each student)

Activity: Part One

Display a collection of small objects that you can use to illustrate a backward number sequence. Give students a purpose for counting the objects to make the activity more meaningful. For example, say:

- We need six paper plates for a class project. I have ten paper plates. Let us count backward from ten until we have six paper plates.
- We also need twelve pieces of construction paper for the project. I have twenty pieces of construction paper. Let us count backward from twenty until we have twelve pieces of construction paper.
- We will use twenty stickers for the project. I will give one sticker to each of twenty students. Let us count backward from twenty as I pass out the stickers.

Now, place fifty dried beans (or other counters) on a large, floor chart (one bean per square from 1 to 50). Ask one student to remove the bean from the "50" square, and ask:

- How many beans are there now?

Have students count backward as you continue to remove beans one at a time.

Remove all beans from the chart. Select a student to throw one bean onto the chart. Now, ask that student to start at the number where the bean landed and walk on the chart in a backward number sequence while the rest of the students count aloud.

Activity: Part Two

Give each of several students a numeral card in a sequenced range between 1 and 50 (for example, 9, 10, 11, 12, 13, 14, 15). Ask students to arrange themselves in order, from the largest number to the smallest number, and again from the smallest number to the largest number.

Unit 5 • Number Concepts

2

Have students practice repeating the backward number sequence aloud. Use different numeral cards in different sequenced ranges, and repeat the activity.

Hang a clothesline (length of string) at a height students can reach somewhere in the classroom. Again, distribute to each student one numeral card in a sequenced range between 1 and 50. Also, give each student one clothespin. Randomly call up one student, and have him/her hang his/her card on the clothesline. Call up a second student, and ask him/her to hang his/her card on the clothesline in relation to the first card to create a *backward* sequence. Continue randomly calling up students until all students have hung their cards on the clothesline.

Note: As students add more cards to the clothesline, you may need to help them adjust or move hanging cards to make room for remaining cards.

Once students have completed the backward number sequence, ask them to count aloud, backward and forward. Point to the cards as they count. Take this opportunity to talk about number placement.

Now, turn around all except one of the hanging numeral cards so that the numbers on these cards are not visible to students (be sure to keep the cards in sequence). Point to a reversed card. Have students use the number on the card they *can* see to determine which number is on the front of the card you are pointing to, as in the following diagram:

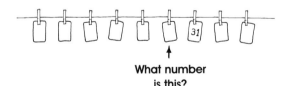

What number is this?

When students identify the card, turn it around so it is facing forward again. Now, point to another reversed card. Have students use the numbers on the two cards they can see to help them determine which number is on the front of the reversed card. Continue until all cards are facing forward. Have students count the backward number sequence aloud.

Activity: Part Three

On the overhead projector, display the backward-counting skipping rhyme from 20 (5.2.1). Read through the verse together with students, ensuring that they are comfortable with the backward number sequence.

Divide the class into pairs of students, and give each pair a skipping rope. Have partners chant the rhyme together; when the counting part begins, the first student skips in time to the backward number sequence and counts aloud. If the student misses a skip, his/her partner takes over skipping and counting from that number until he/she reaches 0. If the first student gets to 0 without missing a skip, the partners chant the rhyme again, and the second student skips and counts when the counting part begins. As students progress, introduce the backward-counting skipping rhyme from 50 (5.2.2).

Activity: Part Four

Divide the class into pairs of students and provide each pair with a "Drop of Doom" game board – 0-20 (5.2.3), scissors, glue, a number cube, and two paper clips.

Have students cut out their game boards. Then, tell each student to attach a paper clip to one side of the game board at the 20. Partners take turns rolling the number cube and sliding their paper clips down the Drop of Doom the number of spaces rolled. Play continues until one partner reaches the bottom.

Next Step

As students progress, introduce the "Drop of Doom" game board – 0-50 (5.2.4). Have students cut out the two parts of their game boards and glue them together to create the 0-50 game board. The game is then played in the same way as with the 0-20 board.

Problem Solving

Choose a number between 10 and 20. Beginning with the number you chose, print ten numbers in a backward sequence on a strip of paper, but leave out one number. Trade number sequences with a classmate, and see if he/she can figure out which number you missed. If your classmate gets it right, have him/her sign the back of your paper. Collect at least ten signatures.

Extensions

- Play bingo with students. When you call out each number, challenge students to use bingo chips to cover the number that *precedes* that number in a normal counting sequence.

- Have students use the constant feature on their calculators to create backward number sequences. Beginning at a starting point between 10 and 20, count slowly as students press the buttons, stopping to draw their attention to the patterns of the backward number sequence. As students progress, have them begin at a starting point between 40 and 50.

Note: Different calculators activate the constant feature in different ways. A common way to create a backward number sequence using the constant feature is to start with a number (for example, 9), press "– 1," and then press the equal sign repeatedly. Before doing this extension activity with students, be sure to experiment with the calculators they will be using.

Unit 5 • **Number Concepts**

375

Backward Counting Skipping Rhyme from 20

I can count backward

I can count backward

Starting at 20.

I have learned plenty!

I am a hero,

All the way to 0!

20, 19, 18, 17, 16, 15, 14, 13, 12,
11, 10, 9, 8, 7, 6, 5, 4, 3, 2, 1, 0.

Backward Counting Skipping Rhyme from 50

I can count backward

I can count backward

Starting at 50.

I am so nifty!

I am a hero

All the way to 0!

50, 49, 48, 47, 46, 45, 44, 43, 42, 41,

40, 39, 38, 37, 36, 35, 34, 33, 32, 31,

30, 29, 28, 27, 26, 25, 24, 23, 22, 21,

20, 19, 18, 17, 16, 15, 14, 13, 12, 11,

10, 9, 8, 7, 6, 5, 4, 3, 2, 1, 0

Drop of Doom
0-20

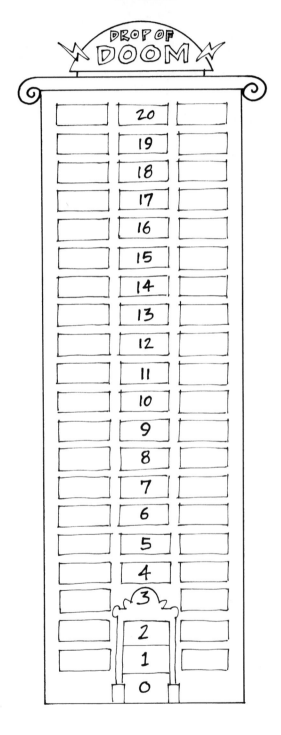

Drop of Doom
0-50

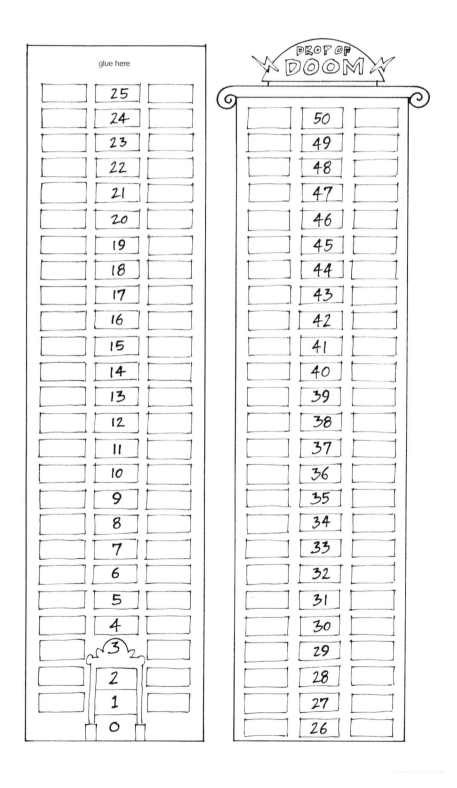

3 | Skip-Counting by 2s

Background Information for Teachers

Introduce skip-counting to students in a progressive manner, ensuring first that they can skip-count by 2s to 100, then moving gradually to 200. Do the same for skip-counting by 5s and 10s, moving progressively beyond 100 as students master each level.

Providing students with plenty of opportunities to skip-count in meaningful ways throughout the year will help them master this task. For example, before a field trip, count bus partners by 2s; count students' shoes and boots by 2s, and so on.

Materials

- large, floor hundred chart (use a vinyl tablecloth or a piece of vinyl fabric. Use a permanent marker to create a 10 x 10 grid. Fill in the grid with the numbers 1 to 100.)
- hundred charts (included with part 1, unit 1, lesson 10. Make one photocopy for each student.) (1.10.1)
- chart paper
- markers
- number line, 0-100 (Use adding machine or cash register tape, available at office supply stores. On the tape, record calibrations and numbers from 0 to 100. Number lines are also available for purchase at teacher supply stores.)
- tape
- metre stick or pointer
- calculators (one for each student)
- *How Many Feet in the Bed?* a book by Diane Johnston Hamm
- *The Crayon Counting Book*, a book by Pam Muñoz Ryan and Jerry Pallotta

Activity: Part One: Reviewing Skip-Counting by 2s

Read with students the book *How Many Feet in the Bed?*, which explores both forward and backward skip-counting-by-2s number sequences.

Activity: Part Two: Practicing Skip-Counting by 2s

Have students sit in a large circle with their feet out in front of them. Squat in the middle of the circle, and count students' feet by tapping each foot one at a time; as you tap each foot, have students count together by 1s: "1, 2" (first student), "3, 4" (second student), and so on.

Now, have students count aloud again as you tap their feet, but this time tell students to say each odd number quietly and say each even number loudly ("1, **2**, 3, **4**..."). Repeat the tapping and counting again, this time having students "think" each odd number and say each even number aloud.

Have students return to their desks. Count together with them, by 1s, to 20. Have students remain seated (or sit down again) for the odd numbers and stand for the even numbers. Extend this activity to counting to 50, then to 100.

Now, have students repeat the activity, this time using a backward number sequence. Beginning at 20, have students count backward; ask them to sit for the odd numbers and stand for the even numbers. Extend this challenge by beginning the counting sequence at higher numbers (50, 80, 100).

▶

380   **Hands-On Mathematics • Grade 2**

Activity: Part Three: Skip-Counting by 2s Using a Floor Hundred Chart

Using a large, floor hundred chart, have students take turns counting by 2s as they walk through the counting sequence on the chart. Encourage the rest of the class to also quietly recite the number sequence as each student does his/her counting walk.

Then, have students take turns walking through the backward number sequence on the floor chart, beginning at 20 and counting backward by 2s. Again, encourage the rest of the class to also quietly recite the backward number sequence as each student does his/her counting walk. Progress to counting backward from 50, then from 100.

Provide students with hundred charts. Have students count aloud by 2s as they "finger walk" on their hundred charts. Do this for both forward and backward number sequences.

Activity: Part Four: Skip-Counting by 2s Using Odd Numbers

To review skip-counting by 2s and to introduce skip-counting by 2s beginning at odd numbers, read *The Crayon Counting Book* with students.

Activity: Part Five: Skip-Counting by 2s Using a Number Line

Display a 0-to-100 number line by taping it to a wall. Select one student as the "pointer." Ask the pointer to use a metre stick to point to each number said as the rest of the class skip-counts forward or backward by 2s to (or from) 100. Repeat the activity a number of times, beginning the counting sequence at (or ending it at) various numbers.

Activity: Part Six: Skip-Counting by 2s Using the Constant Feature

Show students how to use the constant feature on their calculators to skip-count by 2s.

Note: Remember that different calculators activate the constant feature in different ways. A common way to skip-count by 2s using the constant key is to press "+2" and then press the "=" sign repeatedly. Before doing this activity with students, be sure to experiment with the calculators they will be using.

Distribute Activity Sheet A (5.3.1), and have students fill in the missing numbers. Then, have students count by 2s and draw a circle around each number they say.

Activity Sheet A

Directions to students:

Fill in the missing numbers. Skip-count by 2s, and draw a circle around each number that you say (5.3.1).

Next Steps

Continue with similar activities that allow students to practice skip counting by 2s, progressively moving to the next hundred number sequences beyond 100. Activity Sheet B (5.3.2) is included for students to complete as they gain mastery of these counting sequences.

Activity Sheet B

Directions to students:

Fill in the missing numbers. Then, skip-count by 2s, and draw a circle around each number that you say (5.3.2).

Extension

Add the term *skip-count(ing)* to your classroom Math Word Wall.

Unit 5 • **Number Concepts**

Skip-Counting by 2s

1	2	3	4		6	7	8	9	
	12	13	14		16	17	18	19	
21		23	24		26	27	28	29	30
31	32		34		36	37	38	39	
41	42	43			46	47	48	49	
51	52	53	54		56	57	58	59	
61	62	63	64		66	67	68	69	
71	72	73	74		76	77	78	79	
81		83	84		86	87	88	89	
	92	93	94		96	97	98		

Date: _____   **Name:** _____

Skip-Counting by 2s – from 101 to 200

101	102	103	104		106	107	108		
111	112	113		115	116	117	118		120
121	122		124		126	127			130
131	132	133		135	136		138		140
141	142	143	144	145		147	148		150
									160
161	162	163		165		167	168		170
171	172		174	175		177	178		180
181		183	184	185	186	187	188		190
	192	193	194	195	196	197	198		

3B   Portage & Main Press, 2006, Hands-On Mathematics, Level 2, ISBN: 978-1-55379-091-4   5.3.2 – 383

4 Skip-Counting by 5s, 10s, and 25s

Materials

- large, floor hundred chart (see lesson 3)
- hundred charts (included with part 1, unit 1, lesson 10. Make one photocopy for each student.) (1.10.1)
- chart paper
- markers
- number line, 0-100 (see lesson 3)
- tape
- metre stick or pointer
- calculators (one for each student)
- 60-cm lengths of string (one for each student. Tie a knot at one end of each piece of string.)
- 1-metre lengths of string (two for each student. Tie a knot at one end of each piece of string.)
- beads with large holes (two colours. You will need at least fifty beads of each colour for each student.)
- nickels, dimes, and quarters

Activity: Part One: Reviewing Skip-Counting by 5s

Use the following activities to practice skip-counting by 5s with students:

Note: Some of the following activity descriptions are brief, because they are modified repeats of the activities conducted for skip-counting by 2s. Refer to lesson 3 for more details on these activities.

- Have students sit in a circle and take turns counting all five fingers (i.e., fingers and thumb) on one hand aloud. Ask students to count cumulatively, each student beginning where the previous student left off (for example, Sarah: "1, 2, 3, 4, 5," Jason: "6, 7, 8, 9, 10," and so on). Tell students to say the first four numbers quietly and the fifth number more loudly. Work toward having students "say" the first four numbers in their heads and say only the multiples of five aloud.

- Have students count by 1s, slowly and in unison, to 50. Ask students to stand up briefly when they reach each multiple of 5. Extend this activity by counting to 100.

- Have students repeat the previous activity using the backward number sequence. Extend this activity by beginning at higher numbers (80, 100).

- Have students take turns counting aloud by 5s as they walk through the counting sequence on a large, floor hundred chart. Encourage the rest of the class to also quietly recite the number sequence as each student does his/her counting walk.

- Have students walk through the backward number sequence, beginning at 50 and counting backward by 5s, while the rest of the students also quietly recite the numbers. Progress to counting backward beginning at 75, then 100.

- Provide students with hundred charts. Have them count by 5s as they "finger walk" on their hundred charts, counting both forward and backward.

- Display a 0-100 number line by taping it to the wall. Have students use the number line to practice skip counting by 5s, forward and backward, to 100. Select individual students to use a metre stick to point to the numbers as the rest of the class says them.

- Have students count collections of nickels to practice skip-counting by 5s.

- Show students how to use the constant feature on their calculators to show patterns of skip-counting by 5s.

4

Note: Remember that different calculators activate the constant feature in different ways. A common way to skip-count by 5s using the constant key is to press "+5" and then press the "=" sign repeatedly. Before doing this activity with students, be sure to experiment with the calculators they will be using.

Activity: Part Two: Practicing Skip-Counting by 5s

Note: For this activity, students will be stringing beads. Tie a knot at one end of each piece of string before distributing the string to students.

Provide each student with a 60-cm piece of string and at least fifty beads in two colours, at least twenty-five of each colour. Have students create bead patterns that show skip-counting by 5s. For example:

AAAAABBBBB (red, red, red, red, red, blue, blue, blue, blue, blue)

Encourage students to make at least five repeats of their bead patterns. Once they have completed their patterns, help each student tie a knot at the top of the piece of string. Be sure there is enough room on the string to move the beads up and down slightly.

Now, have students use their bead strings to practice skip counting by 5s, both forward and backward. Ask them to move the beads up and down, counting and pointing as they say the number sequences.

Extend this activity by having students make bead strings with 100 beads and practice skip-counting by 5s to 100, both forward and backward.

Activity: Part Three: Using an Empty Number Line to Skip-Count by 5s

Use an "empty" number line to skip-count by 5s. Draw a horizontal line on chart paper, and record a 0 at the far, left end. Then, have students skip-count aloud by 5s to 50, and draw a "jump" for each number as they say it. Once students have completed the skip-counting number sequence, record the numerals below the number line, as in the following example:

0 5 10 15 20 25 30 35 40 45 50

Continue to use empty number lines to practice with students both forward and backward skip-counting from 0 to 50.

Extend this activity to skip-count by 5s to 100 from starting points other than 0, as in the following example:

60 65 70 75 80 85 90 95 100

Distribute Activity Sheet A (5.4.1), and have students fill in the missing numbers and then skip-count by 5s, drawing a square around each number they say.

Activity Sheet A

Directions to students:

Fill in the missing numbers. Skip-count by 5s. Draw a square around each number that you say (5.4.1).

Next Step

As students progress, continue with activities that have them skip-counting by 5s to 200. Distribute Activity Sheet B (5.4.2), and have students practice this skill by filling in the missing numbers.

▶

4

Activity Sheet B

Directions to students:

Fill in all the missing numbers to show skip-counting by 5s (5.4.2).

Activity: Part Four: Reviewing Skip-Counting by 10s

Use the following activities to practice skip-counting by 5s with students:

- Have students sit in a circle and take turns counting all ten of their fingers (i.e., fingers and thumbs) aloud. Ask students to count cumulatively, each student beginning where the previous student left off (for example, April: "1, 2, 3...9, 10," Mark: "11, 12, 13, 14..." and so on.). Tell students to say the first nine numbers quietly and then say the tenth number more loudly. Work toward having students "say" the first nine numbers in their heads and say only the multiples of ten aloud.

- Have students count by 1s, slowly and in unison, to 100. Ask students to stand up briefly when they reach each multiple of 10.

- Have students repeat the previous activity using the backward number sequence. Beginning at 100, ask students to count backward and stand up briefly when they reach the multiples of 10.

- Have students take turns counting aloud by 10s as they walk through the counting sequence on a large, floor hundred chart. Encourage the rest of the class to quietly recite the number sequence while each student does his/her counting walk.

- Have students walk through the backward number sequence, beginning at 100 and counting backward by 10s, while the rest of the students quietly recite the numbers.

- Provide students with hundred charts. Have students count by 10s as they "finger walk" on their hundred charts, counting both forward and backward.

- Display a 0-100 number line by taping it to a wall. Have students use the number line to practice skip-counting by 10s, both forward and backward, to 100. Select individual students to use a metre stick to point to the numbers as the rest of the class says them.

- Have students count collections of dimes to practice skip-counting by 10s.

- Show students how to use the constant feature on their calculators to show patterns of skip-counting by 10s.

Note: Remember that different calculators activate the constant feature in different ways. A common way to skip-count by 10s using the constant key is to press "+10" and then press the "=" sign repeatedly. Before doing this activity with students, be sure to experiment with the calculators they will be using.

Activity: Part Five: Practicing Skip-Counting by 10s

Note: For this activity, students will be stringing beads. Tie a knot at one end of each piece of string before distributing them to students.

Provide each student with a 1-metre piece of string and at least 100 beads of two different colours, at least fifty of each colour. Have students create bead patterns that show skip-counting by 10s. For example:

AAAAAAAAAABBBBBBBBBB (*red, red, red, red, red, red, red, red, red, red, blue, blue, blue, blue, blue, blue, blue, blue, blue, blue*)

Encourage students to make at least five repeats of their bead patterns. Once they have completed their patterns, help students tie knots

386   Hands-On Mathematics • Grade 2

at the tops of their pieces of string. Be sure there is enough room on the string to move the beads up and down slightly.

Now, have students use their bead strings to practice skip counting by 10s, both forward and backward. Ask them to move the beads up and down, counting and pointing as they say the number sequences.

Activity: Part Six: Using an Empty Number Line to Skip-Count by 10s

Use an empty number line to skip-count by 10s. Draw a horizontal line on chart paper, and record a 0 at the far, left end. Then, select one student to draw a "jump" for each number as the rest of the students skip-count aloud by 10s to 100. Once students have completed the skip-counting number sequence, have them help you determine the numbers that should go below the number line, and record them, as in the following example:

0 10 20 30 40 50 60 70 80 90 100

Continue to use empty number lines to practice with students both forward and backward skip-counting by 10s from 0 to 100.

Extend this activity to skip count by 10s to 100 from starting points other than 0, as in the following example:

47 57 67 77 87 97

Distribute Activity Sheet C (5.4.3), and have students fill in the missing numbers and then skip-count by 10s, drawing a rectangle around each number they say.

Activity Sheet C

Directions to students:

Fill in the missing numbers. Skip-count by 10s. Draw a rectangle around each number that you say (5.4.3).

Next Steps

Continue with similar activities of skip counting by 10s, progressively moving to different number sequences to 200. As students gain mastery of each counting sequence, use Activity Sheet D (5.4.4) to practice this skill.

Activity Sheet D

Directions to students:

Fill in all the missing numbers to show skip-counting by 10s (5.4.4).

Activity: Part Seven: Skip-Counting by 25s

Use the following activities to introduce students to skip-counting by 25s:

- Use quarters to give students a real-life example of counting by 25s to 100 ($1). Students should become familiar with the values of one, two, three, and four quarters. Create problems for students such as the following:
  - Stacie earned one quarter doing chores. How much money does she have?
  - How much money will Stacie have if she earns one more quarter? Another quarter? Even one more?
- Have students count by 1s, slowly and in unison, to 100. Ask students to stand up briefly when they reach each multiple of 25.

Unit 5 • Number Concepts

- Have students repeat the previous activity using the backward number sequence. Beginning at 100, ask students to count backward and stand up briefly when they reach each multiple of 25.

- Have students take turns counting aloud by 25s as they walk through the counting sequence on a large, floor hundred chart. Encourage the rest of the class to quietly recite the number sequence as each student does his/her counting walk.

- Have students walk through the backward number sequence, beginning at 100 and counting backward by 25s, while the rest of the students quietly recite the numbers.

- Provide students with hundred charts. Have students count by 25s as they "finger walk" on their hundred charts, counting both forward and backward.

- Display a 0-100 number line by taping it to a wall. Have students use the number line to practice skip-counting by 25s, both forward and backward, to 100. Select individual students to use a metre stick to point to the numbers as the rest of the class says them.

- Show students how to use the constant feature on their calculators to show patterns of skip-counting by 25s.

Note: Remember that different calculators activate the constant feature in different ways. A common way to skip-count by 25s using the constant key is to press "+25" and then press the "=" sign repeatedly. Before doing this activity with students, be sure to experiment with the calculators they will be using.

Activity: Part Eight: Skip-Counting by 25s with Beads

Note: For this activity, students will be stringing beads. Tie a knot at one end of each piece of string before distributing them to students.

Provide each student with a 1-metre piece of string and at least 100 beads in two different colours – at least fifty of each colour. Have students create bead patterns that show skip-counting by 25s. Once they have completed their patterns, help students tie knots at the tops of their pieces of string. Be sure there is enough room on the string to move the beads up and down slightly.

Now, have students use their bead strings to practice skip-counting by 25s, both forward and backward. Ask them to move the beads up and down, counting and pointing as they say the number sequences.

Activity: Part Nine: Using an Empty Number Line to Skip-Count by 25s

Use an empty number line to skip-count by 25s. Draw a horizontal line on chart paper, and record a 0 at the far, left end. Then, select one student to draw a "jump" for each number as the rest of the students skip-count aloud by 25s to 100. Once students have completed the skip-counting number sequence, have them help you determine the numbers that should go below the number line, and record them, as in the following example:

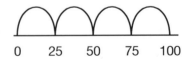

Continue to use empty number lines to practice with students both forward and backward skip-counting by 25s to 100.

Distribute Activity Sheet E (5.4.5), and have students fill in the missing numbers and then skip-count by 25s, drawing a triangle around each number they say.

▶

4

Activity Sheet E

Directions to students:

Fill in the missing numbers. Count by 25s. Draw a triangle around each number that you say (5.4.5).

Problem Solving

Use a hundred chart to help you answer these questions:

- How many numbers do you say when you count from 1 to 100 by 2s?

- How many numbers do you say when you count from 1 to 100 by 5s?

- How many numbers do you say when you count from 1 to 100 by 10s?

- What are all the numbers that you say *both* when you count by 5s *and* when you count by 10s?

- What are all the numbers that you say *both* when you count by 2s *and* when you count by 10s?

- How many numbers do you say when you count from 1 to 100 by 25s?

Note: A reproducible master for these problems can be found on page 514.

Activity Centre

Safety Note: This activity has students making trail mix. Consider any student allergies before proceeding with this activity, and select foods with this in mind.

Provide ten frames (included, 5.4.6), five frames (included, 5.4.7), and two frames (included, 5.4.8) at an activity centre. Also provide small paper cups, scrap paper, pencils, plastic sandwich bags, a container filled with Cheerios, a container filled with raisins, and a container filled with small marshmallows (or any other food items appropriate for making trail mix).

Have students use a paper cup to take one scoop of Cheerios and then use ten frames to count the Cheerios by 10s. Tell students to record the number of Cheerios they count and put them into a plastic sandwich bag. Next, have students use a paper cup to take one scoop of raisins and then use five frames to count the raisins by 5s. Tell students to record the number of raisins they count and add them to the bag. Finally, have students repeat with the marshmallows but use the two frames to count the marshmallows by 2s.

When students have completed making their trail mix, discuss the counting processes they used. Ask:

- Which was easiest to count, Cheerios, raisins, or marshmallows? Why?
- Which did you count the fastest? Why?

Extension

Review skip-counting with students by reading *The King's Commissioners*, a book by Aileen Friedman. In the story, the commissioners are counted by 2s, 5s and 10s, with remainders.

Unit 5 • **Number Concepts**

Skip-Counting by 5s

1	2		4		6	7	8	9	
11	12	13		15	16	17		19	20
21		23	24	25		27			30
31		33	34	35		37	38		
	42	43	44		46		48	49	50
51		53	54	55	56	57		59	60
61			64	65		67	68		
		73	74	75		77		79	80
	82		84	85			88		90
	92	93		95	96	97		99	

Date: _____   **Name:** _____

Skip-Counting by 5s

101	102	103	104	◯
106	107	108	109	◯
111		113		◯
	117		119	◯
121		123		◯
126				◯
	132	133		◯
	137			◯
		143		◯
	147		149	◯

4B

Portage & Main Press, 2006, Hands-On Mathematics, Level 2, ISBN: 978-1-55379-091-4

5.4.2 – 391

Skip-Counting by 10s

1		3		5			8	9	10
11	12		14	15	16		18		20
	22	23	24		26		28	29	30
	32		34	35		37	38	39	40
41	42	43		45		47	48	49	
	52	53				57	58	59	
	62	63		65		67	68	69	
71	72				76		78		80
81	82		84	85			88	89	90
91		93	94	95	96		98	99	100

392 – 5.4.3   Portage & Main Press, 2006, Hands-On Mathematics, Level 2, ISBN: 978-1-55379-091-4

4C

Name: _____ **Date:** _____

Skip Counting by 10s

101	102	103	104	105	106	107	108	109	◇	111	112	113	114	115	116	117	118	119	◇
	122					127		129	◇		132						138		◇
141			144				148		◇				154			157		159	◇
161		163		165		167		169	◇					175			178		◇
	182		184		186		188		◇		192		194			197		199	◇

Portage & Main Press, 2006, Hands-On Mathematics, Level 2, ISBN: 978-1-55379-091-4

4D

Date: _____   **Name:** _____

Skip-Counting by 25s

	2	3	4		6	7			
11		13	14		16	17		19	
21	22	23		25		27	28	29	
31		33	34		36	37	38		40
	42	43	44				48	49	50
	52	53		55	56	57	58		
61		63	64	65			68	69	70
71		73		75	76	77		79	
81	82	83		85	86	87	88	89	
91	92	93	94	95	96	97	98	99	

Ten Frames

Portage & Main Press, 2006, Hands-On Mathematics, Level 2, ISBN: 978-1-55379-091-4

Five Frames

396 – 5.4.7

Portage & Main Press, 2006, Hands-On Mathematics, Level 2, ISBN: 978-1-55379-091-4

Two Frames

Portage & Main Press, 2006, Hands-On Mathematics, Level 2, ISBN: 978-1-55379-091-4   5.4.8 – 397

5 | Number Words to Twenty

Materials

- number word cards, zero to twenty (included. Photocopy, cut out, and mount on sturdy tagboard.) (5.5.1)
- numeral cards, 0-20 (included in unit 1, lesson 12. Photocopy, cut out, and mount on sturdy tagboard.) (1.12.1)
- pocket chart
- foam letters or letter tiles; or individual chalkboards or whiteboards (with corresponding writing utensils; one for each student); or sheets of paper and pencils
- *Ten Black Dots*, a book by Donald Crews
- other simple number books of your choice
- sheets of 11" x 14" white paper (six pieces for each student.)
- crayons, pencil crayons, or markers
- stapler

Activity: Part One

Display the numeral cards (1.12.1), in order, in the pocket chart. Count together with students from 0 to 20. Then, mix up the cards, and have students sequence them.

Below the numeral cards in the pocket chart, display the number word cards (5.5.1) in order. Read the number words together with students, and talk about any patterns they see or what they notice about the spelling of the words. For example, ask:

- Which of the numbers that are greater than ten end with "teen"?
- In which of these "teen" numbers can you see smaller numbers? (fourteen, sixteen, and so on)

Now, mix up the number word cards in the pocket chart, and challenge students to sequence them.

Remove the number word and numeral cards from the pocket chart. Randomly select half as many number word cards as there are students in your class, and match these with the corresponding numeral cards. Distribute one of these number word or numeral cards to each student, and have each student find the classmate with the corresponding card. Repeat several times.

Activity: Part Two

Show students one number word card. Have students use foam letters or letter tiles to record the number word, or have them print the word on individual whiteboards or chalkboards or on pieces of paper.

Next, show students one numeral card, and have students record the number word in the same way.

Finally, show students a number word card, and have them draw a corresponding set of objects (for example, nine triangles).

Activity: Part Three

Read with students several simple number books such as *Ten Black Dots*. Tell students that they will now create their own number books. Students can model any number book they have explored but must follow these criteria:

- show the numbers 1-20
- show one number on each page
- use numerals to show the number
- use words to show the number
- use (a) picture(s) to show the number

▶

398　　　　　　　　　　　　　　　　　　Hands-On Mathematics • Grade 2

5

Distribute six sheets of 11" x 14" white paper to each student. Have students fold each page in half horizontally.

Note: To create a book that includes a cover page and 20 pages of numbers, each student will need six pieces of paper folded in half. There will be three pages left over; students can decide for themselves how to fill the remaining blank pages (for example, include an inside cover page, a back cover page, a table of contents page, a single blank page at the front, and/or a single blank page at the back).

Have students use crayons, pencil crayons, or markers to create their books. Help students staple their books together along the fold lines. Have students read their books to various classmates several times before sharing the books with students from other classes or with relatives.

Distribute Activity Sheet A (5.5.2), and have students print the appropriate numeral on each engine car, a corresponding dot pattern on each boxcar (middle car), and a corresponding number word on each caboose.

Activity Sheet A

Directions to students:

In the correct order down each page, print a numeral on each engine car, a dot pattern on each boxcar (middle car), and a number word on each caboose (5.5.2).

Problem Solving

Unscramble the following number words:

- eesnv
- ihegt
- wto
- urfo
- weetlv

Note: A reproducible master for this problem can be found on page 514.

Activity Centre

Have blank index cards and writing utensils at an activity centre. Ask students to work with partners to make sets of paired number word and numeral cards (0 through 20). Tell students to write a number word on one card and the corresponding numeral on a second card. One student in each pair can make the number word and numeral cards for 0 through 10; the other can make the cards for 11 through 20. Ask partners to check each other's cards for spelling and number formation. Finally, have partners use their cards to play "Memory" ("Concentration") or "Go Fish" (for these games, a number word card and its corresponding numeral card are considered a "match").

Extensions

- Add the number words *zero* through *twenty* to your classroom Math Word Wall.

- Use the number words in regular classroom spelling drills.

- Use any number rhyme or poem to help students practice writing number words. Prepare an activity sheet for students by writing out the rhyme or poem but leaving blanks where number words should be, as in the Extension Activity Sheet called "One, Two, Buckle My Shoe" (5.5.3).

- Have students draw their own picture outlines or use uncoloured colouring-book pages to create simple paint/colour-by-number pictures. Ask them to use number words on their colour legends and numerals on their picture outlines (numbering the spaces to be coloured). Have students exchange their paint/colour-by-number pictures with partners to colour them.

Unit 5 • **Number Concepts**

399

Number Word Cards

zero	one
two	**three**

400 – 5.5.1   Portage & Main Press, 2006, Hands-On Mathematics, Level 2, ISBN: 978-1-55379-091-4

four	five
six	**seven**

Portage & Main Press, 2006, Hands-On Mathematics, Level 2, ISBN: 978-1-55379-091-4

eight	nine
ten	**eleven**

402 – 5.5.1

twelve

thirteen

fourteen

fifteen

Portage & Main Press, 2006, Hands-On Mathematics, Level 2, ISBN: 978-1-55379-091-4

| sixteen | seventeen |

| eighteen | nineteen |

twenty

404 – 5.5.1

Date: _____ **Name:** _____

Number Trains

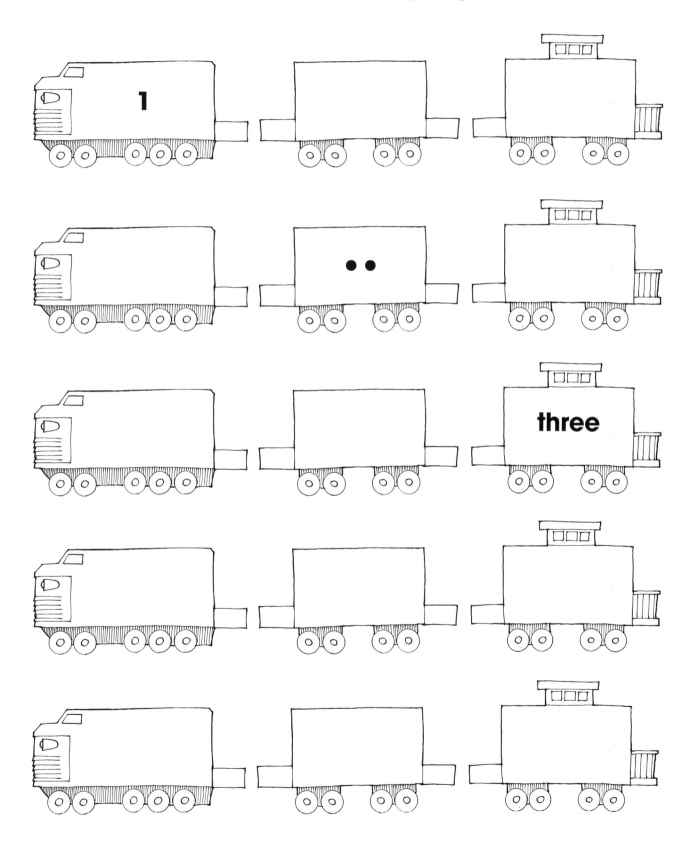

5A

Date: _____ Name: _____

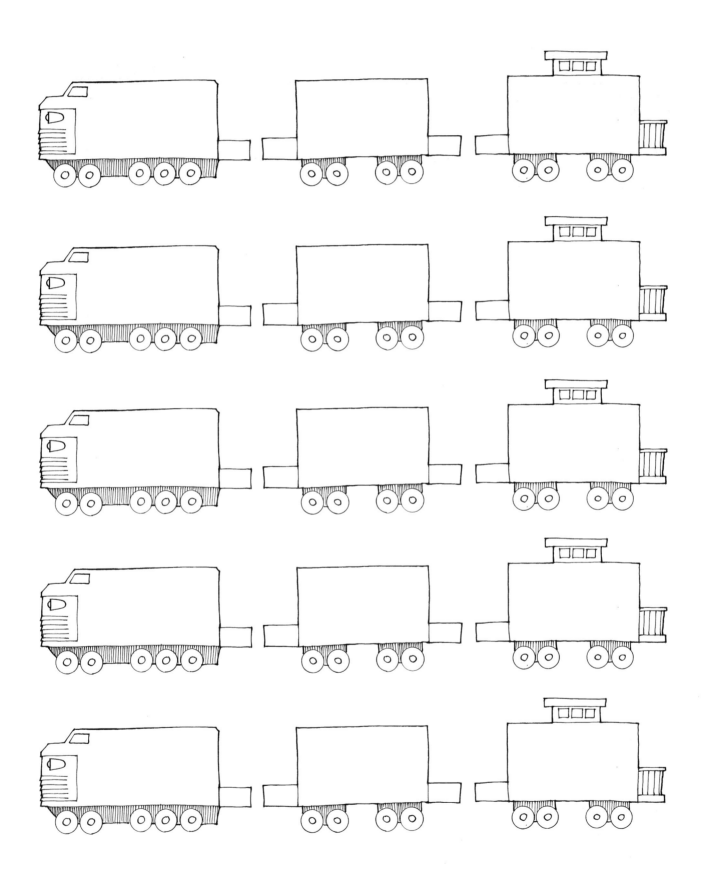

406 – 5.5.2   Portage & Main Press, 2006, Hands-On Mathematics, Level 2, ISBN: 978-1-55379-091-4   **5A**

Date: _____ Name: _____

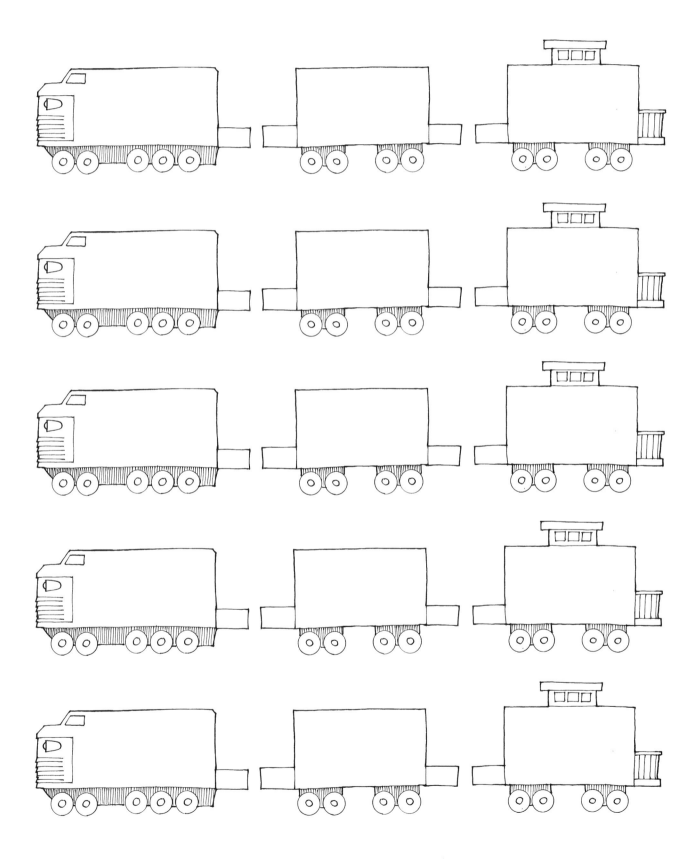

5A

5.5.2 − 407

Date: _____ Name: _____

5A

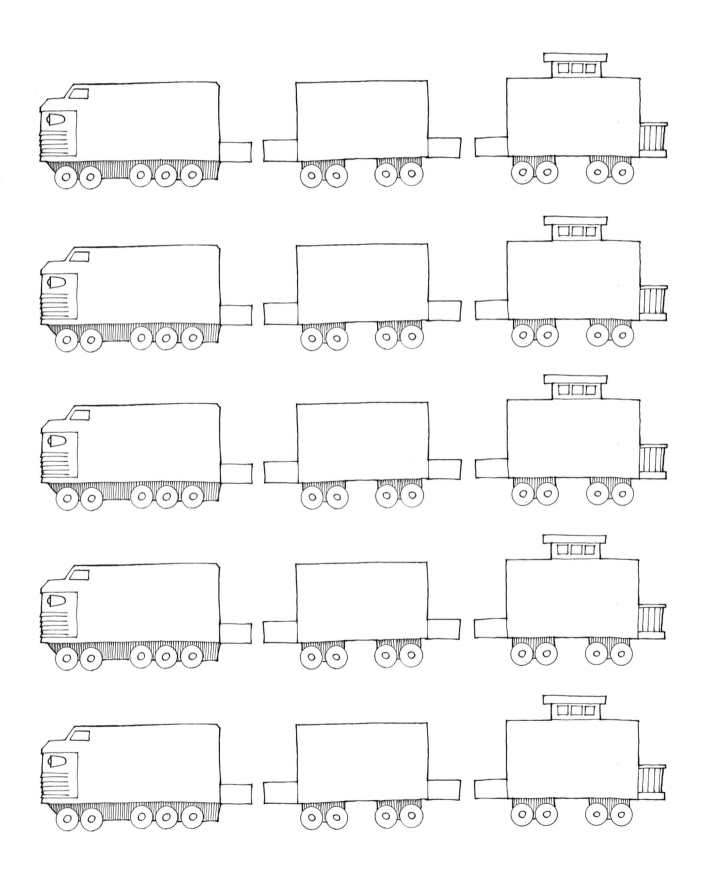

408 – 5.5.2

Date: _____ **Name:** _____

One, Two, Buckle My Shoe

_____, _____, buckle my shoe;

_____, _____, close the door;

_____, _____, pick up sticks;

_____, _____, lay them straight;

_____, _____, a big, fat hen;

_____, _____, dig and delve;

_____, _____, maids a' courting;

_____, _____, maids in the kitchen;

_____, _____, maids in waiting;

_____, _____, my plate's empty!

Extension

6 Ordinal Numbers

Background Information for Teachers

Note: Although ordinal numbers to 31st are introduced in the grade one Ontario curriculum, this lesson is included for review and reinforcement.

Ordinal numbers identify position in a series or order. For example, first (1st), second (2nd), third (3rd), and so on.

You can effectively demonstrate ordinals to students using daily, classroom situations. For example, use a daily calendar routine to model the language of ordinals, asking students questions such as:

- Which day is the first day of the week?
- Which day is the fifth day of the week?

A classroom lineup provides another good opportunity to discuss ordinals. Ask questions such as:

- Is the fourth student in line wearing blue jeans?
- Who is sixth in line?

Regular use of ordinal numbers during daily classroom routines will help solidify students' understanding of them.

Materials

- ordinal number cards (included. Photocopy, cut out, and laminate several sets. Keep sets in envelopes.) (5.6.1)
- pocket chart
- *The Button Box*, a book by Margarette S. Reid
- collection of buttons
- button train frames (included. Photocopy, and cut out one frame for each student.) (5.6.2)
- blank calendar month (included. Make at least one photocopy for each student.) (5.6.3)
- crayons, pencil crayons, or markers
- current wall calendars (one for each pair or small group of students. Many businesses distribute free calendars toward the end of the year. Have students and their families collect these for classroom use).

Note: Try to obtain calendars that include significant Canadian dates (for example, Canadian Thanksgiving, Canada Day).

Activity: Part One

Display a set of ordinal number cards (5.6.1), in sequence, in the pocket chart. Practice reading the words aloud with students, and discuss their meaning. Mix up the cards, and have students put them in the correct order again.

Distribute one ordinal number card to each student.

Note: Be sure the cards you distribute are in consecutive order.

Have students hold up their cards and line themselves up in sequence, using gestures (if necessary) but without talking.

Note: If you have a large class and/or a small classroom, conduct this activity in a location where students can line up in a straight and single line (for example, in a school hallway or in the gymnasium).

Then, have students take turns reading their ordinal number cards aloud, in sequence. Ask:

- Who is the twenty-fifth student in line?
- In which place in line is the student who is wearing the Spiderman t-shirt?
- How many students come before the fifth student in line?
- How many students come after the tenth student in line?

Redistribute the cards, and repeat the activity.

410   Hands-On Mathematics • Grade 2

6

Activity: Part Two

Read *The Button Box* with students. Then, divide the class into working groups, and provide each group with a collection of buttons. Also, give each student a button train frame (5.6.2). Have students make button trains by placing one button into each box of their frames. Once students have completed their trains, ask:

- What colour button is in the third space on your button train?
- What colour button is in the tenth space?
- Who has a white button in the fifth space of his/her button train?
- What colour button is in the space just before the ninth space on your button train?
- How many buttons come before the button in the sixth space?

Activity: Part Three

Distribute current wall calendars to pairs or small groups of students. Model for students how they can ask each other questions using ordinal numbers. For example, ask:

- What is the fifth month of the year?
- What special day falls during the second (or third, depending on the year) week of February?
- What special day is on the first day of the seventh month?
- In what month is your birthday? Use an ordinal number in your answer.
- When is Halloween? Use an ordinal number in your answer.

In pairs or in their small groups, have students ask each other questions similar to the ones you modeled.

Distribute a blank calendar month (5.6.3) to each student, and have students complete them for the current month by printing the month name at the top, and printing the number dates in the appropriate boxes. Be sure students know on which day of the week the month begins. Then, have students use crayons, pencil crayons, or markers to do the following:

- Draw a red circle around the first day of the month.
- Draw a green triangle around the twentieth day of the month.
- Draw a blue line under the last day of the month.
- Draw a yellow diamond around the thirteenth day of the month.
- Draw a black line above the twenty-seventh day of the month.

Repeat the activity during various months of the year.

Distribute Activity Sheet A (5.6.4), and have students complete the sentences using ordinal numbers. To help them, have students draw pictures of their families in the large box at the bottom of the sheet. Then, distribute Activity Sheet B (5.6.5), and have students add colour and drawings to the sheet to make each statement true.

Activity Sheet A

Directions to students:

Use ordinal numbers to complete the sentences. To help you, draw a picture of your family in the large box at the bottom of the sheet (5.6.4).

Activity Sheet B

Directions to students:

Make each of the following statements true by adding to and colouring the drawing:

- The first person is wearing blue pants.
- The third person is carrying an umbrella.
- The tenth person has a red cap on his head.
- The twelfth person has black hair.

Unit 5 • **Number Concepts**   411

6

- The eighteenth person has a number 18 on her shirt.
- The nineteenth person is carrying a bag.
- The twenty-first person has a green belt on.
- The twenty-fifth person is wearing a striped shirt (5.6.5).

Problem Solving

Abby is twelfth in line, Carmina is sixteenth in line. Linda is in front of Carmina. Nicole is behind Abby. Randy is between Linda and Nicole. In what place in line is Randy? Draw a picture.

Note: A reproducible master for this problem can be found on page 514.

Extensions

- Add the ordinal numbers to your classroom Math Word Wall.

- As a class, use the tune from "The Twelve Days of Christmas" ("A Partridge in a Pear Tree") to create a song. Record the song on chart paper, and have students copy the lyrics into booklets to illustrate and then read and share. An example might be:

On the first day of second grade
My teacher gave to me
A pencil in red box.

On the second day of second grade
My teacher gave to me
Two pink erasers and a pencil in red box.

On the third day of second grade
My teacher gave to me
Three funny books, two pink erasers, and a pencil in red box.

On the fourth day of second grade
My teacher gave to me
Four yellow crayons, three funny books, two pink erasers, and a pencil in red box.

On the fifth day of second grade my teacher gave to me
Five golden stars, four yellow crayons, three funny books, two pink erasers, and a pencil in red box.

- Together with students, use ordinal numbers to write directions for art or cooking activities. For example:

First, cover the table with newspaper.
Second, pour the water-colour paint into containers.
Third, paint your picture. Include a sky in your picture.
Fourth, sprinkle salt on your painted sky while the paint is still wet.
Fifth, watch as the salt makes patterns on your painted sky.

412   **Hands-On Mathematics • Grade 2**

Ordinal Number Cards

first

1st

second

2nd

third

3rd

fourth

4th

fifth

5th

sixth

6th

seventh

7th

eighth

8th

ninth

9th

414 – 5.6.1

Portage & Main Press, 2006, Hands-On Mathematics, Level 2, ISBN: 978-1-55379-091-4

tenth	eleventh
10th	11th

twelfth	thirteenth
12th	13th

fourteenth
14th

fifteenth	sixteenth
15th	16th

seven-teenth	eighteenth
17th	18th

nineteenth 19th

416 – 5.6.1

Portage & Main Press, 2006, Hands-On Mathematics, Level 2, ISBN: 978-1-55379-091-4

twentieth

20th

twenty-first

21st

twenty-second

22nd

twenty-third

23rd

Portage & Main Press, 2006, Hands-On Mathematics, Level 2, ISBN: 978-1-55379-091-4

5.6.1 – 417

twenty-
fourth

24th

twenty-fifth

25th

twenty-
sixth

26th

twenty-
seventh

27th

twenty-eighth 28th	**twenty-ninth** 29th
thirtieth 30th	**thirty-first** 31st

Portage & Main Press, 2006, Hands-On Mathematics, Level 2, ISBN: 978-1-55379-091-4

Button Train Frames

420 – 5.6.2

Portage & Main Press, 2006, Hands-On Mathematics, Level 2, ISBN: 978-1-55379-091-4

Date: _____

Name: _____

Calendar

Month: _____

Sunday	Monday	Tuesday	Wednesday	Thursday	Friday	Saturday

Portage & Main Press, 2006, Hands-On Mathematics, Level 2, ISBN: 978-1-55379-091-4

5.6.3 – 421

Date: _____   **Name:** _____

Using Ordinal Numbers

I was the _____ child born in my family.

My birthday is on the _____ day of the _____ month.

I am the _____ one to get up in the morning.

My favourite thing to do happens on the _____ day of the week.

My favourite season begins in the _____ month of the year.

I am the _____ youngest person living in my home.

Here is a picture of my family.

Name:

Date:

Waiting in Line

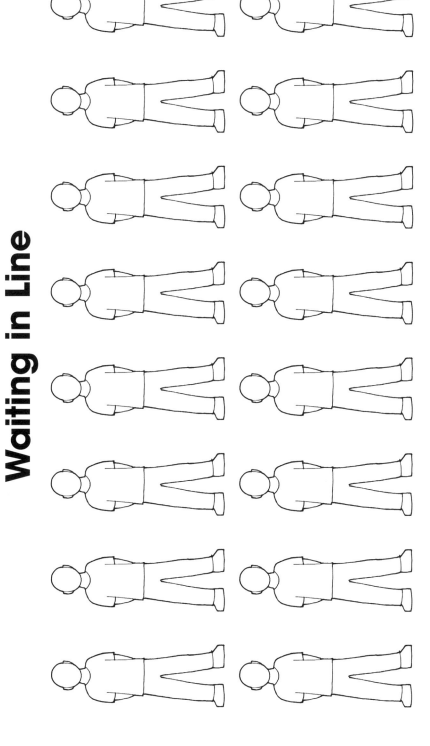
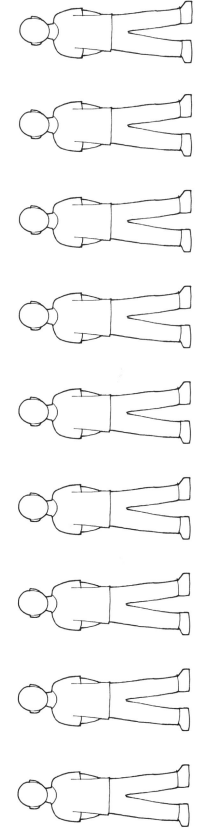

7 Reading and Writing Numbers to 100

Materials

- poster paper
- markers
- pencils
- sketchbooks or clipboards with paper
- digital camera (optional)
- number response cards (included with lesson 1) (5.1.1)
- hundred charts (included with part 1, unit 1, lesson 10. Make one photocopy for each student as well as one overhead transparency for demonstration.) (1.10.1).
- blank hundred charts (included in unit 1, lesson 10 as Activity Sheet A. Make one photocopy for each student as well as an overhead copy for demonstration.) (1.10.2)
- small, opaque counters, or other items for screening numbers on the overhead hundred chart
- scissors
- glue
- tagboard square (large enough to cover a three-unit x three-unit area on the overhead hundred chart. Cut out the middle square (one-unit x one-unit) so that one number on the hundred chart is visible through the hole, as in the following diagram):

36	37	38	39	40
46				50
56		58		60
66				70
76	77	78	79	80

Activity: Part One

Note: Before beginning this lesson, record, on poster paper, a collection of numbers that are significant to you in your personal life. For example: the street number on your house, ages of people in your family, the year you were born, the number on your licence plate, your telephone number, your date of birth.

Display the poster paper with your "personal numbers." Ask students to look carefully at the numbers and guess what each one might represent. Then, have students use markers to record some of their own personal numbers on poster paper. Ask students to read their numbers to partners or share them with the rest of the class.

Note: Take this opportunity to remind students that although it is appropriate to share personal numbers like addresses, phone numbers, and birthdates with friends, they should never share these numbers with strangers, even online, without parental consent. There are special circumstances when it might be necessary to share these numbers with strangers (for example, when ordering a magazine subscription), but they should always check with a parent or guardian before doing so.

Activity: Part Two

Go on a number hunt, first around the classroom, then around the school, and finally through the surrounding community. Provide students with pencils and sketchbooks or clipboards and paper, and have them record all the numbers that they see or draw sketches of the number locations. You may also consider taking digital photos of these number locations for display purposes.

Once students have completed their number hunt, discuss locations where numbers are often found and why the numbers are used there.

7

Activity: Part Three

Display the transparency of the hundred chart on the overhead. Use counters to screen some of the numbers in one column or row. Point to a screened number and ask students:

■ What number do you think this is?

Have students use their number response cards to show what number they think is screened. Then, ask:

■ How did you know what the number was?
■ What strategy did you use to determine what the number was?

Repeat this for several different numbers on the hundred chart.

Place the tagboard square on the overhead hundred chart to reveal one number while screening the other numbers around it. Have students use their number response cards to answer the following:

■ What number can you see?
■ What number is to the left of this number?
■ What number is to the right?
■ What number is below this number?
■ What number is above?

Repeat for several numbers.

Next, display a blank hundred chart (1.10.2) on the overhead, and distribute blank hundred charts to students. Challenge students to point to the square on their blank charts where the number 20 would go.

Note: Encourage students to use what they already know about numbers, number sequences, and the hundred chart to determine their answers, rather than simply to guess.

Now, lay the hundred-chart transparency over the blank hundred-chart transparency to reveal for students where the number 20 goes. Have

students print the number 20 in the correct space on their blank hundred charts. Repeat for several different numbers.

Distribute Activity Sheet A (5.7.1), Activity Sheet B (5.7.2), and Activity Sheet C (5.7.3) for students to complete.

Activity Sheet A

Note: This is a two-page activity sheet.

Directions to students:

Find all the numbers at the candy store. Record each number in one of the stars on the activity sheet. (Do not break up two- or three-digit numbers. Record each two- or three-digit number in one star.) Read the numbers to yourself, and then read them to a classmate (5.7.1).

Note: For Activity Sheet B and Activity Sheet C, students will need scissors and glue.

Activity Sheet B

Note: This is a two-page activity sheet.

Directions to students:

Cut out the puzzle pieces. Fill in the missing numbers. Put the puzzle pieces together on the blank hundred chart. Glue the puzzle pieces onto the blank hundred chart (5.7.2).

Activity Sheet C

Note: This is a two-page activity sheet.

Directions to students:

Cut out the puzzle pieces. Fill in the missing numbers. Put the puzzle pieces together on the blank hundred chart. Glue the puzzle pieces onto the blank hundred chart (5.7.3).

▶

Unit 5 • **Number Concepts**

425

7

Problem Solving

A grade-two class is making a number line. Each day, the students add a few more numbers to the number line. On Tuesday, the students stopped at number 34. On Wednesday, they added 20 more numbers to the number line. Draw a number line, and write the 20 numbers the students added to it on Wednesday.

Note: A reproducible master for this problem can be found on page 515.

Extensions

■ Have students create pictures by shading or colouring in the boxes for a series of numbers on a hundred chart. For example, shading the following numbers will create a tree:

3, 4, 5, 6, 7, 8, 12, 19, 21, 30, 31, 40, 42, 49, 53, 54, 55, 56, 57, 58, 65, 66, 75, 76, 85, 86, 95, 96.

Call out the numbers one by one while students shade them, or have a student call out the numbers. Also, have students plan and record their own number series that will create pictures when the boxes are shaded. Then, have students work in pairs: one student reads aloud his/her number series for the other to shade.

■ Have students look through newspapers or magazines to find two-digit numbers. Ask them to cut out 10 two-digit numbers and paste them onto blank sheets of paper. Have students work with partners and take turns reading each other's numbers aloud.

■ Have students work in pairs. Ask one student from each pair to select a number from the hundred chart and read it to his/her partner. Have the partner enter that number on a calculator. Ask students to make sure their numbers are the same. Then, have partners switch roles.

■ Send students home to look for specific numbers, treasure-hunt style. For example, have students find:

■ a penny with a 7 on it
■ a telephone number with a 9 in it
■ an item in a flyer with a 3 in the price
■ a nutritional listing on a food item with a 6 in it

Name: _____

Date: _____

Candy Store Number Hunt

7A

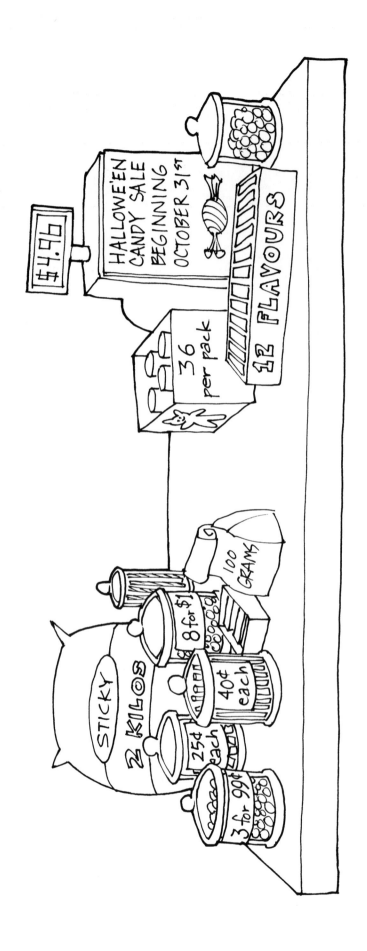

Date: _____   **Name:** _____

5.7.2 – 429

Hundred Chart Jigsaw

7B

Portage & Main Press, 2006, Hands-On Mathematics, Level 2, ISBN: 978-1-55379-091-4

7B

25 19 38 42 69 47 67 99 18 93 2 71

Date: _____ Name: _____

Hundred Chart Jigsaw 2

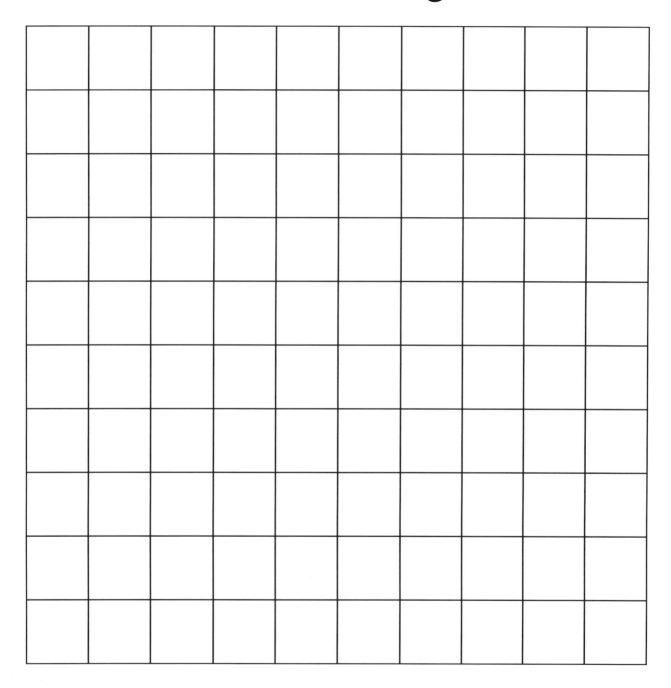

7C

7C

10 45 38 22 59 58 90 85 3 82 12 61

8 Number Lines

Materials

- masking tape, painters' tape, or adding-machine tape
- marker
- small sticky notes
- large hundred chart
- index cards displaying numbers 0 through 50
- long piece of string or clothesline
- paper clips or clothespins
- rulers (one for each pair of students)
- paper
- pencils

Activity: Part One

Run a 4- to 5-metre strip of tape along the floor where all students can see it clearly. Use a marker to mark a 0 at the far, left end of the strip of tape and a 50 at the far, right end. Select a student to come up and point to the middle of the strip of tape. Ask students:

- What number would this be?

Discuss with students which number would be in the middle of a 1-50 number line. Have students use the large hundred chart for reference. Write the number 25 on a sticky note, and place it at the midpoint of the strip of tape.

Together with students, continue adding numbers to the number line, beginning with multiples of 10. Write the numbers 10, 20, 30, and 40 on sticky notes, and have students help you place them in the appropriate places on the strip of tape.

Now, write the remaining numbers on sticky notes. Divide the class into pairs of students, and provide each pair with one or more of these numbered sticky notes. Have the pairs discuss where their number(s) should go, verbalizing their reasoning to each other. Model the language for them. For example, say:

- I think 22 should go here because it is only 2 away from 20 and 8 away from 30.

Once students have decided where their numbers should go, have the pairs come up, one at a time, to place their number(s) on the number line.

Distribute Activity Sheet A (5.8.1), and have students look at the number in each star and write it on the number line where they think it belongs.

Activity Sheet A

Directions to students:

Look at the number in each star. Record the number on the number line where you think it belongs (5.8.1).

Activity: Part Two

Hang a long piece of string or a clothesline somewhere in the classroom that is accessible to all students. Give each of ten random students an index card displaying a number from 0 to 50. Have students imagine that the string is a number line and use paper clips or clothespins to attach their cards to it where they think they belong.

Then, have the rest of the class check for accuracy by comparing the number line to a hundred chart or to another number line. Make any necessary changes to the number line.

▶

Unit 5 • **Number Concepts**

433

8

Next Step

As students progress, introduce similar number-line activities to 100. To reinforce these activities, distribute Activity Sheet B (5.8.2). Have students record each number in the correct place on the corresponding number line.

Activity Sheet B

Directions to students:

Look at the number in each star. Record the number on the number line where you think it belongs (5.8.2).

Problem Solving

Work with a partner. Use a ruler to draw a line on a piece of paper. Record 0 at one end of the line, and record 20 at the other end. Draw a dot in the middle of the line. Now, record the number that goes in the middle of the line, where you drew the dot. Then, fill in the rest of the numbers from 1 to 20.

Note: A reproducible master for this problem can be found on page 515.

Extension

Extend Activity: Part One by creating a number line on tape with an endpoint of 100. Challenge students to find the midpoint, number it, locate the multiples of 10, and complete the number line.

Date: _____   Name: _____

Number Lines

 0 ─────────────────────── 50

 0 ─────────────────────── 50

 0 ─────────────────────── 50

 0 ─────────────────────── 50

 0 ─────────────────────── 50

8A Portage & Main Press, 2006, Hands-On Mathematics, Level 2, ISBN: 978-1-55379-091-4   5.8.1 – 435

Name: _____

Date: _____

More Number Lines

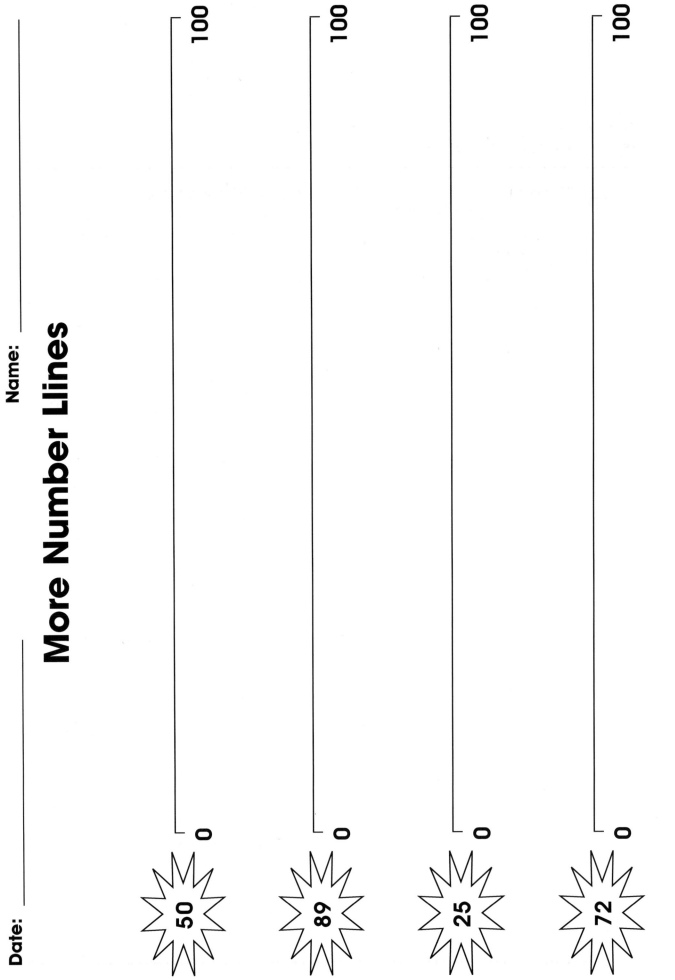

436 – 5.8.2

Portage & Main Press, 2006, Hands-On Mathematics, Level 2, ISBN: 978-1-55379-091-4

8B

9 Sets of 100

Materials

- collections of 100 items (for example, 100 pencils, 100 canned goods. See Activity: Part One.)
- *The Wolf's Chicken Stew*, a book by Keiko Kasza
- *One Hundred Ways to Get to 100*, a book by Jerry Pallotta
- egg-carton ten frames (Cut off two egg cups from one end of each egg carton, as in the diagram below. You will need one egg-carton ten frame for each pair or small working group of students.)

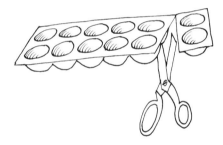

- small, paper ten frames (included. Photocopy, and cut out. You will need one small ten frame for each pair or small working group of students.) (5.9.1)
- large, paper ten frames (included. Photocopy, and cut out. You will need one large ten frame for each pair or small working group of students.) (5.9.2)
- small objects that are packaged in 100s (paper clips, screws, beads, and so on. You will need one package of objects for each pair or small working group of students.)
- *How Much Is a Million?* a book by David Schwartz
- variety of items for counting (see Activity: Part Three)
- crayons, pencil crayons, or markers
- stapler
- camera (optional)

Activity: Part One

Make collections of 100 items with students. Consider collections for which students can see immediate purpose. For example:

- Set up 100 chairs for a school event.
- Collect 100 pencils to send to needy school children.
- Collect 100 dog biscuits to donate to an animal shelter.
- Bake 100 cookies for a bake sale.
- Plant 100 tulip bulbs on school grounds.
- Collect 100 canned goods for a food bank.
- Measure 100 metres for a race.
- Prepare a bandage container with 100 bandages.

Activity: Part Two

Read *The Wolf's Chicken Stew* and/or *One Hundred Ways to Get to 100*. Have students examine the pictures of 100 in the books.

Display several packages of products that indicate that they contain a quantity of 100. Ask students:

- Do you think there are exactly 100 paper clips (or screws, beads) in this package?
- How can we check?
- What would be the fastest and easiest way to count the paper clips?
- What do we need to count the paper clips?

Divide the class into pairs or small working groups of students. Provide each pair with an egg-carton ten frame, a small, paper ten frame (5.9.1) and a large, paper ten frame (5.9.2). Also, give each pair a package of 100 objects. Have students choose the most appropriate ten frame to use for counting the objects in their packages. For example, the egg-carton ten frame might be the most appropriate tool to use for counting objects that roll, such as beads.

9

Have students use the ten frames to count the objects. Discuss their results, and ask students:

- How did you count your objects?
- Would you count your objects in a different way next time?
- Were there 100 objects in your package?

Activity: Part Three

Note: This activity has students working together in pairs or small groups. Before beginning the activity, review with students what cooperative work looks and sounds like.

Read *How Much Is a Million?* with students. As a class, design a book called *How Huge Is a Hundred?* Begin by brainstorming ways to illustrate counting to 100 by modelling the language used in *How Much Is a Million?* For example:

- If you pick 100 blades of grass…
- If you fill a bucket with 100 stones…
- If you stack 100 books…
- If you print your name 100 times…
- If you line up 100 drinking straws…
- If you do 100 jumping jacks…
- If you roll 100 balls of Plasticine…

Note: You may want to set the following criteria for items you will include in the book:

1. The task (for example, picking 100 blades of grass) must be completed in a supervised place (for example, in the school playground, in the classroom).
2. If objects (for example, books) are needed to complete the task, the objects must be easy to obtain.
3. The task must be one that can be completed in one afternoon.
4. The task must be safe and fun.

Divide the class into pairs or small working groups of students. Ask each pair to choose one idea (task) from the brainstormed list of ideas (be sure you have brainstormed enough ideas to allow for plenty of choice). Then, ask students to suggest ways of keeping track of the counting for their task (for example: tallies, grouping, skip-counting, ten frames). Have students discuss all the possibilities with their partners/groups and come up with a plan for counting, encouraging them to use one or more of the ideas shared.

Assist students in gathering their materials and finding a space to work. Allow plenty of time for students to complete their tasks. Consider taking photographs of students completing their tasks to include in the book.

Note: You may decide to carry out some tasks as a class.

Distribute Activity Sheet A (5.9.3), and have students draw pictures of the tasks they completed to illustrate counting to 100. Also, have students record statements about how huge one hundred is, again modelling the language used in *How Much Is a Million?* For example:

- If you fill a bucket with 100 stones…it is too heavy to lift.
- If you do 100 jumping jacks…your heart will beat faster.

Partners/groups may decide on their statements together, or individual students may come up with their own statements.

Activity Sheet A

Directions to students:

Draw a picture of the task you completed to illustrate counting to 100. Record a statement about how huge one hundred is. Decide on your statement together with your partner/group or come up with your own statement (5.9.3).

Staple together students' completed activity sheets, and make a cover to complete the book.

Problem Solving

Draw 100 objects in a way that a classmate can count them without having to count by 1s.

Note: A reproducible master for this problem can be found on page 515.

Activity Centre

Place wooden craft sticks, glue, and a large container of dried beans at an activity centre, and have students make "bean sticks." Ask each student to count out 100 beans. Have students glue ten beans onto each of ten wooden craft sticks.

Note: Keep students' bean sticks for place-value activities in subsequent lessons.

Extensions

- Add the terms *hundred* and *ten frame* to your classroom Math Word Wall.

- Have each student use 100 pattern blocks to create a design. Ask each student to record the quantity of each type of block (triangle, hexagon, and so on) he/she used.

Assessment Suggestions

- Observe students as they complete their tasks for the *How Huge Is a Hundred?* book. Focus on their abilities to work together. Use the Cooperative Skills Teacher-Assessment sheet, found on page 27, to record results.

- Have students complete Cooperative Skills Self-Assessment sheets, found on page 29, to reflect on their abilities to work together.

Unit 5 • **Number Concepts**

Small Ten Frames

440 – 5.9.1

Portage & Main Press, 2006, Hands-On Mathematics, Level 2, ISBN: 978-1-55379-091-4

Large Ten Frames

Portage & Main Press, 2006, Hands-On Mathematics, Level 2, ISBN: 978-1-55379-091-4

Date: _____   **Name:** _____

How Huge Is 100?

442 – 5.9.3

Portage & Main Press, 2006, Hands-On Mathematics, Level 2, ISBN: 978-1-55379-091-4

9A

10 | Greater Than and Less Than

Materials

- greater than/less than mat (included. Copy one mat for each student.) (5.10.1)
- > or < symbols (included. You will need one symbol for each student and one for teacher demonstration.) (5.10.2)
- bingo chips, dried beans, or other small counters
- chart paper
- markers
- butterfly paper fasteners (one for each student)
- numeral cards, 0-100 (included in unit 1, lesson 12. You will need two or three sets of cards.) (1.12.1)

Activity: Part One

Begin the activity by reviewing the terms *greater than* and *less than* with students. Provide each student with a greater than/less than mat (5.10.1) and a collection of bingo chips (or other small counters). Have each student put between one and ten bingo chips into the left box on the mat. Then, ask each student to put a smaller amount of bingo chips into the right box on the mat. Ask students:

- Which box has a greater amount of bingo chips?
- What does "greater" mean?
- Which box has less bingo chips?
- What does "less" mean?

On chart paper, record:

_____ is greater than _____.
_____ is less than _____.

Have students complete the statements with numbers that correspond to the amounts of beans they put on their mats. Then, ask students to take turns reading their statements. For example:

Nine is greater than four.
Two is less than five.

Have students clear their mats. Now, ask them to put beans in the boxes again, this time putting the greater amount in the right-hand box.

Again, record on chart paper:

_____ is greater than _____.
_____ is less than _____.

Again, have students complete the statements with numbers that correspond to the amounts of beans they put on their mats. Have students take turns reading their statements.

Extend the activity using quantities of beans between one and twenty.

Activity: Part Two

When students are comfortable with the concepts of greater than and less than, introduce the greater than and less than symbols: > and <. Explain that these symbols are used to show which number is greater and which number is less.

Provide each student with a greater than/less than mat (5.10.1), a > or < symbol (5.10.2), a butterfly paper fastener, and a collection of bingo chips. Have students use the butterfly paper fasteners to attach their > or < symbols to their greater than/less than mats so that they can turn the symbols in either direction.

On chart paper, draw a large, demonstration version of the greater than/less than mat. Draw ten bingo chips in the left box and five bingo chips in the right box. Have students copy your example by placing ten bingo chips in the left box on their mats and five bingo chips in the right box.

Now, display the enlarged, demonstration version of the > or < symbol for students to see. Discuss the positioning of the symbol. Ask:

▶

Unit 5 • **Number Concepts**   **443**

10

- Which group of bingo chips has the greater amount?
- Which group of chips has less?
- Which way do you think the symbol should go?

Discuss students' ideas, and explain that the pointed part of the symbol points to the smaller number and the open end points to the larger number. Have students position their own > or < symbols in this way.

Repeat this activity several times, with different amounts of beans. Allow students plenty of time to practice the concept of greater than/less than and the correct positioning of the > or < symbol.

Activity: Part Three

Provide each student with a greater than/less than mat, a > or < symbol, and a collection of numeral cards (approximately ten cards each). Have each student select two numeral cards to place in the boxes on the mat and then position the > or < symbol so that it correctly indicates which number is greater than and which number is less than. Have students repeat the activity several times with different numeral cards. Students can also exchange cards with classmates to continue the activity.

Distribute Activity Sheet A (5.10.3) and Activity Sheet B (5.10.4), and have students put the correct symbol (> or <) between each set of two numbers.

Activity Sheet A

Note: This activity sheet focuses on numbers between 0 and 50.

Directions to students:

Put the correct symbol (> or <) between each set of two numbers (5.10.3).

Activity Sheet B

Note: This activity sheet focuses on numbers between 0 and 100.

Directions to students:

Put the correct symbol (> or <) between each set of two numbers (5.10.4).

Next Steps

As students gain confidence using the > and < symbols, provide them with more challenging tasks. For example, on chart paper, display number sentences that use more than one symbol, such as the following:

___ > ___ > ___
___ < ___ < ___
___ < ___ > ___
___ > ___ < ___

Have students work together to place number cards in the correct order to make each statement true.

Problem Solving

Find all the numbers that are greater than 5 but less than 20. Make a number line to help you.

Note: A reproducible master for this problem can be found on page 515.

Activity Centre

At an activity centre, provide small cubes, blocks, or tiles, as well as paper and pencils. Also provide several containers of various sizes (yoghurt cups, fruit-cup tins, margarine containers, and so on). Label the containers A, B, C, D and so on. Have students choose two containers and fill them both with cubes. Tell students to count the cubes as they fill each of the two containers, and record how many cubes

10

each container holds. Finally, have students record greater than/less than statements using words and symbols. For example:

A holds 23 blocks.
C holds 42 blocks.
$A < C$.

Extensions

■ Add the terms *greater than* and *less than* to your classroom Math Word Wall.

■ Repeat Activity: Part One and Activity: Part Two with students, but have them place coins rather than beans on their greater than/less than mats. Ask students to add the coin values in each box to determine which box has a greater or lesser value.

■ Have students use the > or < symbols with addition and subtraction facts. For example:

$1 + 3 < 2 + 4$
$5 - 1 > 9 - 8$

Unit 5 • **Number Concepts**

445

Greater Than/Less Than Mat

> or < Symbols

Portage & Main Press, 2006, Hands-On Mathematics, Level 2, ISBN: 978-1-55379-091-4   5.10.2 – **447**

Date: _____ **Name:** _____

Greater Than or Less Than?

4 ◯ 7		10 ◯ 6		17 ◯ 20			
5 ◯ 1		10 ◯ 3		15 ◯ 20			
8 ◯ 1		10 ◯ 11		24 ◯ 20			
8 ◯ 9		10 ◯ 15		11 ◯ 20			
2 ◯ 8		10 ◯ 0		22 ◯ 20			

14 ◯ 16		25 ◯ 30		26 ◯ 27			
15 ◯ 16		22 ◯ 30		29 ◯ 22			
19 ◯ 16		35 ◯ 30		15 ◯ 25			
11 ◯ 16		31 ◯ 30		36 ◯ 24			
18 ◯ 16		24 ◯ 30		27 ◯ 37			

448 – 5.10.3   Portage & Main Press, 2006, Hands-On Mathematics, Level 2, ISBN: 978-1-55379-091-4   **10A**

Date: _____   **Name:** _____

Greater Than or Less Than? Part 2

3 ◯ 63   11 ◯ 71   2 ◯ 100

99 ◯ 9   65 ◯ 55   80 ◯ 0

16 ◯ 36   4 ◯ 13   14 ◯ 36

49 ◯ 79   29 ◯ 88   69 ◯ 96

18 ◯ 8   7 ◯ 4   12 ◯ 72

56 ◯ 65   12 ◯ 92   18 ◯ 96

86 ◯ 11   92 ◯ 12   5 ◯ 44

13 ◯ 63   19 ◯ 99   90 ◯ 11

63 ◯ 13   34 ◯ 64   22 ◯ 44

15 ◯ 55   65 ◯ 5   6 ◯ 88

10B   Portage & Main Press, 2006, Hands-On Mathematics, Level 2, ISBN: 978-1-55379-091-4   5.10.4 – 449

11 Equal and Not Equal

Materials

- chart paper
- markers
- equal/not-equal frame (included. Photocopy onto an overhead transparency.) (5.11.1)
- overhead projector
- non-permanent overhead marker
- small counters such as bingo chips or dried beans (you will need sixty for each pair of students)
- index cards or small pieces of paper (two for each student)
- scissors
- glue
- number cubes

Activity: Part One

Record the term *equal* on chart paper for students to see. Discuss the meaning of the word, and have students share their ideas of what it means. Record students' ideas and definitions on chart paper. Use these to come up with a class definition for the term.

Note: Be sure to stress that the = symbol means that what is on the left side is the same as what is on the right side.

Provide each student with a collection of bingo chips (or other small counters). Place a number of bingo chips on the overhead, arranging them in a way that will help students count them quickly, such as in groups of two or five. Discuss strategies for counting the chips.

Now, have students make a set with their own bingo chips that is equal in quantity to the set of chips on the overhead. On chart paper, record the number sentence using the equal symbol. For example:

16 = 16

Place the equal/not-equal frame (5.11.1) transparency on the overhead, and put a set of counters in each box. Use a non-permanent overhead marker to record an equal or not-equal symbol (≠) in the centre circle. Now, ask students to tell you whether the statement displayed on the overhead is true or false by showing you a "thumbs-up" sign for true and a "thumbs-down" sign for false. Come to a class consensus on whether the statement is true or false. If it is false, change the symbol to show the appropriate answer.

Repeat this activity several times. Then, replace the counters with numbers. Record a number between 0 and 100 in each box, and record an equal or not-equal symbol in the centre circle. Again, have students show the thumbs-up or thumbs-down sign to indicate whether the statement is true or false.

Activity: Part Two

Provide each student with two index cards or small pieces of paper. Have each student record a large equal symbol on one card and a not-equal symbol on the other.

Again, use the overhead equal/not-equal frame, but extend the activity by printing number sentences in each box, beginning with addition facts to 10. For example, record 4 + 5 in one box, and 9 in the other box. Have students hold up one of their cards to show whether the boxes are equal or not equal.

Divide the class into pairs of students, and distribute number cubes, sixty counters, scissors, glue, and a copy of Activity Sheet A (5.11.2) to each pair. The activity sheet becomes a game board for the game "Equal/Not Equal." Have students cut along the dotted lines on their activity sheets and cut out both = symbols and both ≠ symbols. Ask them to glue each = symbol to the back of each ≠ symbol to make

11

two =/≠ chips. Each chip should have = on one side and ≠ on the other side.

Have students put twenty counters into the centre twenty frame of their game board, one counter in each box. Also, ask students to put one =/≠ chip into each empty circle, ≠ side up. Explain the rules of the game (below) to students, and have them play.

Activity Sheet A

Note: This activity sheet is a game for two players.

Directions to students:

Work in pairs. Cut along the dotted lines of your activity sheet. Cut out the two = symbols and the two ≠ symbols. Glue each = symbol to the back of each ≠ symbol to make two =/≠ chips. Each chip should have = on one side and ≠ on the other side.

Put twenty counters into the centre twenty frame, one counter in each box. Put one =/≠ chip into each empty circle, ≠ side up.

Have Player A roll the number cube and put that number of counters into the twenty frame on his/her side of the game board. Have Player B do the same. Play continues until one player has an amount of counters in his/her twenty frame that is equal to the amount in the centre. That player then flips over his/her =/≠ chip to display the = symbol and wins the game.

Note: Players must roll the exact amount needed to complete the twenty frame.

Play the game again with a different number of counters in the centre twenty frame.

Next Steps

As students gain confidence using the equal and not-equal symbols, challenge them to answer more complex questions. For example, on index cards, record several correct and incorrect addition and subtraction stories such as the following:

$5 + 3 = 4 + 4$

$3 + 5 = 5 + 3$

$10 + 6 = 8 + 5$

$3 + 3 \neq 5 + 4$

$4 + 9 \neq 3 + 10$

Show students the cards, one at a time, and have them give you a thumbs-up sign if the story is correct and a thumbs-down sign if the story is incorrect.

Problem Solving

- You are sharing a box of chocolates with your friend. If there are 20 chocolates in the box, do you each get an equal amount? Record a number sentence to show whether or not the two sets of chocolates are equal. Use the = or ≠ sign.

- Now, you are sharing a box of 25 chocolates with your friend. Do you each get an equal amount? Record a number sentence to show whether or not the two sets of chocolates are equal. Use the = or ≠ sign.

Note: A reproducible master for these problems can be found on page 515.

Extension

Add the terms *equal* and *not equal* to your classroom Math Word Wall.

Unit 5 • **Number Concepts**

451

Equal/Not-Equal Frame

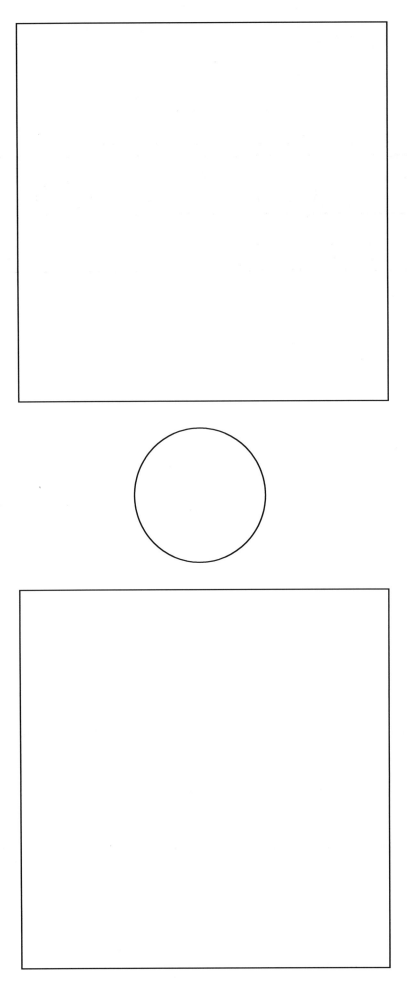

452 – 5.11.1   Portage & Main Press, 2006, Hands-On Mathematics, Level 2, ISBN: 978-1-55379-091-4

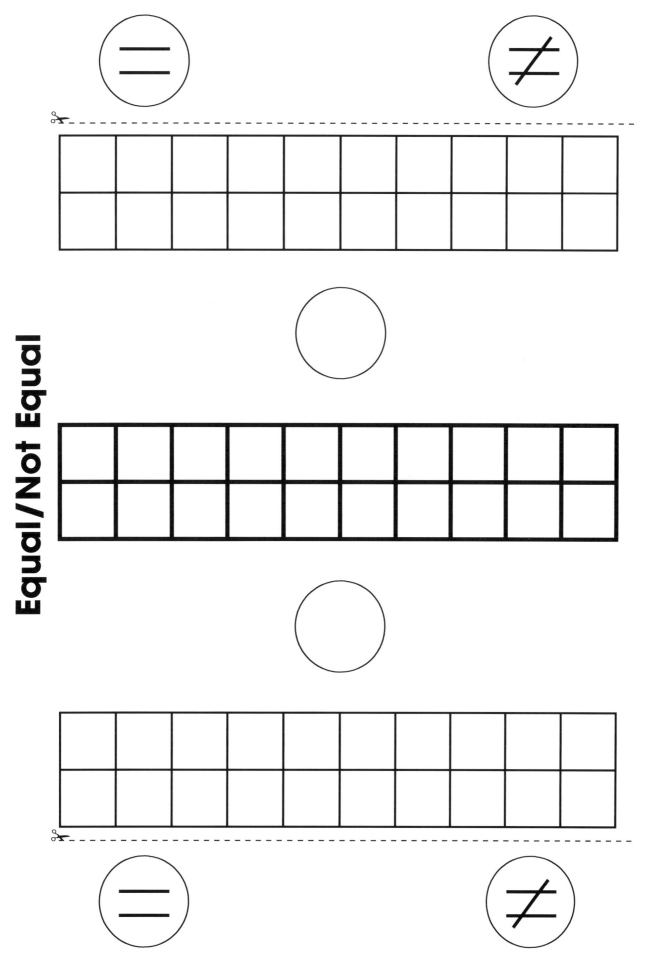

12 Even and Odd

Background Information for Teachers

In this lesson, students learn about even versus odd numbers. Although this concept is not specific to the Ontario curriculum, it reinforces skip-counting by 20 and helps students understand different conceptions of numbers. While you are doing the following activities, have a large, paper hundred chart visible to students. As students discover which numbers are even and which numbers odd, colour the numbers: use one colour for even numbers and a different colour for odd numbers. Discuss any emerging patterns with students.

Materials

- chart paper
- markers
- *Missing Mittens*, a book by Stuart J. Murphy
- large, paper hundred chart
- twenty-frame mat (included. Photocopy onto an overhead transparency.) (5.12.1)
- bingo chips or other small objects to use as counters
- hundred charts (included with part 1, unit 1, lesson 10. Make one photocopy for each student.) (1.10.1)
- crayons
- number cubes

Activity: Part One

Present to students the terms *even* and *odd*, recording them on chart paper. Ask students:

- What does the word *even* mean?
- What does the word *odd* mean?

Explain to students that numbers that can be divided into two equal halves, with no leftovers, are called "even" numbers. Numbers that have 1 left over when they are divided in half are called "odd" numbers.

Now, tell students they can also think of even numbers as numbers that can be divided into partners or pairs with no leftovers. Numbers that have 1 left over when they are divided into partners are called "odd" numbers.

Have students discuss these concepts, and create a class definition for each term. Record the class definitions on chart paper. Read *Missing Mittens,* a story about animals that are each missing a mitten. Have students identify the even and odd numbers in the story.

Activity: Part Two

Have students hold up both hands into fists, closed fingers facing each other. Now, ask each student to stick out one thumb from one hand. Explain that since one thumb has no partner, 1 is an odd number. Next, have each student stick out the thumb from his/her other hand, matching it to the first thumb. Explain that since each of the two thumbs has a pair, 2 is an even number. Now, tell each student to stick out one index finger (forefinger) from one hand (be sure students leave their two thumbs sticking out). Ask students to count how many fingers they have sticking out now.

Note: For the purpose of this activity, consider the thumbs to be fingers.

Point out that each student has three fingers sticking out. Although students' thumbs have partners, their index fingers do not (they are left over). So, 3 is an odd number. Continue in this way until you reach the number 10 and students have partnered up all fingers on both hands.

Distribute Activity sheet A (5.12.2), and have students complete the Venn diagram by recording even and odd numbers from 1 to 10. Extend the activity by having students add more numbers to each Venn circle as they learn more even and odd numbers.

454 Hands-On Mathematics • Grade 2

12

Activity Sheet A

Directions to students:

Complete the Venn diagram by recording odd and even numbers from 1 to 10. Add more numbers to each circle as you learn more even and odd numbers (5.12.2).

Activity: Part Three

Distribute hundred charts and crayons to students. Display the twenty-frame transparency (5.12.1) on the overhead. Place one bingo chip in the bottom, left box of the first twenty frame. Ask students:

- Is 1 an even number or an odd number?
- How do you know? (It doesn't have a partner/pair.)

Remind students that even numbers can be divided into partners or pairs and odd numbers have 1 left over.

As a class, determine a colour for odd and a colour for even numbers. Have students colour the number 1 on their hundred charts in the colour designated for odd numbers.

Note: If you have already begun colouring even and odd numbers on the large, class hundred chart, have students use the same colours on their own hundred charts.

One at a time, add more bingo chips to the overhead transparency of the twenty-frame. Each time you add a bingo chip, have students identify the number of bingo chips on the frame and then decide whether that number is even or odd (i.e., can be divided into partners, or has 1 left over).

Note: When placing chips on the twenty frames, always place the first chip at the bottom left of the frame. Place the second chip beside the first one so students can readily see the pairs. Place the third chip above the first, and so on, as in the following diagram:

For each number you explore as a class, have students colour that number on their hundred charts in the designated colour for even or odd. Continue until students begin to see patterns on their hundred charts. Ask students:

- What patterns do you see on your hundred chart?
- What do you notice about all the even numbers?
- What do you notice about all the odd numbers?
- How many odd numbers are there on the hundred chart?
- How many even numbers are there?
- What is the smallest/largest even number on the hundred chart?
- What is the smallest/largest odd number?
- Do you think the number 102 (114, 126, 138, 150) is an even or an odd number?
- Do you think the number 111 (125, 167, 183) is an even or an odd number?

Have students colour all the numbers on their hundred charts in the designated even/odd colours.

Unit 5 • **Number Concepts**

12

Divide the class into pairs of students and distribute to each pair one number cube, two bingo chips, and a copy of Activity Sheet B (5.12.3). Explain the rules to the game "To the Candy Store," and have students play.

Activity Sheet B

Directions to students:

Play the game in pairs. Decide who will play on the even side of the street and who will play on the odd side. Place a bingo chip on each "Start" space (house). Have the "Even" player roll the number cube. If the number rolled is even, he/she moves the chip on the "Even" side of the board one space. If the number rolled is odd, he/she does not move. Then, have the "Odd" player roll the number cube and move his/her chip one space only if the number rolled is odd. Players only move on their own turns (when they have rolled the number cube). Play continues until one player reaches the candy store (5.12.3).

Problem Solving

The Rabbit family is going snowshoeing. Mrs. Rabbit found 15 snowshoes in the closet. Mr. Rabbit found 21 snowshoes in the basement. Together, do they have an even number of snowshoes or an odd number? How many rabbits can go snowshoeing?

Note: A reproducible master for this problem can be found on page 516.

Extension

Add the terms *odd, even, pair,* and *partner* to your classroom Math Word Wall.

456　　　　　　　　　　　　　　　　　　　　　**Hands-On Mathematics • Grade 2**

Twenty-Frame Mat

Portage & Main Press, 2006, Hands-On Mathematics, Level 2, ISBN: 978-1-55379-091-4

5.12.1 – 457

Name:

Date:

Even and Odd Numbers

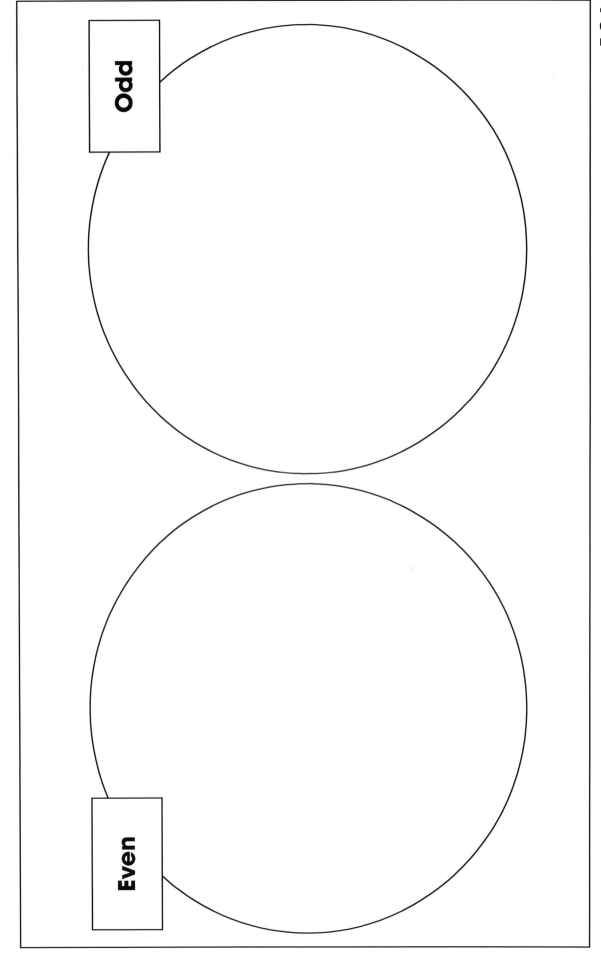

To the Candy Store

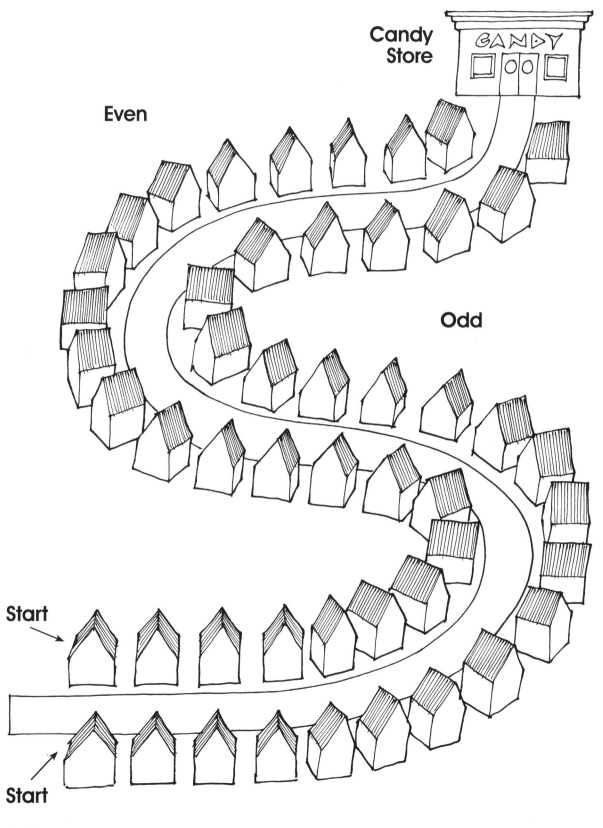

12B

13 Rounding Off to the Nearest Ten

Materials

- painter's tape or masking tape
- marker
- Plasticine
- toothpicks
- tape
- ten small, cardboard squares
- small toy car
- number line, 0-100 (see lesson 3)
- number response cards (included with lesson 1) (5.1.1)

Activity: Part One

Use tape and a marker to make a 0-100 number line on the floor. Make sure the space between each number is at least as long as the toy car you will be using (i.e., the number line should be at least 100 cars long).

Make ten small street signs by taping each of ten squares of cardboard to a toothpick and sticking the toothpick into a small Plasticine ball. Use the signs to mark each decade as a "10 town" on your number line. Place the toy car on the number line. Present students with various scenarios. For each scenario, ask students: "To which 10 town is the car closest?" For example:

Jay is driving to the beach. When he reaches number 32 on Number Line Road, he realizes he has forgotten to bring sunscreen. He decides to stop and buy some sunscreen at a nearby town. To which 10 town is Jay closest?

Mr. Ross is driving to the store. He is at number 16 on Number Line Road when he sees that he is almost out of gas. To which 10 town should Mr. Ross drive to fill his car with gas?

After presenting students with several scenarios, encourage them to create their own scenarios for the rest of the class to solve.

Note: Explain to students that if the car is at a number with a 5 in the ones place (for example, 15, 45) the rule is to go to the higher 10 town rather than to the lower 10 town. For example, if Casey is at number 75 and wants to stop for lunch, she should go to 80 town, not to 70 town. Discuss this concept in detail with students. Students may understand that 5 is just as close to 1 as it is to 10 or that 5 is halfway between 1 and 10. But the "5 rule" must be followed so that everyone gets the same results.

Activity: Part Two

Review the 10 town activity with students. Explain that the action of determining what is the nearest 10 is called "rounding off to the nearest 10." Tell students that rounding off to the nearest 10 is a strategy many people use to help them come up with solutions quickly and/or approximately. Provide students with the following rounding-off scenario:

Jacob is putting new tile in his kitchen. He needs about 35 tiles for the cooking area and about 27 tiles for the eating area. To be sure he has enough tiles, and just in case some of the tiles break while he is installing them, he decides to round off the tiles he needs to the nearest 10. He rounds off 35 to 40 tiles and 27 to 30 tiles. Then, he adds 40 and 30 together and buys 70 tiles.

Hang a number line in the classroom where all students can see it, and continue to practice rounding off with students. For example, point to the number 65, and ask students:

- Which is the nearest ten?

Have students use their number response cards to show the nearest ten.

13

Distribute Activity Sheet A (5.13.1), and have students use the classroom number line to help them round off each number to the nearest 10.

Activity Sheet A

Directions to students:

Use the classroom number line to help you round off each number to the nearest 10 (5.13.1).

Problem Solving

There are four grade-two classes at Sunnybrook School. Room 2A has 18 students, room 2B has 23 students, room 2C has 25 students, and room 2D has 26 students. Use rounding off to estimate how many grade-two students go to Sunnybrook School.

Note: A reproducible master for this problem can be found on page 516.

Extensions

■ Add the term *rounding off* to your classroom Math Word Wall.

■ Present students with various three-digit numbers, and have students round off each number to the nearest 10.

Unit 5 • **Number Concepts**

Date: _____   **Name:** _____

Rounding Off

29		72	
17		52	
52		66	
31		94	
76		45	
22		13	
91		16	
88		57	
45		95	
93		48	
34		81	
46		99	
22		65	
16		83	
31		38	

14 | Estimating

Background Information for Teachers

The ability to estimate is based on a background knowledge of and familiarity with the objects or measure being estimated. For example, in Activity: Part One, students estimate how many objects are in a jar. By using different objects and different jars to repeat this activity with students several times, students will begin to learn about capacity (how much each jar holds), volume (how much space objects take up), and the relationship of each to the number of objects in the jar.

It is best to provide students with a referent before they estimate in order to help them understand that making an estimation is not just making a *guess*. For example, for the activity referred to above, students are each provided with five bingo chips to help them estimate how many chips are in the jar.

To encourage students to think and speak like mathematicians and use proper terminology, teachers should refrain from using the terms *guess* or *guesstimate* when *estimate* is the appropriate term.

Materials

- variety of small objects (bingo chips, large, dried beans, centimetre cubes, small tiles)
- small, clear, unbreakable jar with lid
- number response cards (included with lesson 1) (5.1.1)
- large floor tile (or a piece of paper)
- chart paper
- overhead projector
- estimation game cards (included. Copy, and cut out a set for each pair of students.) (5.14.1)
- *Counting Wildflowers*, a book by Bruce McMillan
- Hula-Hoop
- dandelion patch mat (included. Make a photocopy for each student.) (5.14.2)
- rubber jar rings, pipe-cleaner loops, or dollar-store bracelets

Activity: Part One

Note: Do this activity over a period of time to allow students time to develop estimation skills.

Fill a small, clear "estimation jar" with small objects such as bingo chips or large, dried beans. Provide each student with a few of the objects to use as a referent. Be sure the referent is a simple number that they can easily use for making an estimate. For example, give each student five lima beans, and say:

- You have five lima beans in your hand. How many beans do you think are in the jar?

Or:

- You have ten lima beans in your hand. How many beans do you think are in the jar?

Ask students to use their number response cards to show their estimates. Then, have students explain how they determined their responses. Ask:

- How did you decide on that estimate?

Discuss the strategies students used to make their estimates. Now, as a class, count the number of beans in the jar, encouraging students to practice their skip-counting and rote number-sequencing skills.

Repeat this activity on a regular basis, using different objects in the jar. Or, select a jar of a different size, but use objects already explored.

Use a large floor tile as an "Estimation Tile," and repeat the previous activity. Place a collection of objects on the tile. Provide students with a few objects to use as referents, and have them estimate how many objects are on the tile.

Unit 5 • **Number Concepts**

14

Activity: Part Two

Display a collection of bingo chips (five, ten, or twenty) on the overhead projector for students to use as a referent. Then, shut off the projector, and add or remove some bingo chips. Turn the projector back on, leaving it on long enough for students to see the collection, but not long enough for students to count it. Ask students to give you a "thumbs-up" sign if they think the new collection has more chips than the referent collection or a "thumbs-down" sign if they think the new collection has less chips.

Now, have students estimate how many chips are on the overhead and use their number response cards to show their estimates. Ask:

- How did you decide on your estimate?
- What were you thinking in order to make that estimate?

Clarify students' thinking so that other students may learn efficient ways to estimate.

Activity: Part Three

Divide the class into pairs of students, and have them play "The Estimation Game." Provide each pair with a set of estimation game cards (5.14.1) and a copy of Activity Sheet A (5.14.3). Identify for students which is the "helper card" within their sets, pointing out that this card has 10 stars. Explain to students that the helper card will help them make good estimates. Have the pairs put their helper cards off to one side. Then, ask students to turn all the other cards facedown and put them into a pile.

Have Player A in each pair turn over the top card in the pile and count quietly for five seconds while Player B looks at the card.

Note: Give students suggestions for counting to five fairly and *quietly*, so as not to disturb their partners. For example, suggest that they touch their knees, then their shoulders, five times.

Then, have Player A return the card to a facedown position. Ask Player B to estimate how many stars are on the card and record the estimate on the activity sheet.

Now, have pairs turn over the card again. Ask them to count the collection of stars together and record the actual amount on the activity sheet. Then, have players switch roles.

Activity Sheet A

Directions to students:

Have Player A turn over the top card in the pile and count quietly for five seconds while Player B looks at the card. Then, have Player A return the card to a facedown position. Have Player B estimate how many stars are on the card and record the estimate on the activity sheet. Now, turn over the card again, and count the collection of stars together. Record the actual amount on the activity sheet. Switch roles (5.14.3).

Activity: Part Four

Read the book *Counting Wildflowers*.

Weather/season-permitting, take students on a walking tour of the community to locate a dandelion or clover patch. Use a Hula-Hoop to enclose an area of the patch, and have students estimate how many dandelions/clovers are inside the Hula-Hoop. Count the actual number of plants.

Return to the classroom, and provide each student with a dandelion patch mat (5.14.2), a copy of Activity Sheet B (5.14.4), and a rubber jar ring (or pipe-cleaner loop, or dollar-store bracelet). Have students toss their rings onto their dandelion patch mats. Ask students to estimate, but not count, how many dandelions are in their samples (rings). Have them record

464   Hands-On Mathematics • Grade 2

14

their estimates on their activity sheets. Then, ask students to count the dandelions in their samples and record the actual amounts. Tell them to repeat the activity four more times.

Activity Sheet B

Directions to students:

Toss your ring onto your dandelion patch. Estimate, but do not actually count, how many dandelions are inside the ring. Record your estimate on your activity sheet. Count the dandelions inside the ring, and record the actual amount. Repeat four more times (5.14.4).

Problem Solving

Estimate how many letters there are in the first names of all students in the class. Record your estimate. Now, count how many letters there actually are in the first names of all students in the class. Show how you came up with your estimate.

Note: You can simplify this problem by asking students to estimate how many letters there are in the first names of five or ten friends combined. A reproducible master for this problem can be found on page 516.

Activity Centre

At an activity centre, have a collection of animal cards (cut out animal pictures from magazines and calendars, and mount them on large index cards or pieces of cardboard). Write the name of the animal on each card. Punch a hole in each card, and attach a piece of string that is the actual length of an average animal of this type (gather this information from reference books/ CDs or the Internet), as in the following diagram:

At the centre, also include a large quantity of interlocking cubes, 30-cm rulers, metre sticks, copies of the Activity Centre sheet called "Estimating and Measuring Animal Lengths (5.14.5)," and pencils.

For each animal card, have students look at the length of string and estimate either how long it is in interlocking cubes (non-standard unit of measure) or in centimetres, decimetres, or metres (standard units of measure).

Note: If students choose to use a standard unit of measure, it is important that they consider which one would be most appropriate for each animal. For example, students would measure the length of a caterpillar in centimetres and the length of a horse in metres.

Then, have students use the cubes or the 30-cm rulers/metre sticks to measure the animal's (string's) actual length. Have students record their estimates and the actual measurements on the activity centre sheets.

Extensions

- Add the terms *estimate* and *estimation* to the Math Word Wall.

- Have students estimate how many pages there are in a book before they open it.

Assessment Suggestion

Observe students as they estimate quantities of various objects. Focus on each student's ability to:

- take risks (necessary for estimation)
- estimate
- make a sound estimation using the objects and containers provided

Use the Anecdotal Record sheet, found on page 22, to record your results.

Unit 5 • **Number Concepts**   **465**

Estimation Cards

Helper Card

466 – 5.14.1

Portage & Main Press, 2006, Hands-On Mathematics, Level 2, ISBN: 978-1-55379-091-4

Dandelion Patch Mat

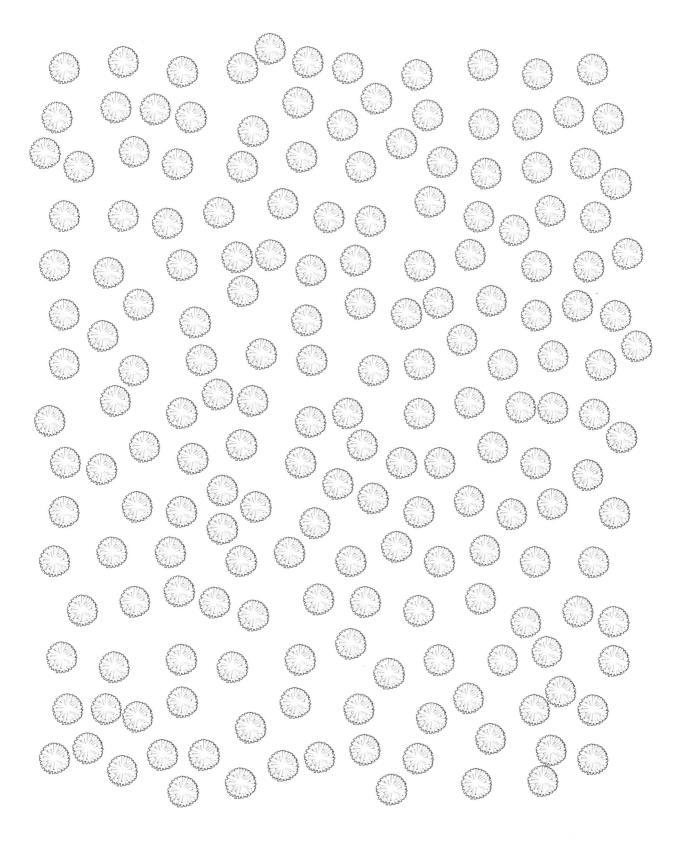

Names: _____

Date: _____

The Estimation Game

Player A _____

My Estimate	Actual

Player B _____

My Estimate	Actual

14A

468 – 5.14.3

Portage & Main Press, 2006, Hands-On Mathematics, Level 2, ISBN: 978-1-55379-091-4

Date: _____   **Name:** _____

Estimating Dandelions

My Estimate	Actual

Estimating and Measuring Animal Lengths

Animal	Unit of Measure	Estimate of Length	Actual Length

470 – 5.14.5   Portage & Main Press, 2006, Hands-On Mathematics, Level 2, ISBN: 978-1-55379-091-4   **Activity Centre**

15 Zero as a Place Holder

Materials

- two very long strips of paper such as adding-machine or cash-register tape (divide the paper strip into three, long columns by drawing two vertical lines down the middle)
- small paper cups or muffin-tin liners
- two large box lids (for example, from photocopy or printer paper. Label one lid "Tens" and the other lid "Ones.")
- clothespin (optional)
- number cubes (ten-sided cubes will work best for the activity. You will need one number cube for each student.)
- dried lima beans (or other dried beans. You will need 100 beans for each student.)
- place-value arrows (included. Photocopy one set for each student and an extra set for demonstration.) (5.15.1)
- scissors

Activity: Part One

Divide a set of 100 beans among students so that each student has an equal amount. Keep any extras for yourself. Sit with students in a circle, and place the "Ones" box lid in the centre. Tell students that as a class, you will use the beans to count to 100. Explain that when you clap your hands, the student on your left will toss a single bean into the box while all students say, "one." When you clap again, the next student will toss a bean into the lid while all students say, "two."

As students toss their beans, record the number of beans on the strip of paper divided into three columns. Begin at the bottom of the strip, recording the numbers 1 through 9 in the right-hand column of the strip.

When the tenth bean has been tossed, select a student to put the ten beans into a paper cup or muffin-tin liner and place the cup in the "Tens" box lid. Record the number 10 on the paper strip with the 1 in the middle column (1 ten) and the 0 in the right-hand column (0 ones). Then, continue with number 11, having the next student toss a bean into the "Ones" lid.

Discuss with students the patterns emerging on the strip of paper, paying particular attention to the 0s, as they appear in the right-hand column. For example, at 30 ask students:

- Which part of the number 30 shows 3 tens?
- Where is the 0 in the number 30?
- What does the 0 represent? (0 ones)

Note: If the paper strip becomes cumbersome, you may consider rolling it up as you go and clipping it with a clothespin. Be sure to leave enough of the strip visible for students to see the patterns. When you have completed the activity, unroll the strip for students to investigate the entire set of numbers.

Encourage students to look for patterns on the numbered paper strip.

Activity: Part Two

Repeat the previous activity, but begin with 100 beans (the first student tosses a single bean into the box while all students say, "one hundred") and count backward, breaking tens as you go (i.e., remove each set of ten beans and put it into the paper cup, for deposit into the "Tens"

Unit 5 • Number Concepts

15

lid). Record the numbers on a similar strip of paper, but begin recording numbers at the top of the strip.

Distribute to each student 100 dried beans, a number cube, and a copy of Activity Sheet A (5.15.2). Have each student roll the number cube and count beans to match the number rolled. Ask students to keep running tallies of how many tens and ones they have until they reach 100. For example, if students roll an 8, they count out eight beans and record an 8 in the "Ones" column of their activity sheets. If they roll a 5 next, they count out five more beans. They now have thirteen beans, so they record a 1 in the "Tens" column and a 3 in the "Ones" column.

In the large box on the activity sheet, have students draw pictures of their collections of beans, arranged as tens and ones, adding to their pictures as they go.

Activity Sheet A

Directions to students:

Roll a number cube. Count beans to match the number you rolled. On your activity sheet, keep a running tally of how many tens and ones you have. Keep rolling until you reach 100. In the large box on the activity sheet, draw a picture of your collection of beans, arranged as tens and ones. Add to the picture as you go (5.15.2).

Activity: Part Three

Note: The following activity reinforces the idea of place value for students as well as the concept of zero as a place holder. It also gives students an opportunity to practice reading numbers.

Provide each student with a set of place-value arrows (5.15.1) and a pair of scissors. Have students cut out all of their arrows.

Use the demonstration set of place-value arrows to show students how to build numbers to 999. Demonstrate how to build the number 135 by selecting the 100 arrow and placing the 30 arrow on top of it so that they overlap. Then, place the 5 arrow on top of the 30 arrow, again so that the triangles overlap. Ask students to build the number 135 in the same way. Then, have students continue to use their place-value arrows to build a variety of other numbers.

Problem Solving

There are 84 cookies. You need to put the cookies into packages of 10. How many packages of 10 cookies can you make? Are there any leftovers? How many?

Note: A reproducible master for this problem can be found on page 516.

Activity Centres

Note: Each of the following activity centres gives students the opportunity to further explore both the concepts of place value and of zero as a place holder.

- At a centre, place several boxes filled with different quantities of cubes, to a maximum of 100 cubes. Also, provide paper and pencils. Have students choose one box of cubes, group the cubes into sets of tens and ones, and record the results. For example, if a box contains 86 cubes, the student makes 8 groups of ten cubes and 6 groups of one cube.

- On each of several sheets of 11" x 17" paper, draw a long and curvy or zigzag line. Place these sheets at a centre along with paper clips, paper, and pencils. Have students line up paper clips, end to end, along one of the lines on the sheet of paper. Then, tell

472   Hands-On Mathematics • Grade 2

15

students to group the paper clips into sets of tens and ones and record the length of the line in paper clips.

- At a centre, provide a large container of dried beans and a variety of cups, ladles, and spoons to use as scoops. Also, provide paper and pencils. Have students fill one of the scoops with beans, group the beans into sets of tens and ones, and record the results.

- On each of several sheets of construction paper, draw a large and simple geometric shape. Place these sheets at the centre along with tiles, paper, and pencils. Have each student select a shape, cover the shape with tiles, group the tiles into sets of tens and ones, and record the results.

- At a centre, provide bingo dabbers, large sheets of paper, and pencils. Have students use bingo dabbers to make as many spots (dabs) on one sheet of paper as they can in ten seconds. Tell students their spots should not overlap and they should be in a pattern that makes them easy to count. Then, have students circle sets of ten spots and record the number in tens and ones. For example, if a student makes 14 spots with the dabber, he/she circles 1 set of ten spots and then records the number as 1 ten and 4 ones.

Extensions

- Add the terms *ones, tens*, and *hundreds* to your classroom Math Word Wall.

- Have students use the "bean sticks" they made in the Activity Centre in lesson 9 (see page 439) to repeat Activity Part: One. When the tenth bean has been tossed, rather than having a student put the ten beans into a paper cup or muffin-tin liner, have a student put a bean stick into the "Tens" box lid. (Return the ten "Ones" beans to the container.) Then, continue with number 11, having the next student toss a bean into the "Ones" lid.

Note: Once students have completed the activity, be sure to keep students' bean sticks for place-value activities in subsequent lessons.

Assessment Suggestion

Observe students as they work at the various Activity Centres. Focus on each student's ability to:

- count sets of objects
- group objects into sets of ten
- identify sets of tens and ones
- record sets of tens and ones

List these criteria on the Rubric sheet, found on page 25, and record your results.

Unit 5 • **Number Concepts**

473

Place-Value Arrows

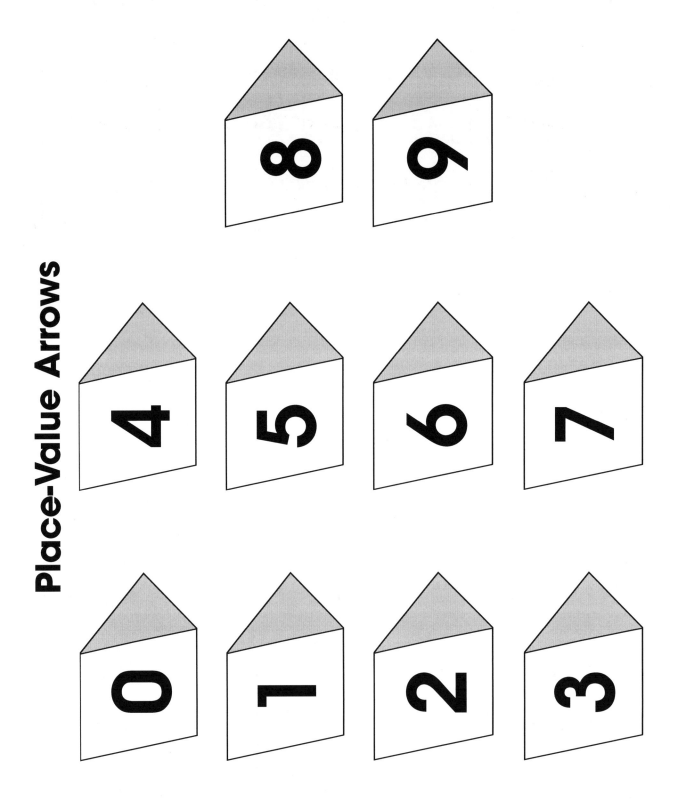

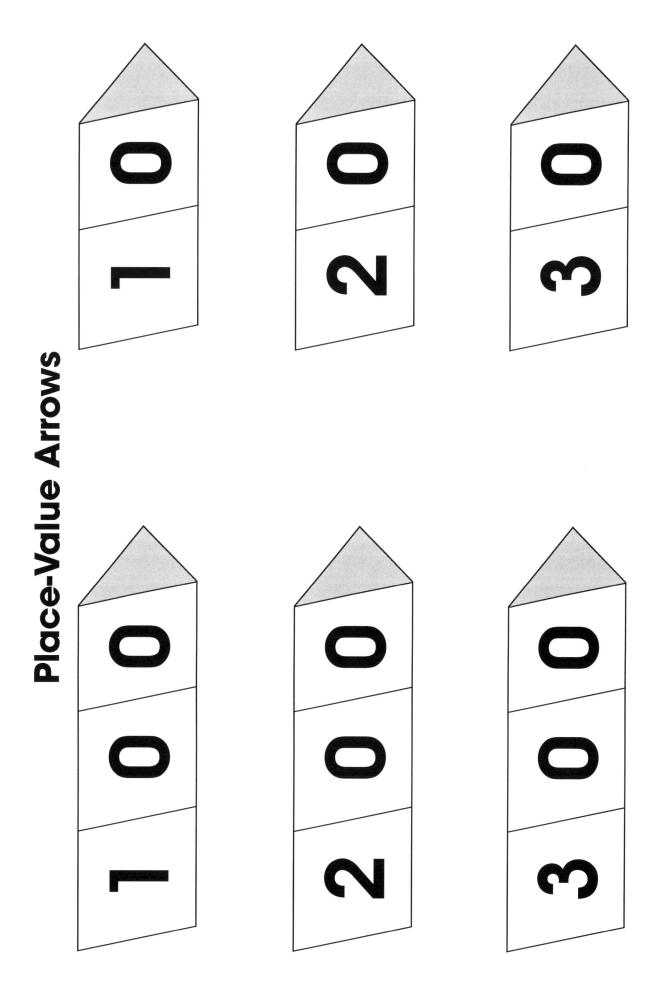

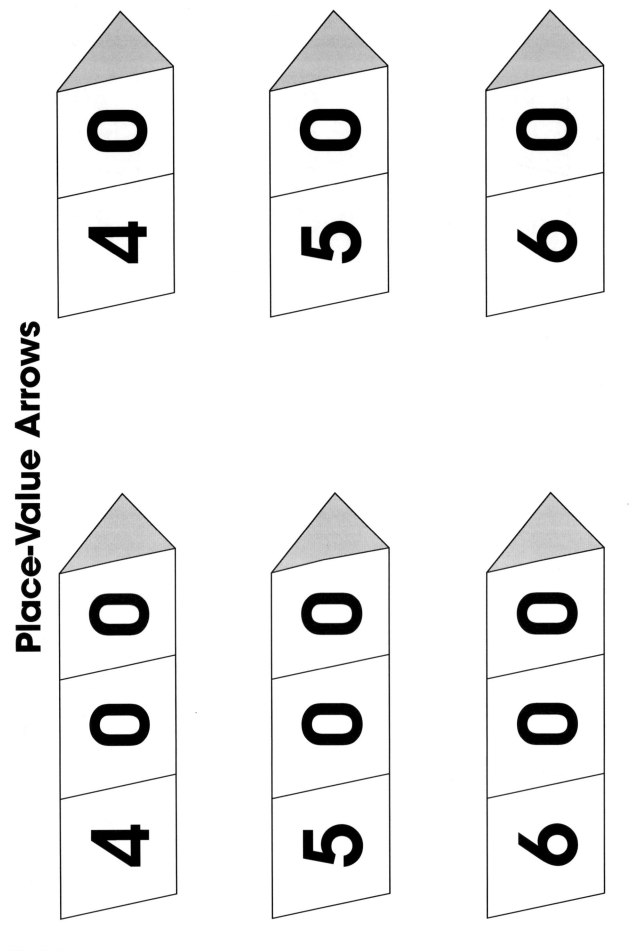

Place-Value Arrows

476 – 5.15.1

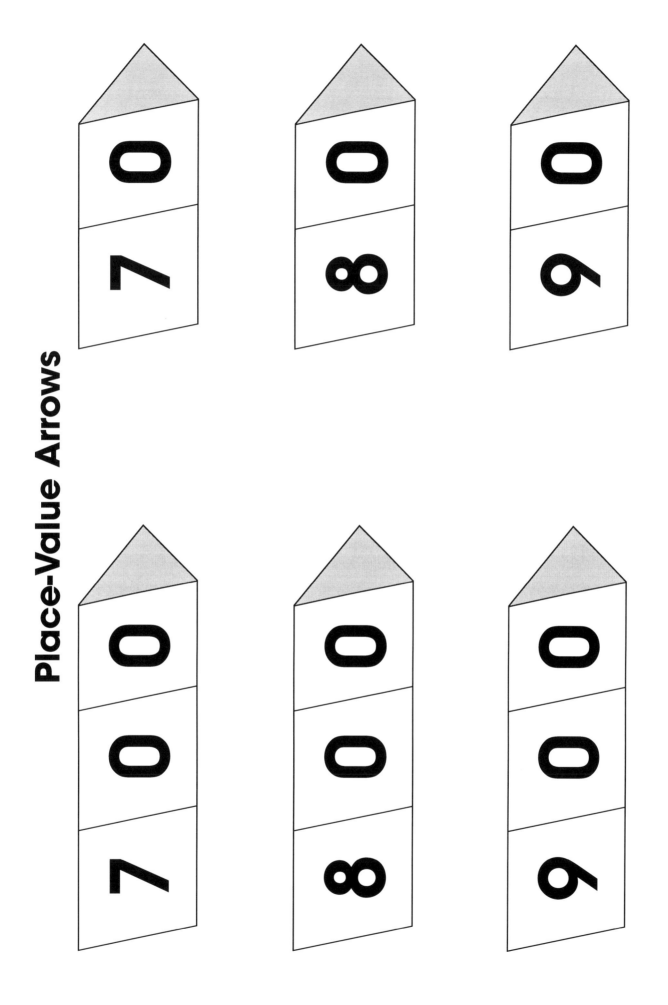

Name: _____

Date: _____

Roll to 100

Tens	Ones

15A

478 – 5.15.2

Portage & Main Press, 2006, Hands-On Mathematics, Level 2, ISBN: 978-1-55379-091-4

16 | Representing Numbers to 100

Materials

- tens and ones mats (included. Make one photocopy for each student.) (5.16.1)
- dried beans (you will need a large quantity of beans)
- plastic containers (empty margarine or yoghurt containers work well. Be sure each container is large enough to hold about 100 dried beans. You will need one container for each student.)
- bean sticks (made by students in lesson 9)
- interlocking cubes
- stir sticks or wooden craft sticks
- elastic bands
- dimes and pennies
- chart paper
- markers

Activity: Part One

Provide each student with a tens and ones mat (5.16.1), several bean sticks, and a plastic container filled with dried beans. Ask students to use their bean sticks and beans to make the number 54 on their tens and ones mats. Then, determine how students made the number 54. Ask:

- Did anyone use 5 bean sticks (5 tens) and 4 single beans (4 ones) to make 54?

Explain that this is one way to make the number 54, but there are other ways. Ask:

- Did anyone use 54 beans (54 ones) to make the number 54?

Point out that this is another way of making 54. Both ways are correct.

Ask students to explore any other ways of making the number 54, using different combinations of tens and ones. On chart paper, make a tens and ones chart like the one that follows, and have students look for patterns:

Number	Tens	Ones
54	5	4
54	4	14
54	3	24
54	2	34
54	1	44
54	0	54

Repeat using different numbers to 100.

Activity: Part Two

Repeat the previous activity using different materials such as interlocking cubes (in chains and "singles"), stir sticks and elastic bands (use elastic bands to bundle stir sticks in groups of tens), or dimes and pennies. Continue to discuss the various ways to build and represent a given number using both manipulatives and symbolic representations.

Distribute to students beans and bean sticks (or interlocking cubes) as well as copies of Activity Sheet A (5.16.2). Tell students to use the beans and bean sticks to make the number 34 in as many ways as they can. Have students draw each way they made 34 on their activity sheets.

Activity Sheet A

Directions to students:

Use beans and bean sticks (or interlocking cubes) to make the number 34 in as many ways as you can. On your activity sheet, draw each way you made the number 34 (5.16.2).

Distribute to students beans and bean sticks as well as copies of Activity Sheet B (5.16.3). Have students choose their own numbers (less than 100) to represent in as many ways as they can, using the beans and bean sticks. Ask students

▶

Unit 5 • **Number Concepts**

479

16

to draw each way on their activity sheets. Also, have students print their numbers in the blank in the title found at the top of their activity sheets.

Activity Sheet B

Directions to students:

Choose a number that is less than 100. Use the beans and bean sticks to make your number in as many ways as you can. Draw each way you made your number. Also, print your number in the blank in the title at the top of the activity sheet (5.16.3).

Problem Solving

Make a chart to show all the ways you can make 43 cents using only pennies and dimes.

Note: A reproducible master for this problem can be found on page 516.

Extension

Have students create a concrete representation of a hundred chart. Use a permanent marker to draw a 10 x 10 grid on a large, vinyl tablecloth. Have students use bean sticks and beans or commercial tens and ones blocks to build each number on the hundred chart.

480   **Hands-On Mathematics • Grade 2**

Tens and Ones Mat

Tens	Ones

5.16.1 – **481**

Portage & Main Press, 2006, Hands-On Mathematics, Level 2, ISBN: 978-1-55379-091-4

Date: _____

Name: _____

Making the Number 34

Number	Tens	Ones
34		
34		
34		
34		

482 – 5.16.2

Portage & Main Press, 2006, Hands-On Mathematics, Level 2, ISBN: 978-1-55379-091-4

16A

Date: _____

Name: _____

Making the Number _____

Number	Tens	Ones

16B

5.16.3 – **483**

Portage & Main Press, 2006, Hands-On Mathematics, Level 2, ISBN: 978-1-55379-091-4

17 Fractions: Halves

Background Information for Teachers

Provide many opportunities for students to use the language of fractions in natural settings, such as while they are measuring and sharing, while you are passing out materials, and so on. Be sure to focus on both:

- the fractional part of a whole, such as parts of an object. For example: half of the pizza
- the fractional part of a set, such as components of a group of objects. For example: half of the dozen eggs

Materials

- *Give me Half!* a book by Stuart Murphy
- fraction cards A (included. Make one photocopy for each student.) (5.17.1)
- crayons (five crayons for each student including one orange, one yellow, one green, one brown, and one red)
- envelopes
- small paper plates (or cardboard circles of the same size. You will need two plates for each student.)
- pipe cleaners (six pipe cleaners for each student)
- scrap paper
- glue
- red poster paint
- paintbrushes (one for each student)
- plastic containers for holding water (one for each pair of students)
- black markers (one for each pair of students)
- small, black construction-paper circles (approximately the diameter of a cardboard toilet-paper roll. You will need one circle for each student.)
- black dot stickers (ten stickers for each student)
- scissors
- 10-centimetre squares of construction paper, in two colours (one square for each student. Have half as many squares in one colour as there are students in your class, and half as many squares in the other colour as there are students in your class.)

Activity: Part One

Provide each student with a copy of fraction cards A (5.17.1), which shows shapes or pictures divided into either two equal parts or two unequal parts. Have students cut apart their cards and then examine the shape or picture on each card. Ask:

- Into how many parts is each shape divided?
- Are all of the shapes divided into two *equal* parts?

Challenge students to sort the pictures into two groups: equal and not equal. Check their sorting, then have students put aside their unequal cards.

Together as a class, discuss the shapes that are divided equally into two parts. Explain to students that each of these cards shows a shape or picture divided into *halves*.

Now, distribute crayons to students, and provide them with the following instructions:

- Find your picture of the Popsicle. Colour one half of the Popsicle orange.
- Find your picture of the cracker. Colour one half of the cracker yellow.
- Find your oval shape. Colour one half of the oval green.
- Find your picture of the cookie. Colour one half of the cookie brown.
- Find your heart shape. Colour one half of the heart red.

Distribute envelopes, and have students store their fraction cards A (both the "halves" cards and the unequal cards) in the envelopes.

17

Activity: Part Two

Read the book, *Give Me Half!* Now, show students the one-half symbol ($\frac{1}{2}$). Have students retrieve their set of fraction cards A from their envelopes. Have students again sort the pictures into two groups: equal and not equal. On each "equal" card, ask students to record the one-half symbol on the uncoloured half of the shape/picture.

Activity: Part Three

Note: The following activity has students making paper ladybugs. Although the instructions suggest that the craft is completed all at once, it is best completed in three stages: (A) gluing stage (steps 1-3, below); (B) painting stage (step 4); and (C) decorating stage (steps 5-7).

Have students work in pairs. Distribute to each pair four small paper plates (or cardboard circles of the same size), two small, black construction-paper circles, twenty dot stickers, twelve pipe cleaners, and two sheets of scrap paper. Ask the pairs to divide their craft supplies in half so that each student gets an equal amount. Encourage students to use the language of fractions as they divide the supplies. Have students record several sentences on scrap paper to describe how they divided their materials in half.

Now, distribute glue, red poster paint, paintbrushes, plastic containers filled with water, and black markers to the pairs, and tell students they will be making paper ladybugs. Explain to students the instructions for the craft:

1. Place in front of you one paper plate, right side up, for the ladybug's body. Put plenty of glue around the edge of the plate.
2. While the glue is still wet, stick six pipe cleaners to the edge of the paper plate as the ladybug's legs. Be sure that about half of each pipe cleaner sticks outside of the paper plate and the other half rests on the inside of the plate.
3. Before the glue dries, place the second paper plate upside-down on top of the first paper plate, edge to edge. Rearrange the pipe cleaners as necessary so that half of each pipe cleaner is still sticking out from between the edges of the two plates. Hold the two plates together while the glue sets.
4. Once the glue is completely dry, paint the top of the ladybug body with red poster paint.
5. When the paint has dried, use a black marker to draw a line down the middle of the top of the ladybug's body.
6. Stick one half of the dot stickers on one side of the top of the ladybug's body and one half of the stickers on the other side of the top of the ladybug's body.
7. Glue the small, black circle to the edge of the top paper plate as the ladybug's head. Be sure that a good portion of the black circle is sticking out beyond the plate, as in the following diagram:

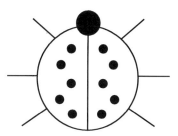

Distribute Activity Sheet A (5.17.2), scissors, and glue, and have students divide the picnic food in half. Tell students to cut out each food item and then glue half of all the food onto one side of the tablecloth and the other half onto the other side.

▶

Unit 5 • **Number Concepts**   485

17

Activity Sheet A

Note: This is a two-page activity sheet.

Directions to students:

You are having a picnic with a friend. You must divide the food in half so that everything is shared equally. Cut out all of the food. Glue half of the food onto your side of the tablecloth and the other half onto your friend's side of the tablecloth (5.17.2).

Problem Solving

Distribute to each student a pair of scissors and a 10-centimetre square of construction paper in one of two colours. Half of the class should have squares in one colour, and half of the class should have squares in the other colour.

Have students fold their squares diagonally in half, from corner to corner, and then cut along the folded lines to make two halves. Ask students:

- How many different ways can you put the triangles together so that the edges that are touching are the same length?

Have students work independently to solve this problem.

Now, pair up students so that each pair has two triangles in each colour.

Note: If you have an odd number of students in the class, work with the remaining student for this activity.

Tell the pairs of students to combine their triangle halves (each pair should have four halves, two halves in one colour and two halves in a second colour). Pose a second challenge for the pairs to solve by asking:

- How many different ways can you put four triangles together so that the edges that are touching are the same length?

Note: Students should be putting all four triangle halves together to form one new shape, in as many different ways as possible.

When the pairs of students have solved this problem, have them use their scissors to cut each of their triangles in half again. Each pair should now have eight triangles, four in one colour and four in the other colour. Ask:

- How many different ways can you put eight triangles together so that the edges that are touching are the same length?

Activity Centre

Divide the class into groups of two to four players. Provide each group with copies of "The Hexagon Race" game board (one copy for each player), a number cube, yellow hexagon pattern blocks, and red trapezoid pattern blocks (each player will need ten yellow hexagons and twenty red trapezoids).

Have players take turns rolling the number cube and taking as many red trapezoids as the number rolled. At the end of their turns, players may also trade any two red trapezoids (halves) for one yellow hexagon (whole). The first player to fill his/her board with yellow hexagons is the winner (5.17.13).

Extension

Add the terms *half/halves, equal,* and *unequal* to your classroom Math Word Wall.

486   **Hands-On Mathematics • Grade 2**

Fraction Cards A

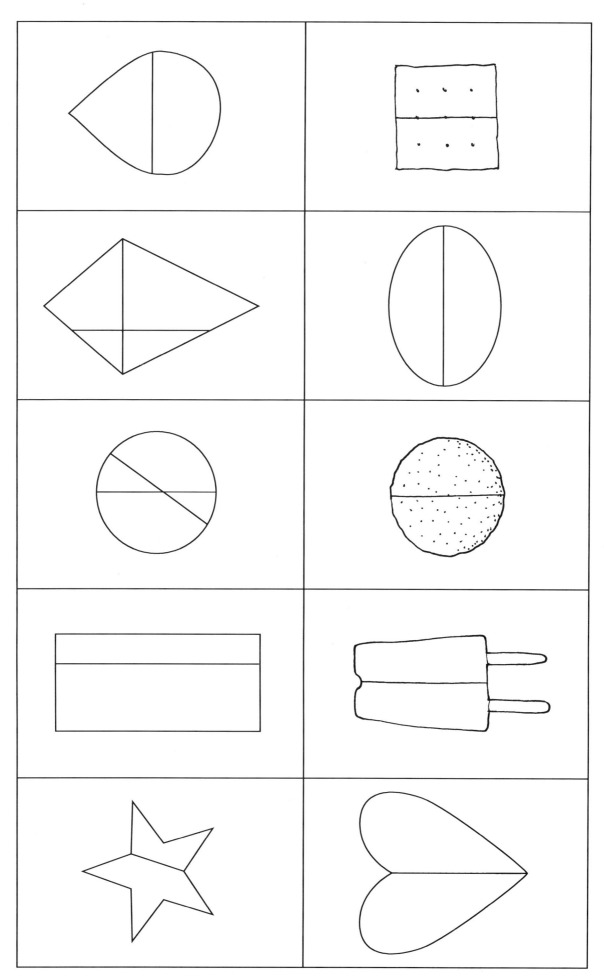

Name: _____

Date: _____

Our Picnic

My Food

$$\frac{1}{2}$$

My Friend's Food

$$\frac{1}{2}$$

17A

488 – 5.17.2

Portage & Main Press, 2006, Hands-On Mathematics, Level 2, ISBN: 978-1-55379-091-4

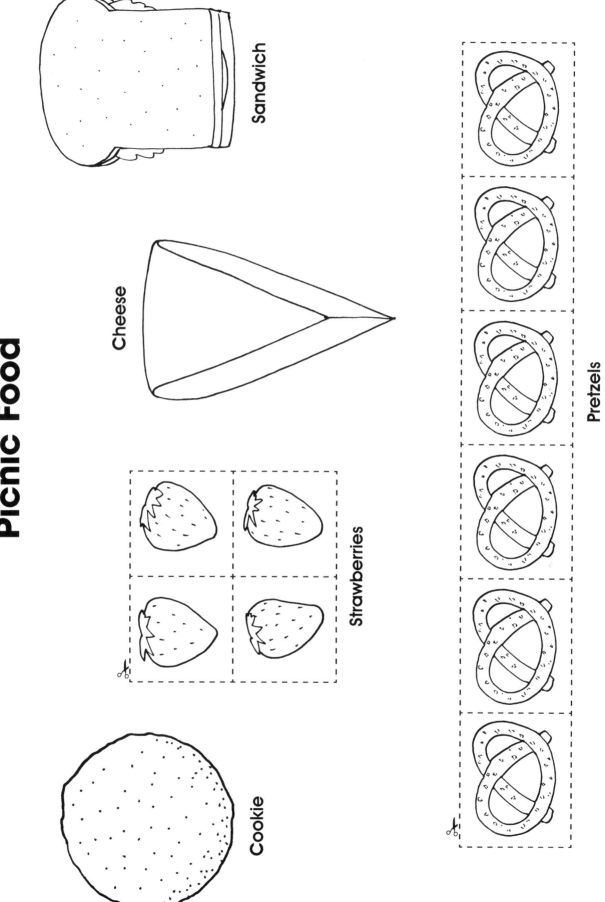

The Hexagon Race Game Board

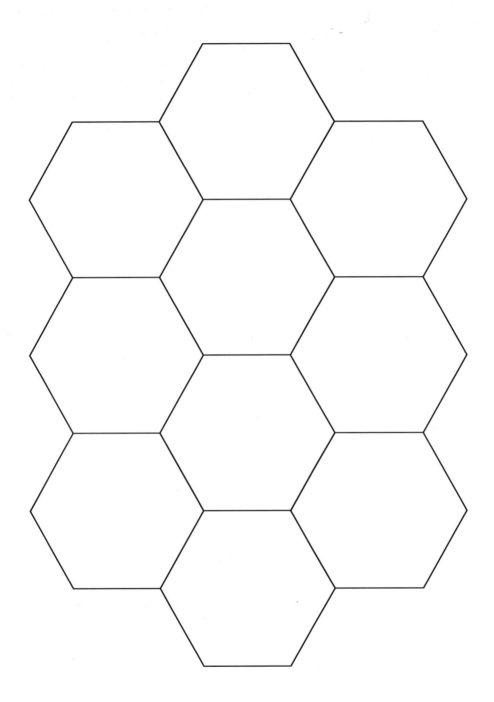

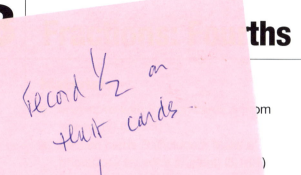

Record ½ on their cards

nd
...arger
...eet of 8½" x 11" construction paper. You will need one of each shape for each group of four students.)
- 8½" x 11" construction paper (of a different colour than the shapes, above. You will need one piece of paper for each group of four students.)
- variety of pasta shapes (macaroni, rotini, shells, bowties, penne, and so on)
- glue
- scissors
- geoboards (one for each student)
- elastic bands (four for each student)

Activity: Part One

Have students sort their sets of fraction cards A into groups of halves and not halves. Review with students that a half is one of two *equal* parts of a divided whole. Have students put aside the cards that do not show halves. Collect these cards.

Provide each student with a set of fraction cards B (5.18.1) and a pair of scissors. Have students cut apart the cards. Ask:

- What can you tell me about how the shapes/pictures on these cards are divided?
- Is each shape divided into the same number of parts?
- Into how many parts are the shapes divided?

Have students sort their set of fraction cards B into shapes that are divided into fourths and shapes that are not. Ask students to put aside the shapes that are not divided into fourths and to focus on the shapes that are divided into fourths. Draw a circle on chart paper. Ask:

- What would one fourth of the circle look like?

Have students share their ideas. Then, divide the circle into fourths, and shade one fourth of the circle. Record the $\frac{1}{4}$ symbol on (or near) each quarter, as in the following diagram:

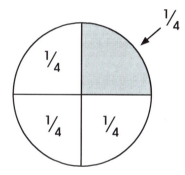

Have students colour in one fourth of each of their "fourths" fraction cards and record the $\frac{1}{4}$ symbol on (or near) each fourth.

Note: Have each student store all of his/her fraction cards (halves, thirds, and fourths) in an envelope.

Activity: Part Two

Divide the class into working groups of four students. Provide each group with one construction-paper circle, one construction-paper square, one construction-paper rectangle, scissors, twenty pieces of rotini, twelve pieces of macaroni, sixteen pasta shells, and eight pasta bowties.

Note: You may substitute different pasta shapes based on their availability.

Challenge groups to divide the materials equally among all group members. As a class, discuss

Unit 5 • **Number Concepts**

18

how the groups divided their materials, or have students write sentences on chart paper to describe how they shared their materials among group members.

Now, distribute a sheet of construction paper and some glue to each group. Have each group create a "Pasta Creature" by arranging all of their materials (pasta and paper shapes) into a character and gluing them onto the sheet of construction paper.

Distribute Activity Sheet A (5.18.2), scissors, and glue to students, and have them divide the birdhouse-making supplies in fourths. Tell students to cut out each item and then glue one fourth of all the supplies onto each workbench.

Activity Sheet A

Note: This is a two-page activity sheet.

Directions to students:

You and three friends are building a birdhouse. Cut out all of the supplies. Divide the supplies into fourths. Glue each person's supplies onto a separate workbench (5.18.2).

Problem Solving

Use four elastic bands to find as many ways as you can to divide a geoboard into fourths. Be sure that you create four equal parts.

Note: A reproducible master for this problem can be found on page 516.

Extension

Add the terms *fourth(s)* and *quarters* to your classroom Math Word Wall.

492

Hands-On Mathematics • Grade 2

Fraction Cards B

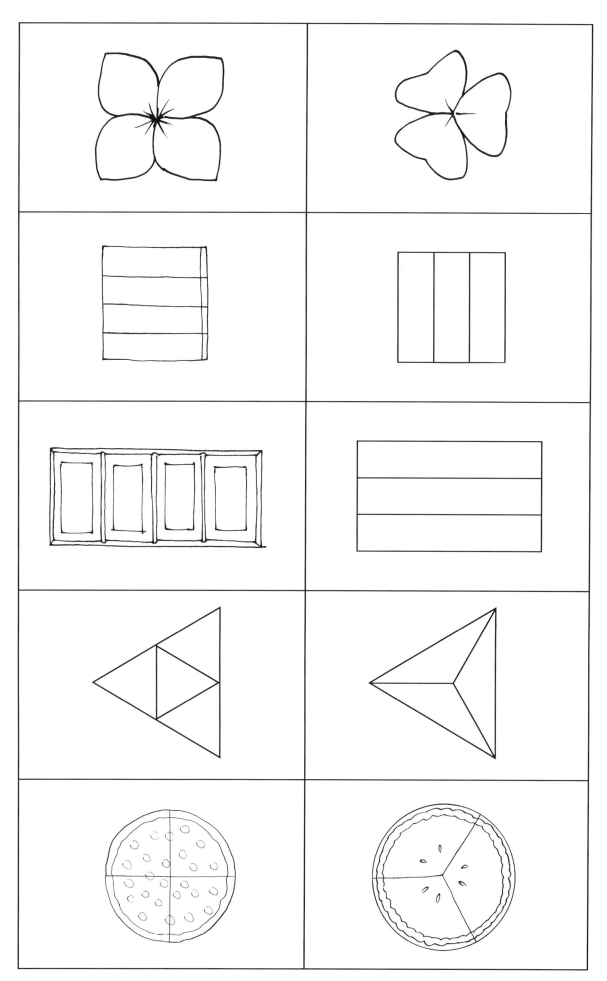

5.18.1 – 493

Name: _____

Date: _____

Building a Birdhouse
Workbenches

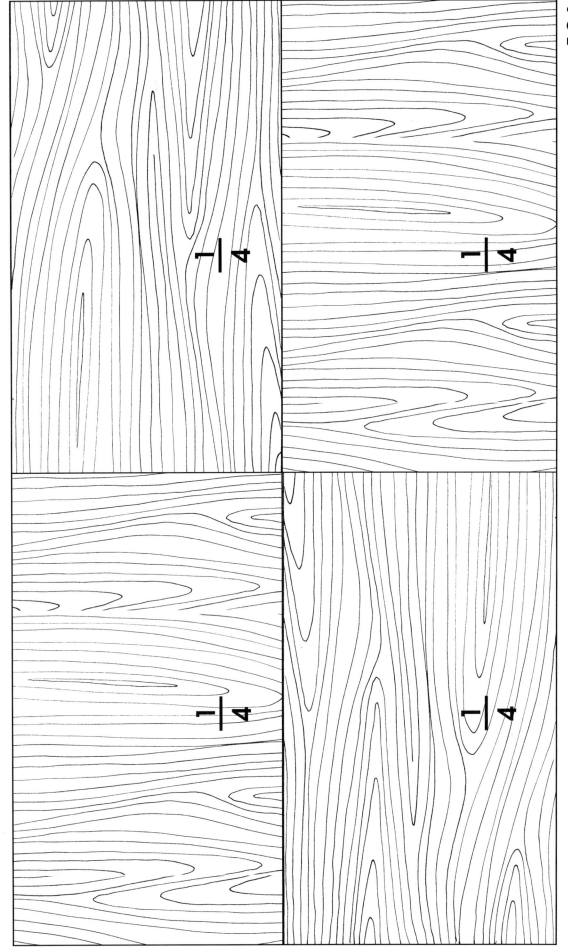

18A

494 – 5.18.2

Portage & Main Press, 2006, Hands-On Mathematics, Level 2, ISBN: 978-1-55379-091-4

Birdhouse Supplies

Wooden Boards

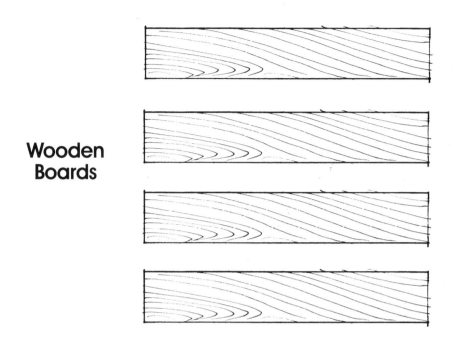

Dowel

Nails

Wooden Triangles

Sandpaper

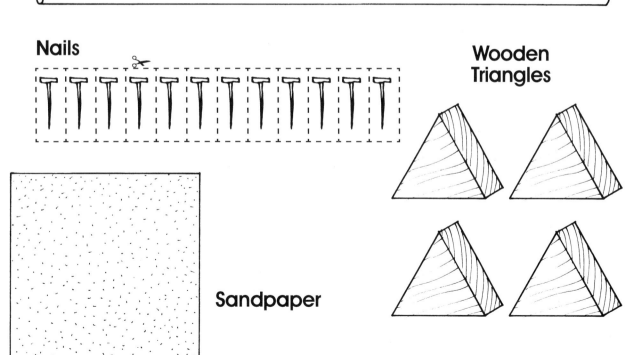

18A

19 Fractions: Thirds

Materials

- fraction cards (both sets *A* and *B*, one set for each student, in envelopes, from lessons 17 and 18)
- chart paper
- markers
- crayons
- paper circles, squares, and rectangles (each shape should be no larger than $1/3$ of a sheet of $8½$" x 11" construction paper. You will need one of each shape for each group of three students.)
- toothpicks
- mini marshmallows
- dried kidney beans
- wooden craft sticks
- construction paper (one piece for each student)
- glue
- scissors

Activity: Part One

Distribute envelopes of fraction cards (*A* and *B*) to students. Have students examine and sort their fraction cards into groups. Then, ask students:

- How did you sort your cards?
- How are the cards in each of your groups different from the cards in your other groups?

Discuss the different ways students sorted their cards. Ask students who did not already sort their cards by fractions to do so now. Ask students:

- Can you point to the cards that show halves?
- Can you point to the cards that show fourths or quarters?
- What does the third group of cards show?

Have students focus on the shapes/pictures divided into thirds. Draw a square on chart paper. Ask students:

- Can you show me one third of the square?

Have students share their ideas. Then, divide the square into thirds, and shade one third of the square. Record the $1/3$ symbol on (or near) each third of the square.

Have students use crayons to colour in one third of each of their "thirds" fraction cards and record the $1/3$ symbol on each part.

Note: Have students store all of their fraction cards in envelopes.

Activity: Part Two

Divide the class into working groups of three students. Provide each group with the following materials: one paper circle, one paper square, one paper rectangle, eighteen toothpicks, fifteen mini marshmallows, twelve dried kidney beans, nine wooden craft sticks.

Note: You may substitute different materials, based on their availability. Also consider any student allergies when using food items such as marshmallows.

First, challenge each group to divide their materials equally among all group members. As a class, discuss how the groups divided their materials, or have students write sentences on chart paper to describe how they shared their materials among group members.

Once all students have their materials, distribute a piece of construction paper to each student, and have students create collages by arranging and gluing all of the materials onto the paper.

Distribute Activity Sheet A (5.19.1), and have students divide the birthday-party supplies into thirds and glue each person's supplies onto the table.

496   Hands-On Mathematics • Grade 2

19

Activity Sheet A

Note: This is a two-page activity sheet.

Directions to students:

You have invited two friends to your birthday party. Divide your party supplies into thirds so that each person gets the same amount of each party supply. Glue each person's supplies onto the table (5.19.1).

Problem Solving

Use three elastic bands to find as many ways as you can to divide a geoboard into thirds. Be sure that you create three equal parts.

Note: A reproducible master for this problem can be found on page 517.

Extension

Add the term *third(s)* to your classroom Math Word Wall.

Unit 5 • **Number Concepts**

Name: _____

Happy Birthday!

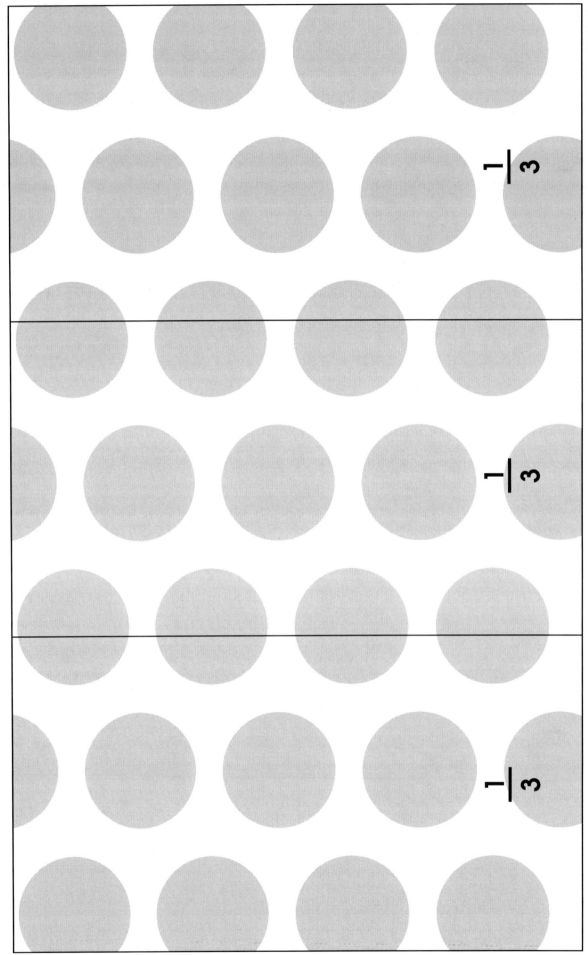

Date: _____

Party Supplies

Birthday Cake

Candies

Pizza

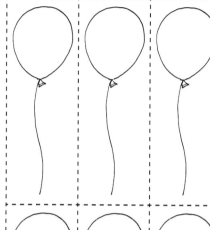

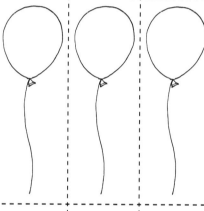

Balloons

Plates

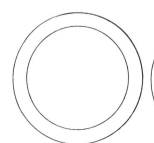 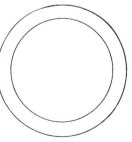 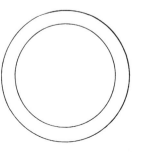

19A

20 More Fractions

Materials

- fraction pieces template (included. Make four photocopies of the sheet for each student, as well as four overhead transparencies of the sheet for demonstration.) (5.20.1)
- large envelopes
- overhead projector
- permanent overhead markers (four different colours)
- chart paper
- markers
- crayons (four different colours for each student)
- scissors
- scrap paper
- construction paper (one sheet for each student)
- small chalkboards or whiteboards
- chalk or whiteboard markers
- bingo chips (thirty-six for each group of five students)
- paper clips (two for each group of five students)
- sharp pencils (two for each group of five students)

Activity: Part One

Before beginning this activity, cut out the overhead-transparency circles from the fraction pieces templates (5.20.1), but do not cut out the individual fraction pieces. You will need one whole circle, two circles showing halves, three circles showing thirds, and four circles showing fourths.

Create a set of overhead fraction pieces (including $1/2$, $2/2$, $1/3$, $2/3$, $3/3$, $1/4$, $2/4$, $3/4$, and $4/4$, as well as one whole circle) by using different coloured permanent overhead markers to colour in different fraction pieces. For example, on a circle showing fourths, colour one quarter of the circle red. On a second circle showing fourths, colour one quarter of the circle red and a second quarter green. On a third circle showing fourths, colour one quarter of the circle red, a second quarter green, and a third circle blue, and so on.

Provide each student with a pair of scissors and four copies of the fraction pieces template (5.20.1). Have students cut out all the fraction-pieces circles (but not the individual fraction pieces).

Display the transparency of the whole circle on the overhead. Ask students:

- Is this circle divided into parts? (no)

Explain that this circle shows one whole. Now, display the circle that shows $1/2$. Ask:

- Is this circle divided into parts?
- Are the parts equal?
- How many parts are shown?
- How many parts are coloured in?

Have each student select a circle showing halves from his/her own set and use a crayon to colour in one half of the circle.

Display the overhead circle that shows $1/3$. Ask students:

- Is this circle divided into parts?
- Are the parts equal?
- How many parts are shown?
- How many parts are coloured in?

Have each student select a circle showing thirds from his/her set and use a crayon to colour in $1/3$ of the circle.

Now, display the overhead circle showing $2/3$. Ask:

- Is this circle divided into parts?
- Are the parts equal?
- How many parts are shown?
- How many parts are coloured in?

500 Hands-On Mathematics • Grade 2

20

Have each student select a circle showing thirds from his/her set and use two different colours of crayons to colour in $\frac{2}{3}$ of the circle (a different colour for each third).

Repeat until each student has created a set of fraction pieces that includes circles showing $\frac{1}{2}$, $\frac{2}{2}$, $\frac{1}{3}$, $\frac{2}{3}$, $\frac{3}{3}$, $\frac{1}{4}$, $\frac{2}{4}$, $\frac{3}{4}$, and $\frac{4}{4}$, as well as one whole circle.

Note: Have students store their fraction pieces in envelopes when not in use.

Activity: Part Two

Provide each student with a sheet of construction paper to use as a work mat. Now, call out a fraction, and record it on chart paper. Have students show the same fraction by finding it among their own fraction pieces and displaying it on their work mats. For example, say:

- Show me one whole. (record on chart paper)
- Show me one fourth.
- Show me two fourths.
- Show me one third.

Repeat the activity, this time having students record the fractions you say on chalkboards or whiteboards.

Distribute Activity Sheet A (5.20.2) and divide students into groups of five to play "Fraction Bingo." Also provide each group with thirty-six bingo chips, two paper clips, two pencils, a pair of scissors, and scrap paper. Have students cut out their fraction bingo cards and spinner templates. Show students how make spinners with the paper clips, pencils and spinner templates. Ask groups to choose one player to be their caller. Have the caller distribute a fraction bingo card and nine bingo chips to each of the other four players. Explain the rules of the game to students.

Activity Sheet A

Note: This is a two-page activity sheet.

Directions to students:

Cut out the four fraction bingo cards. Choose one player to be the caller. Have the caller distribute a fraction bingo card and nine bingo chips to each of the other four players. Cut out the spinner templates. Use paper clips and pencils with the spinner templates to make spinners.

Have the caller spin both the shape spinner and the fraction spinner, one at a time. Then, have the caller call out the fraction and shape he/she spun. For example: "circle, $\frac{1}{3}$." Tell the caller to record the shape/fraction spun on scrap paper. Have players check their fraction bingo cards for shapes with the same fractions shaded. If a player has the correct shape/fraction, have him/her cover it with a bingo chip. Continue until one player fills his/her fraction bingo card and calls out, "Bingo!" Check that player's bingo card against the caller's recorded spins to make sure no errors have been made (5.20.2).

Distribute Activity Sheet B (5.20.3), and have students complete their Carroll diagrams by drawing, dividing, and correctly shading each shape.

Activity Sheet B

Directions to students:

Complete the Carroll diagram: Draw the correct shape in each box. Divide and colour each shape according to the fraction above it (5.20.3).

Unit 5 • **Number Concepts**

20

Problem Solving

■ Draw several squares. Find all the different ways you can divide a square into fourths (four equal parts).

■ Draw a triangle. Find a way to divide the triangle into thirds (three equal parts).

■ Draw a triangle. Find a way to divide the triangle into fourths (four equal parts).

Note: Reproducible masters for these problems can be found on page 517.

Fraction Pieces Template

Date: _____ Name: _____

Fraction Bingo
Fraction Bingo Cards

504 – 5.20.2   Portage & Main Press, 2006, Hands-On Mathematics, Level 2, ISBN: 978-1-55379-091-4   **20A**

Name: _____

Date: _____

Spinner Templates

Fraction Spinner

Shape Spinner

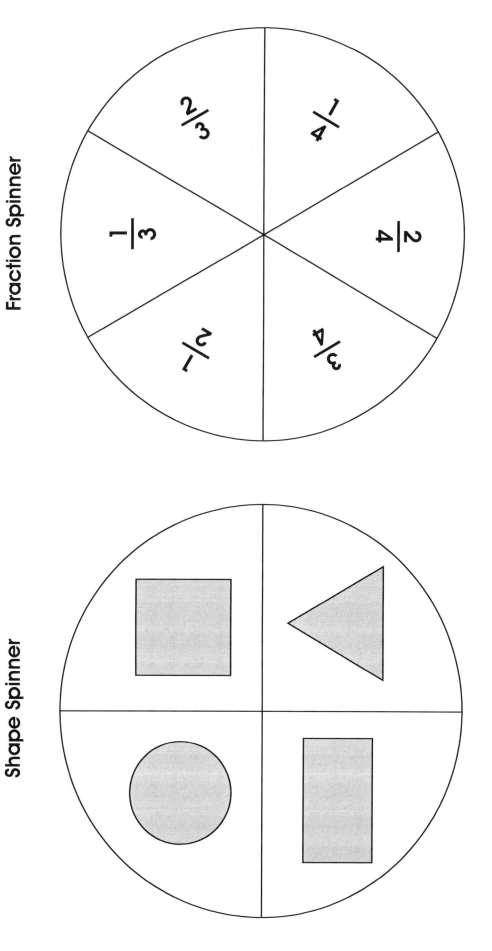

20A

Name: _____

Date: _____

Shape Fractions

	$\frac{1}{4}$	$\frac{1}{3}$	$\frac{1}{2}$	$\frac{2}{4}$	$\frac{2}{3}$	$\frac{3}{4}$
●						
■						
▬						
◄						

506 – 5.20.3

Portage & Main Press, 2006, Hands-On Mathematics, Level 2, ISBN: 978-1-55379-091-4

20B

21 | Comparing Fractions

Background Information for Teachers

At the grade two level, students are not expected to use standard fractional notation when comparing fractions (for example, ¾, ⅝). However, the fraction pieces used in this lesson are identified for clarification (for example, ½, ¼, ⅛).

Materials

- pattern blocks (you will need a large quantity)
- chart paper
- markers (colours to match pattern block pieces)
- fraction pieces (made by students in previous lessons) (5.20.1)
- overhead transparencies of fraction pieces (from lesson 20)
- overhead projector
- paper clips (one for each student)
- pencils (one for each student)

Activity: Part One

Have students sit in a circle. Place a large quantity of pattern blocks in the centre, and ask each student to take one hexagon. Ask:

- How could you cover half of your hexagon?
- Which block could you use to do this?
- Can you think of another way to cover half of the hexagon?

Allow students time to explore ways to cover half of their hexagons. Have students share their solutions, and record their ideas by drawing the shapes on chart paper. For example, draw a yellow hexagon and then draw the red trapezoid inside half of the hexagon. Or, draw the yellow hexagon and then draw three green triangles inside half of the hexagon.

Discuss with students how the area covered by the trapezoid is equal to the area covered by the three triangles.

Now, have students focus on their hexagons again. Ask:

- How could you cover one third of the hexagon?
- Which block could you use to do this?
- Can you think of another way to cover one third of the hexagon?

Allow students time to explore ways to cover one third of their hexagons. Have students share their solutions, and record their ideas by drawing the shapes on chart paper. For example, draw a yellow hexagon and then draw a blue rhombus inside one third of the hexagon.

Note: Ensure that the rhombus you draw is the same shape as the *blue*-rhombus pattern block, not the tan-rhombus pattern block.

Or, draw the yellow hexagon, and then draw two green triangles inside one third of the hexagon.

Discuss with students how the area covered by the trapezoid is equal to the area covered by the three triangles.

Activity: Part Two

Use the overhead fraction pieces (5.20.1) to compare fractions for students. For example, display the circles showing ½ and ²/₄. Say:

- Look carefully at the coloured parts of these two circles. How are these circles different?
- How are these circles the same?
- Is the coloured area on both circles equal?

Overlap one circle on top of the other to show that the coloured areas are equal.

Now, have students use their fraction pieces to compare fractions. Ask students to spread out all of their fraction pieces in front of them. Ask questions such as:

- Can you display the fraction piece that shows ¹/₃?

▶

Unit 5 • **Number Concepts**   507

21

- Can you display the fraction piece that shows $\frac{1}{4}$?
- Which is the larger fraction?

Check for understanding by having students hold up their selected fraction pieces. Display the overhead fraction pieces showing $\frac{1}{3}$ and $\frac{1}{4}$. Overlap one circle on top of the other to show that the shaded area of the $\frac{1}{3}$ fraction piece is larger than the shaded area of the $\frac{1}{4}$ fraction piece.

Repeat this activity by comparing different fraction pieces.

Distribute Activity Sheet A (5.21.1) and scissors, and have students cut out their game boards, spinner templates, and fraction game pieces. Also, ask students to cut apart their fraction game pieces along the dotted lines.

Have students play "The Fraction Race" game in pairs. Distribute paper clips and pencils to students, and show them how to use them with their spinner templates to make spinners. Explain the rules of the game to students.

Activity Sheet A

Note: This is a two-page activity sheet.

Directions to students:

Cut out the game board, the spinner template, and the fraction game pieces. Cut apart the fraction game pieces along the dotted lines. Use a paper clip and a pencil with the spinner templates to make a spinner.

Play "The Fraction Race Game" with a partner. Take turns spinning your spinners, finding fraction game pieces to match the fractions spun, and placing the game pieces in circles on your game boards. The first player to fill in all the circles on his/her game board wins the game (5.21.1).

Problem Solving

You have half a pizza. How would you share it with 2 friends? With 3 friends? Four friends? Show your work.

Note: A reproducible master for this problem can be found on page 517.

Extension

Have students play "The Fraction Race Game" again, this time adding $\frac{1}{8}$ game pieces and a $\frac{1}{8}$ space to the spinner ($\frac{1}{8}$ game pieces and new spinner included). If a player lands on the "Free" space on the new spinner, he/she selects the fraction piece of his/her choice to place on his/her game board (5.21.2).

Assessment Suggestion

Use the Student Self-Assessment sheet, found on page 28, to have students reflect on their learning about fractions.

508

Hands-On Mathematics • Grade 2

The Fraction Race Game
Game Board

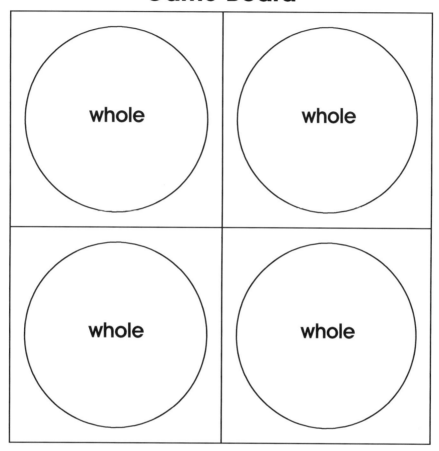

Spinner Template

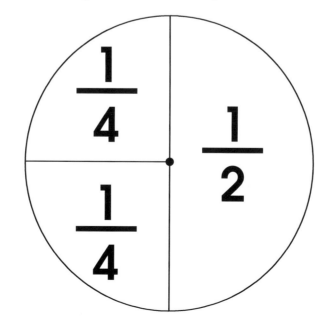

Fraction Game Pieces

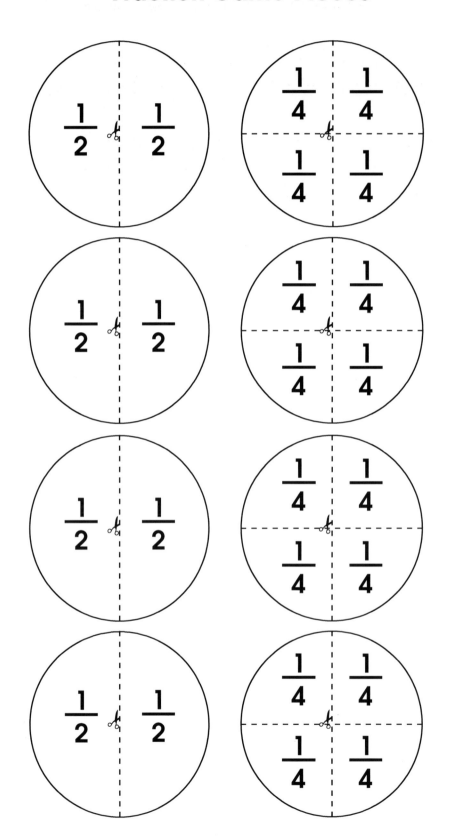

Extension Game Pieces and Spinner

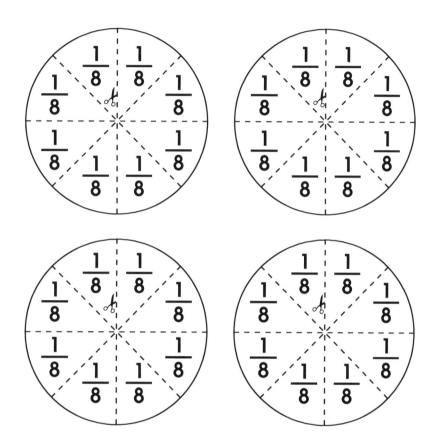

Spinner Templates

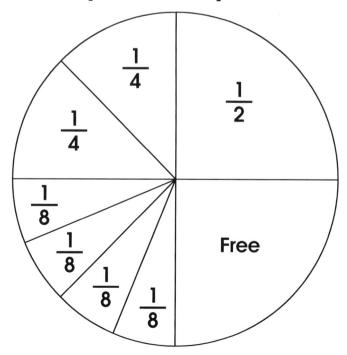

Extension

22 Using What We Know: Number of the Week

Background Information for Teachers

This lesson reviews the concepts on which students have focused throughout the unit. Repeat the activity whenever appropriate throughout the school year.

Activity

Choose a number to explore with students Consider choosing:

- the day of the month
- the number of days students have been in school
- any other number that will successfully challenge students' skills

Use your selected number to explore some or all of the following with students:

- number formation
- the number written in number words
- the number written as an ordinal
- a dot pattern representation of the number
- the number that is 1 less than your selected number
- the number that is 1 more than your selected number
- the number that is 10 less than your selected number
- the number that is 10 more than your selected number
- the number represented with coins
- the number represented as tens and ones
- the number as odd or even
- the number as part of an addition sentence
- the number as part of a subtraction sentence
- a story problem, with this number as the answer

Distribute Activity Sheet A (5.22.1). In the centre box of their activity sheets, have students print the number explored in class. Ask students to fill in the rest of the boxes.

Activity Sheet A

Directions to students:

In the centre box of your activity sheet, print the number explored in class. Fill in the rest of the boxes (5.22.1).

512　　　　　　　　　　　　　　　　Hands-On Mathematics • Grade 2

Name:

Date:

Number of the Week

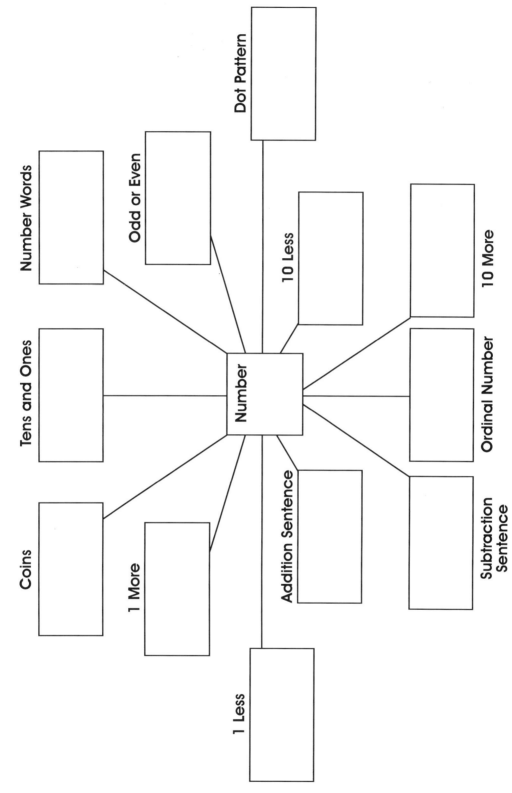

A story problem with this number as the answer: _____

22A

Problem-Solving Black Line Master: Number Concepts

Copy the following four sheets onto overhead transparencies to present to students as daily problem-solving activities. Or, photocopy the pages, and cut them apart for students, problem by problem. Have students paste them into their math journals or agendas for completion independently.

✂ --

Use a hundred chart to help you answer these questions:
- How many numbers do you say when you count from 1 to 100 by 2s?
- How many numbers do you say when you count from 1 to 100 by 5s?
- How many numbers do you say when you count from 1 to 100 by 10s?
- What are all the numbers that you say *both* when you count by 5s *and* when you count by 10s?
- What are all the numbers that you say *both* when you count by 2s *and* when you count by 10s?
- How many numbers do you say when you count from 1 to 100 by 25s?

From unit 5, lesson 4, page 389

✂ --

Unscramble the following number words:
- eesnv
- ihegt
- wto
- urfo
- weetlv

From unit 5, lesson 5, page 399

✂ --

Abby is twelfth in line, Carmina is sixteenth in line. Linda is in front of Carmina. Nicole is behind Abby. Randy is between Linda and Nicole. In what place in line is Randy? Draw a picture.

From unit 5, lesson 6, page 412

▶

514   Portage & Main Press, 2006, Hands-On Mathematics, Level 2, ISBN: 978-1-55379-091-4

A grade-two class is making a number line. Each day, the students add a few more numbers to the number line. On Tuesday, the students stopped at number 34. On Wednesday, they added 20 more numbers to the number line. Draw a number line, and write the 20 numbers the students added to it on Wednesday.

From unit 5, lesson 7, page 426

Use a ruler to draw a line on a piece of paper. Record 0 at one end of the line, and record 20 at the other end. Draw a dot in the middle of the line. Now, record the number that goes in the middle of the line, where you drew the dot. Then, fill in the rest of the numbers from 1 to 20.

From unit 5, lesson 8, page 434

Draw 100 objects in a way that a friend can count them without having to count by 1s.

From unit 5, lesson 9, page 439

Find all the numbers that are greater than 5 but less than 20. Make a number line to help you.

From unit 5, lesson 10, page 444

You are sharing a box of chocolates with your friend. If there are 20 chocolates in the box, do you each get an equal amount? Record a number sentence to show whether or not the two sets of chocolates are equal. Use the = or ≠ sign.

From unit 5, lesson 11, page 451

Now, you are sharing a box of 25 chocolates with your friend. Do you each get an equal amount? Record a number sentence to show whether or not the two sets of chocolates are equal. Use the = or ≠ sign.

From unit 5, lesson 11, page 451

▶

Portage & Main Press, 2006, Hands-On Mathematics, Level 2, ISBN: 978-1-55379-091-4   **515**

The Rabbit family is going snowshoeing. Mrs. Rabbit found 15 snowshoes in the closet. Mr. Rabbit found 21 snowshoes in the basement. Together, do they have an even number of snowshoes or an odd number? How many rabbits can go snowshoeing?

From unit 5, lesson 12, page 456

There are four grade-two classes at Sunnybrook School. Room 2A has 18 students, room 2B has 23 students, room 2C has 25 students, and room 2D has 26 students. Use rounding off to estimate how many grade-two students go to Sunnybrook School.

From unit 5, lesson 13, page 461

Estimate how many letters there are in the first names of all students in the class. Record your estimate. Now, count how many letters there actually are in the first names of all students in the class.

From unit 5, lesson 14, page 465

There are 84 cookies. You need to put the cookies into packages of 10. How many packages of 10 cookies can you make? Are there any leftovers? How many?

From unit 5, lesson 15, page 472

Make a chart to show all the ways you can make 43 cents using only pennies and dimes.

From unit 5, lesson 16, page 480

Use four elastic bands to find as many ways as you can to divide a geoboard into fourths. Be sure that you create four equal parts.

From unit 5, lesson 18, page 492

▶

516   Portage & Main Press, 2006, Hands-On Mathematics, Level 2, ISBN: 978-1-55379-091-4

Use three elastic bands to find as many ways as you can to divide a geoboard into thirds. Be sure that you create three equal parts.

From unit 5, lesson 19, page 497

Draw several squares. Find all the different ways you can divide a square into fourths (four equal parts).

From unit 5, lesson 20, page 502

Draw a triangle. Find a way to divide the triangle into thirds (three equal parts).

From unit 5, lesson 20, page 502

Draw a triangle. Find a way to divide the triangle into fourths (four equal parts).

From unit 5, lesson 20, page 502

You have half a pizza. How would you share it with 2 friends? With 3 friends? Four friends? Show your work.

From unit 5, lesson 21, page 508

References for Teachers

Baratta-Lorton, Mary. *Mathematics Their Way.* Parsippany NJ: Dale Seymour Publications, 1995.

Burns, Marilyn. *Math by All Means: Place Value, Grades 1-2.* Sausalito, CA: Math Solutions Publications, 1994.

Burns, Marilyn, and Bonnie Tank. *A Collection of Math Lessons from Grades 1 through 3.* Sausalito, CA: Math Solution Publications, 1987.

Currah, Joanne, and Jane Felling. *Box Cars and One-Eyed Jacks.* Edmonton: Box Cars and One-Eyed Jacks Publications, 1996.

D'Aboy, Diana. *The Place Value Connection.* Palo Alto, CA: Dale Seymour Publications, 1985.

Fosnot, Catherine Twomey, and Maarten Dolk. *Young Mathematicians at Work: Constructing Number Sense, Addition, and Subtraction.* Portsmouth, NH: Heinemann, 2001.

Friederwitzer, Fredda, and Barbara Berman. *Mathematics Getting in Touch: Activities with Manipulatives.* Vernon Hills, IL: Cuisenaire, 1985.

Reys, Barbara, and Robert Reys. *Number Sense: Simple Effective Number Sense Experiences, Grades 1-2.* Parsippany NJ: Dale Seymour Publications, 1997.

Richardson, Kathy. *Developing Number Concepts: Place Value, Multiplication, and Division.* Parsippany, NJ: Dale Seymour Publications, 1998.

Wright, Robert J., et al. *Teaching Number: Advancing Children's Skills and Strategies.* Thousand Oaks, CA: Paul Chapman, 2002.

Zullie, Matthew E. *Fractions with Pattern Blocks.* Desoto, TX: Creative Publications, 1988.

Unit 6
Number Operations

Books for Children

Aker, Suzanne. *What Comes in 2s, 3s, and 4s?* New York: Simon and Schuster, 1990.

Axelrod, Amy. *Pigs Will Be Pigs*. Toronto: Maxwell Macmillan Canada, 1994.

Boynton, Sandra. *Hippos Go Berserk!* New York: Simon & Schuster Books, 1996.

Buckless, Andrea. *Too Many Cooks*. New York: Scholastic, 2000.

Chorao, Kay. *Number One Number Fun*. New York: Holiday House, 1995.

Chwast, Seymour. *The Twelve Circus Rings*. San Diego: Harcourt Brace Jovanovich, 1993.

Day, Nancy Raines. *Double Those Wheels*. New York: Dutton Children's Books, 2003.

Edens, Cooper. *How Many Bears?* New York: Atheneum, 1994.

Garland, Sherry. *The Lotus Seed*. San Diego: Harcourt Brace Jovanovich, 1993.

Giganti Jr., Paul. *Each Orange Had Eight Slices: A Counting Book*. New York: Mulberry Books, 1994.

Greenberg, Dan. *Mega-Funny Math Poems and Problems*. New York: Scholastic, 1999.

Hong, Lily Toy. *Two of Everything: A Chinese Folktale*. Morton Grove, IL: A. Whitman, 1993.

Hulme, Joy N. *Counting by Kangaroos*. New York: Scientific American Books for Young Readers, 1995.

_____. *Sea Squares*. New York: Hyperion Books for Children, 1991.

Hutchins, Pat. *The Doorbell Rang*. New York: Greenwillow Books, 1986.

Lottridge, Celia Barker. *One Watermelon Seed*. Toronto: Oxford University Press, 1986.

Murphy, Stuart J. *Divide and Ride*. New York: HarperCollins, 1997.

_____. *The Shark Swimathon*. New York: HarperCollins, 2001.

_____. *Too Many Kangaroo Things to Do!* New York: HarperCollins, 1996.

Neuschwander, Cindy. *Amanda Bean's Amazing Dream*. New York: Scholastic, 1998.

Pinczes, Elinor J. *One Hundred Hungry Ants*. Boston: Houghton Mifflin, 1993.

_____. *A Remainder of One*. Boston: Houghton Mifflin, 1995.

Rylant, Cynthia. *The Relatives Came*. New York: Maxwell Macmillan International, 1993.

Silverstein, Shel. *Where the Sidewalk Ends*. New York: Harper and Row, 1974.

Viorst, Judith. Alexander, *Who Used to Be Rich Last Sunday*. New York: Aladdin Books, 1988.

Introduction

The activities in this unit are designed to develop students' understanding of number operations. Story problems are used throughout the unit to provide a purpose for the mathematical tasks. The contexts provided will help students understand the meaning of the operations.

Note: The "Expressions and Equality" expectations from the Patterning and Algebra strand of *The Ontario Curriculum (2005)* are addressed in this unit as they are related to skills and concepts of number operations.

Several lessons in this unit include a section called "Next Step(s)," which guides teachers through a subsequent activity or sequence of activities to carry out with students, following developmentally from the preceding activity or activities.

As new math strategies are introduced in this unit, create wall charts such as the following:

Mental Math Strategies We Know
Doubles
Near doubles (+1, −1)
Count-on
Count back
Think addition

Problem Solving Strategies We Know
Draw a diagram
Guess and check
Make a chart
Look for a pattern
Work backward
Solve with smaller numbers

Throughout this unit, you may also consider including daily target-number activities, in which students are challenged with tasks such as the following:

- generate the number by adding two other numbers
- generate the number by subtracting one number from another number
- double the number
- find the sum of the number plus 20
- find the difference between the number and 5
- determine if the number is even or odd
- determine if the number is said when counting by 2s, 5s, 10s, and 25s

Students may have more suggestions for challenging tasks to complete with the daily target number.

Editorial Note to Teachers

Recent international research suggests that exposing students to *vertical* algorithms too early inhibits their ability to acquire flexible thinking strategies and number sense. Hence, in the **Hands-On Mathematics** books, the horizontal format is used to present addition and subtraction algorithms. You are encouraged to do likewise.

Mathematics Vocabulary

Throughout this unit, teachers should use, and encourage students to use, vocabulary such as: *double, addition, near doubles, subtraction, addend, domino, facts, digit, one digit, two digit, equal, pattern, multiply, multiplication, divide, division,* and *array*.

Continue to use your classroom Math Word Wall as a means of focusing on new vocabulary. As new terms are introduced in the unit, print them on index cards, and display them alphabetically on the Math Word Wall.

Unit 6 • **Number Operations**

1 Addition – Doubles

Background Information for Teachers

The activities in this lesson focus first on addition to 10. As students gain addition skills, next steps include addition to 18.

Materials

- *Double Those Wheels*, a book by Nancy Raines Day
- bingo chips (two colours)
- overhead projector

Activity: Part One

Read the book *Double Those Wheels* with students. Ask:

- In the story, where is the monkey going?
- Why is he going there?
- Why does the monkey keep changing vehicles?
- What happens to the number of wheels each time the monkey changes vehicles?

Read the story again with students. This time, discuss the pictures that show the different vehicles the monkey uses. Help students recognize that adding the number of wheels on both sides of a vehicle or adding the number of wheels on the front half and the back half of a vehicle doubles the number of wheels.

Select one student to name a number that is less than 6. Now, help students double the number by telling them first to hold up fingers on one hand to represent the number named. Then, have students hold up that many fingers on their other hand. For example, if the number is 3, students should hold up three fingers on one hand and then double that by holding up three fingers on the other hand. Ask students:

- How many fingers are you holding up?

Repeat the activity with different numbers that are less than 6.

Activity: Part Two

Before turning on the overhead projector, use two different colours of bingo chips to make a doubles pattern on the screen, as in the following diagram:

Have students focus on the dark screen. Then, turn on the projector long enough for students to see the pattern without being able to count the chips. Ask:

- How many chips are there?
- How do you know?

Repeat the activity for other doubles patterns to 10.

Note: The technique of displaying visual representations of numbers for short periods of time is a strategy called *flash math*. Using flash math techniques helps students develop their abilities to instantly recognize random dot patterns, referred to as *subitizing*.

Next Steps

- Introduce addition doubles to 18.
- Introduce students to the related subtraction facts (subtraction number sentences) that involve doubles to 10. For example:
    - $10 - 5 = 5$
    - $8 - 4 = 4$
    - $6 - 3 = 3$

Discuss with students the patterns that they see in the subtraction facts.

1

Problem Solving

Note: The following problem refers to the book *Double Those Wheels*.

- In the story, the last vehicle the monkey used had 64 wheels. If the monkey changed vehicles one *more* time, how many wheels would the new vehicle have?

- At snack time, each student gets 1 piece of cheese and 2 crackers. Make a chart to find out how many pieces of cheese and how many crackers are needed for 10 students. What about for 20 students? To help you, use the following sample chart for 4 students:

Students	Cheese	Crackers
1	1	2
2	2	4
3	3	6
4	4	8

Note: A reproducible master for the previous problem can be found on page 729.

Activity Centre

Place number cubes and copies of the doubles game scoring sheets (included) at an activity centre, and have students play the "Doubles Game" in pairs or small groups. Each player starts with ten points. Players take turns rolling two number cubes. If players roll doubles, they add to their scores the sum of the two numbers showing on the number cubes. If players do not roll doubles, they lose one point. The first player to get twenty or more points wins. Have each student keep track of his/her own score on a copy of the "Doubles Game" scoring sheet (6.1.1).

Extensions

- Add the term *double(s)* to your classroom Math Word Wall.

- Distribute to students sets of dominos, and ask them to sort the dominos into two groups: doubles and not doubles.

- Provide students with some examples of real-life doubles patterns. For example, each of our fingers (on one hand) has a double (on the other hand); each leg on an insect has a double; each egg cup in an egg carton has a double; each leg on a table has a double. Have students identify other examples of doubles. Keep a running list of students' ideas on chart paper. Then, make a class doubles book, including one example on each page.

- Ask students to solve the following doubles riddles:

  I am thinking of a number.
  The number is between 5 and 10.
  If you double my number, you get 12.
  What is my number?

  I am thinking of a number
  The number is less than 10.
  If you double my number, you get 18.
  What is my number?

  I am thinking of a number.
  It is an odd number.
  If you double my number, you get 14.
  What is my number?

  I am thinking of a number.
  The number is even and is less than 10.
  If you double my number you get 16.
  What is my number?

▶

Unit 6 • **Number Operations**

1

I am thinking of a number.
My number's tens digit is the double
of the ones digit.
What number am I?

Note: The last riddle has many answers. Take the opportunity to discuss with students that in mathematics, there is often more than one possible solution to a problem.

Assessment Suggestion

Ask students:

- What does it mean to double a number?

Have students write the answer to this question in their math journals. In students' answers, look for:

- understanding that a number is doubled when it is added to itself
- appropriate examples

Record your comments on copies of the Anecdotal Record sheet, found on page 22.

Date: _____   **Name:** _____

Doubles Game Scoring Sheet

Roll		Score
Doubles (add sum)	Not Doubles (−1)	
⎯	⎯	10

Activity Centre

Portage & Main Press, 2006, Hands-On Mathematics, Level 2, ISBN: 978-1-55379-091-4

6.1.1 – 525

2 Addition – Near Doubles

Background Information for Teachers

Near doubles, or the doubles-plus-one facts, include all combinations of numbers in which one addend is one more than the other addend (4 + 5; 3 + 2; and so on). The strategy for finding the sum of two near-doubles numbers is to double the smaller number and add one.

Before introducing this strategy to students, conduct one-on-one interviews to make sure they have mastered the doubles facts to 10: 1 + 1; 2 + 2; 3 + 3; 4 + 4; 5 + 5. If students have not mastered them, review and practice these addition facts before moving on to this lesson.

Work first with near-doubles facts to 10 and then progress to near-doubles facts to 18.

Materials

- felt or magnetic board
- felt disks or magnets
- bingo chips
- chart paper
- markers
- red pencils (one for each student)
- green pencils (one for each student)
- number cubes
- dominos (several tiles or cards for each student)
- crayons, markers, or coloured pencils

Activity: Near Doubles to Ten

Distribute a handful of bingo chips to each student. Display the felt/magnetic board where all students can see it. Arrange a set of four felt disks (or magnets) on the board, and have students use their bingo chips to make the same arrangement at their desks, as in the following diagram:

○ ○
○ ○

Add a second set of four disks to the first set, and have students do the same with their bingo chips, as in the following diagram:

○ ○   ○ ○
○ ○   ○ ○

Ask:

- How many bingo chips do you have in each group?
- How many bingo chips do you have altogether?

Write 4 + 4 = 8 on a piece of chart paper.

Next, add one more disk to the second set, and have students do the same with their bingo chips, as in the following diagram:

○ ○   ○ ○
○ ○   ○ ○ ○

Ask students:

- How many bingo chips do you have in your first set?
- How many bingo chips do you have in your second set?
- How many bingo chips do you have altogether?

Write 4 + 5 = 9 on chart paper. Explain to students that 4 + 5 = 9 is called a *near doubles* since it is one more than the double 4 + 4. Repeat the activity for other near doubles

Distribute to each student a copy of Activity Sheet A (6.2.1), a red pencil, and a green pencil. Have students use their red pencils to record answers to the doubles facts and their green pencils to record answers to the near-doubles facts. Tell students *not* to answer the other questions.

526   Hands-On Mathematics • Grade 2

2

Activity Sheet A

Directions to students:

Use a red pencil to record answers to the doubles facts. Use a green pencil to record answers to the near-doubles facts. Do not answer the other questions (6.2.1).

Next Steps

- Have students work in pairs to build near-doubles facts. Distribute to each pair two copies of Activity Sheet B (6.2.2), a number cube, several bingo chips, and some crayons, markers, or coloured pencils. Have students take turns rolling their number cubes. Tell them to use the number rolled to model, say, and then colour a near-doubles fact on one of the twenty frames on their sheets. For example, if a player rolls a 6, he/she uses bingo chips to model 6 + 7 = 13 on the twenty frame. He/she then says the fact and draws 6 + 7 = 13 on the twenty frame.

Note: Be sure students understand that they should first use their bingo chips to make the double of the number rolled and then add one more chip to model the near-double fact.

- Distribute to each student a copy of Activity Sheet C (6.2.3), several dominos, and some crayons, markers, or coloured pencils. Have students find all the dominos in their collections that show near-doubles facts. Tell students to draw each near-doubles domino on their activity sheets. Also have students record the near-doubles (addition) fact that goes with each near-doubles domino as well as its related doubles fact. Finally, have students record their thinking strategy for each near-doubles domino.

- Distribute to each student a copy of Activity Sheet D (6.2.4), a red pencil, and a green pencil. Have students use their red pencils to record answers to the doubles facts and their green pencils to record answers to the near-doubles facts. Tell students *not* to answer the other questions.

Activity Sheet B

Directions to students:

Work with a partner. Take turns rolling the number cube and using bingo chips and the number rolled to model a near-doubles fact on a twenty frame. Then, say the near-doubles fact, and colour it on the twenty frame (6.2.2).

Activity Sheet C

Note: This is a two-page activity sheet.

Directions to students:

Find all the dominos in your collection that show near doubles. Draw each near-doubles domino on your activity sheet. Record the near-doubles (addition) fact that goes with each near-doubles domino. Also, record its related doubles fact. Finally, record your thinking strategy for each near-doubles domino (6.2.3).

Activity Sheet D

Directions to students:

Use a red pencil to record answers to the doubles facts. Use a green pencil to record answers to the near-doubles facts. Do not answer the other questions (6.2.4).

▶

Unit 6 • **Number Operations**

2

Problem Solving

- There are 5 trees in Jason's front yard. There are 4 trees in Jason's backyard. Altogether, how many trees are there in Jason's yard?

- Mandy has 8 pieces of candy. She buys 9 more pieces of candy. How many pieces of candy does Mandy have now?

- Leila read 7 books in March and 8 books in April. How many books did Leila read altogether?

Note: A reproducible master for these problems can be found on pages 729 and 730.

Activity Centre

Prepare a near-doubles bingo card for each student as well as a deck of "thinking-strategy" cards. Use the examples below as models:

Near-Doubles Bingo Card

3 + 4	8 + 7	FREE	2 + 1
4 + 5	6 + 5	9 + 8	4 + 3
2 + 3	8 + 9	6 + 7	5 + 6
7 + 6	FREE	5 + 4	7 + 8

Thinking-Strategy Card

Think 7 + 7
and one more.

Students can also make their own bingo cards by randomly writing near-doubles facts in the squares of 4 x 4 grids.

Distribute to each student a near-doubles bingo card and four bingo chips, and have students play "Near-Doubles Bingo." Read a thinking-strategy card aloud, and have students search their near-doubles bingo cards for the appropriate fact. If they find the fact, have them cover it with a bingo chip. The first player to cover four near doubles in a row (horizontally, vertically, or diagonally) wins.

Note: There may be more than one near-double fact that satisfies a given thinking-strategy card. For example, both 7 + 8 and 8 + 7 are possible answers to the example of the thinking-strategy card provided. Players can only cover one near-double fact for each thinking-strategy card you read.

Extensions

- Add the term *near double(s)* to your classroom Math Word Wall.

- Introduce students to the doubles-plus-two strategy.

- Have pairs of students play "Four-in-a-Row Addition." Distribute to each pair of students a "Four-in-a-Row Addition" game board (included), two paper clips, two colours of bingo chips, and a pair of scissors. Have students cut along the dotted lines on their game boards.

Tell Player A in each pair to begin by clipping each of two paper clips to the game board under each of two numbers in the row of numbers at the bottom. Then, have Player A add those two numbers together and use a bingo chip to cover that number (sum) on the 4 x 4 grid.

Next, have Player B move *one* of the two paper clips to a new number in the row of numbers, leaving the second paper clip where it is. Ask Player B to add together the two numbers marked with paper clips and then use the other colour of bingo chip to

2

cover that number (sum) on the 4 x 4 grid. Play continues until one player has four bingo chips in a row (vertically, horizontally, or diagonally) (6.2.5).

Note: A number can only be covered once on the 4 x 4 grid. If a player builds a sum that is already covered with a bingo chip, he/she does not put down another chip. It is the other player's turn.

Assessment Suggestion

To determine whether or not students recognize different computation strategies, meet with each student individually, and give him/her a set of assessment addition-fact cards (included).

Ask students to sort the cards into three groups: doubles facts; near-doubles facts; and other, as in the following diagram:

Begin with addition facts to 10. If students show appropriate understanding, include addition facts to 18. Use the Individual Student Observations sheet, found on page 23, to record results (6.2.6, 6.2.7).

Unit 6 • Number Operations

Date: _____   **Name:** _____

Fact Finder to 10

4 + 4 = _____   3 + 7 = _____

1 + 4 = _____   1 + 2 = _____

3 + 4 = _____   3 + 3 = _____

6 + 4 = _____   3 + 2 = _____

3 + 4 = _____   5 + 4 = _____

4 + 3 = _____   5 + 5 = _____

2 + 6 = _____   1 + 1 = _____

4 + 5 = _____   2 + 2 = _____

9 + 1 = _____   3 + 3 = _____

3 + 4 = _____   5 + 5 = _____

530 – 6.2.1   Portage & Main Press, 2006, Hands-On Mathematics, Level 2, ISBN: 978-1-55379-091-4   **2A**

Name: _____

Date: _____

2B

Near-Doubles Facts

Portage & Main Press, 2006, Hands-On Mathematics, Level 2, ISBN: 978-1-55379-091-4   6.2.2 – **531**

Date: _____   Name: _____

Doubles and Near Doubles

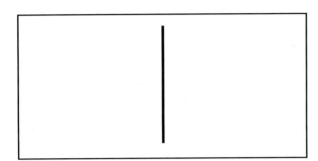

Near-Doubles Fact: ___ + ___ = ___

Doubles Fact: ___ + ___ = ___

Thinking Strategy:

___ + ___ is ___ and 1 more is ___ .

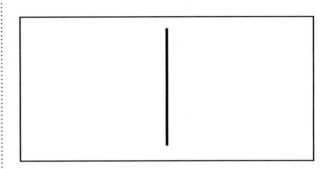

Near-Doubles Fact: ___ + ___ = ___

Doubles Fact: ___ + ___ = ___

Thinking Strategy:

___ + ___ is ___ and 1 more is ___ .

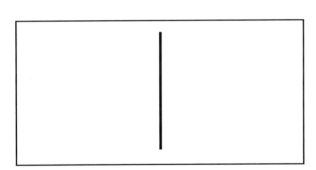

Near-Doubles Fact: ___ + ___ = ___

Doubles Fact: ___ + ___ = ___

Thinking Strategy:

___ + ___ is ___ and 1 more is ___ .

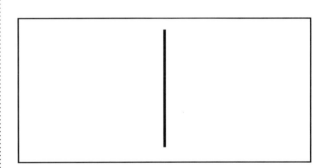

Near-Doubles Fact: ___ + ___ = ___

Doubles Fact: ___ + ___ = ___

Thinking Strategy:

___ + ___ is ___ and 1 more is ___ .

Date: _____   Name: _____

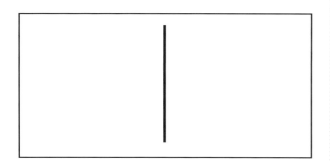

Near-Doubles Fact: ___ + ___ = ___

Doubles Fact: ___ + ___ = ___

Thinking Strategy:

___ + ___ is ___ and 1 more is ___.

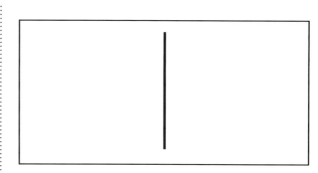

Near-Doubles Fact: ___ + ___ = ___

Doubles Fact: ___ + ___ = ___

Thinking Strategy:

___ + ___ is ___ and 1 more is ___.

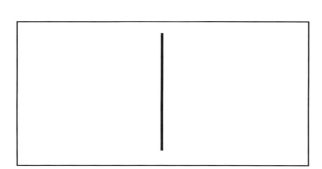

Near-Doubles Fact ___ + ___ = ___

Doubles Fact: ___ + ___ = ___

Thinking Strategy:

___ + ___ is ___ and 1 more is ___.

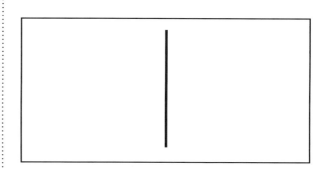

Near-Doubles Fact: ___ + ___ = ___

Doubles Fact: ___ + ___ = ___

Thinking Strategy:

___ + ___ is ___ and 1 more is ___.

2C

Date: _____   **Name:** _____

Fact Finder to 18

3 + 4 = _____	9 + 9 = _____	3 + 7 = _____
1 + 4 = _____	1 + 2 = _____	3 + 4 = _____
3 + 3 = _____	6 + 4 = _____	3 + 2 = _____
8 + 8 = _____	3 + 4 = _____	5 + 4 = _____
5 + 6 = _____	4 + 3 = _____	5 + 5 = _____
7 + 7 = _____	7 + 8 = _____	2 + 6 = _____
6 + 7 = _____	1 + 1 = _____	4 + 5 = _____
2 + 2 = _____	6 + 6 = _____	9 + 1 = _____
8 + 7 = _____	3 + 3 = _____	8 + 8 = _____
3 + 4 = _____	5 + 5 = _____	9 + 9 = _____
8 + 9 = _____	4 + 4 = _____	8 + 4 = _____

534 – 6.2.4   Portage & Main Press, 2006, Hands-On Mathematics, Level 2, ISBN: 978-1-55379-091-4   **2D**

Four-in-a-Row Addition Game Board

14	10	9	18
6	15	12	8
7	17	5	4
13	3	16	11

1   2   3   4   5   6   7   8   9

Extension

Portage & Main Press, 2006, Hands-On Mathematics, Level 2, ISBN: 978-1-55379-091-4

6.2.5 – 535

Assessment Addition-Fact Cards to 10 – Doubles, Near Doubles, and Other

$0 + 0 = \square$

$0 + 1 = \square$

$0 + 2 = \square$

$0 + 3 = \square$

$0 + 4 = \square$

$0 + 5 = \square$

Assessment

$0+6 = \boxed{}$

$0+7 = \boxed{}$

$0+8 = \boxed{}$

$0+9 = \boxed{}$

$0+10 = \boxed{}$

$1+0 = \boxed{}$

Assessment

Portage & Main Press, 2006, Hands-On Mathematics, Level 2, ISBN: 978-1-55379-091-4

6.2.6 – 537

$1 + 1 = \boxed{}$

$1 + 2 = \boxed{}$

$1 + 3 = \boxed{}$

$1 + 4 = \boxed{}$

$1 + 5 = \boxed{}$

$1 + 6 = \boxed{}$

$1 + 7 = \square$

$1 + 8 = \square$

$1 + 9 = \square$

$2 + 0 = \square$

$2 + 1 = \square$

$2 + 2 = \square$

Assessment

Portage & Main Press, 2006, Hands-On Mathematics, Level 2, ISBN: 978-1-55379-091-4

6.2.6 – 539

$2+3 = \square$

$2+4 = \square$

$2+5 = \square$

$2+6 = \square$

$2+7 = \square$

$2+8 = \square$

540 – 6.2.6

Portage & Main Press, 2006, Hands-On Mathematics, Level 2, ISBN: 978-1-55379-091-4

Assessment

$$3+0 = \boxed{}$$

$$3+1 = \boxed{}$$

$$3+2 = \boxed{}$$

$$3+3 = \boxed{}$$

$$3+4 = \boxed{}$$

$$3+5 = \boxed{}$$

Assessment

Portage & Main Press, 2006, Hands-On Mathematics, Level 2, ISBN: 978-1-55379-091-4

$3+6 = \square$

$3+7 = \square$

$4+0 = \square$

$4+1 = \square$

$4+2 = \square$

$4+3 = \square$

542 – 6.2.6

Portage & Main Press, 2006, Hands-On Mathematics, Level 2, ISBN: 978-1-55379-091-4

Assessment

$4+4 = \boxed{}$

$4+5 = \boxed{}$

$4+6 = \boxed{}$

$5+0 = \boxed{}$

$5+1 = \boxed{}$

$5+2 = \boxed{}$

Assessment Portage & Main Press, 2006, Hands-On Mathematics, Level 2, ISBN: 978-1-55379-091-4

$5 + 3 = \boxed{}$

$5 + 4 = \boxed{}$

$5 + 5 = \boxed{}$

$6 + 0 = \boxed{}$

$6 + 1 = \boxed{}$

$6 + 2 = \boxed{}$

544 – 6.2.6   Portage & Main Press, 2006, Hands-On Mathematics, Level 2, ISBN: 978-1-55379-091-4

Assessment

$6 + 3 = \square$

$6 + 4 = \square$

$7 + 0 = \square$

$7 + 1 = \square$

$7 + 2 = \square$

$7 + 3 = \square$

Assessment   Portage & Main Press, 2006, Hands-On Mathematics, Level 2, ISBN: 978-1-55379-091-4   6.2.6 – 545

$8 + 0 = \boxed{}$

$8 + 1 = \boxed{}$

$8 + 2 = \boxed{}$

$9 + 0 = \boxed{}$

$9 + 1 = \boxed{}$

$10 + 0 = \boxed{}$

546 – 6.2.6

Portage & Main Press, 2006, Hands-On Mathematics, Level 2, ISBN: 978-1-55379-091-4

Assessment

Assessment Addition-Fact Cards 11-18 – Doubles, Near Doubles, and Other

$0 + 11 = \boxed{}$

$0 + 12 = \boxed{}$

$0 + 13 = \boxed{}$

$0 + 14 = \boxed{}$

$0 + 15 = \boxed{}$

$0 + 16 = \boxed{}$

Assessment

$$0 + 17 = \boxed{}$$

$$0 + 18 = \boxed{}$$

$$1 + 10 = \boxed{}$$

$$1 + 11 = \boxed{}$$

$$1 + 12 = \boxed{}$$

$$1 + 13 = \boxed{}$$

548 – 6.2.7

Portage & Main Press, 2006, Hands-On Mathematics, Level 2, ISBN: 978-1-55379-091-4

Assessment

$1 + 14 = \boxed{}$

$1 + 15 = \boxed{}$

$1 + 16 = \boxed{}$

$1 + 17 = \boxed{}$

$2 + 9 = \boxed{}$

$2 + 10 = \boxed{}$

Assessment   Portage & Main Press, 2006, Hands-On Mathematics, Level 2, ISBN: 978-1-55379-091-4   6.2.7 – 549

$$2+11 = \boxed{}$$

$$2+12 = \boxed{}$$

$$2+13 = \boxed{}$$

$$2+14 = \boxed{}$$

$$2+15 = \boxed{}$$

$$2+16 = \boxed{}$$

550 – 6.2.7   Portage & Main Press, 2006, Hands-On Mathematics, Level 2, ISBN: 978-1-55379-091-4   **Assessment**

$3 + 8 = \boxed{}$

$3 + 9 = \boxed{}$

$3 + 10 = \boxed{}$

$3 + 11 = \boxed{}$

$3 + 12 = \boxed{}$

$3 + 13 = \boxed{}$

Assessment   Portage & Main Press, 2006, Hands-On Mathematics, Level 2, ISBN: 978-1-55379-091-4   6.2.7 – 551

$3+14 = \boxed{}$

$3+15 = \boxed{}$

$4+7 = \boxed{}$

$4+8 = \boxed{}$

$4+9 = \boxed{}$

$4+10 = \boxed{}$

552 – 6.2.7

Portage & Main Press, 2006, Hands-On Mathematics, Level 2, ISBN: 978-1-55379-091-4

Assessment

$$4 + 11 = \boxed{}$$

$$4 + 12 = \boxed{}$$

$$4 + 13 = \boxed{}$$

$$4 + 14 = \boxed{}$$

$$5 + 6 = \boxed{}$$

$$5 + 7 = \boxed{}$$

Assessment   Portage & Main Press, 2006, Hands-On Mathematics, Level 2, ISBN: 978-1-55379-091-4

$5 + 8 = \boxed{}$

$5 + 9 = \boxed{}$

$5 + 10 = \boxed{}$

$5 + 11 = \boxed{}$

$5 + 12 = \boxed{}$

$5 + 13 = \boxed{}$

Assessment

$6 + 5 = \boxed{}$

$6 + 6 = \boxed{}$

$6 + 7 = \boxed{}$

$6 + 8 = \boxed{}$

$6 + 9 = \boxed{}$

$6 + 10 = \boxed{}$

Assessment Portage & Main Press, 2006, Hands-On Mathematics, Level 2, ISBN: 978-1-55379-091-4

$6+11 = \square$

$6+12 = \square$

$7+4 = \square$

$7+5 = \square$

$7+6 = \square$

$7+7 = \square$

556 – 6.2.7

Portage & Main Press, 2006, Hands-On Mathematics, Level 2, ISBN: 978-1-55379-091-4

Assessment

$7+8 = \boxed{}$

$7+9 = \boxed{}$

$7+10 = \boxed{}$

$7+11 = \boxed{}$

$8+3 = \boxed{}$

$8+4 = \boxed{}$

Assessment   Portage & Main Press, 2006, Hands-On Mathematics, Level 2, ISBN: 978-1-55379-091-4

$$8+5 = \boxed{}$$

$$8+6 = \boxed{}$$

$$8+7 = \boxed{}$$

$$8+8 = \boxed{}$$

$$8+9 = \boxed{}$$

$$8+10 = \boxed{}$$

558 – 6.2.7   Portage & Main Press, 2006, Hands-On Mathematics, Level 2, ISBN: 978-1-55379-091-4   **Assessment**

$9 + 2 = \boxed{}$

$9 + 3 = \boxed{}$

$9 + 4 = \boxed{}$

$9 + 5 = \boxed{}$

$9 + 6 = \boxed{}$

$9 + 7 = \boxed{}$

Assessment Portage & Main Press, 2006, Hands-On Mathematics, Level 2, ISBN: 978-1-55379-091-4

$$9+8 = \boxed{}$$

$$9+9 = \boxed{}$$

$$10+1 = \boxed{}$$

$$10+2 = \boxed{}$$

$$10+3 = \boxed{}$$

$$10+4 = \boxed{}$$

Assessment

$$10 + 5 = \boxed{}$$

$$10 + 6 = \boxed{}$$

$$10 + 7 = \boxed{}$$

$$10 + 8 = \boxed{}$$

$$11 + 0 = \boxed{}$$

$$11 + 1 = \boxed{}$$

Assessment Portage & Main Press, 2006, Hands-On Mathematics, Level 2, ISBN: 978-1-55379-091-4

$11 + 2 = \boxed{}$

$11 + 3 = \boxed{}$

$11 + 4 = \boxed{}$

$11 + 5 = \boxed{}$

$11 + 6 = \boxed{}$

$11 + 7 = \boxed{}$

562 – 6.2.7

Portage & Main Press, 2006, Hands-On Mathematics, Level 2, ISBN: 978-1-55379-091-4

Assessment

$12+0 = \boxed{}$

$12+1 = \boxed{}$

$12+2 = \boxed{}$

$12+3 = \boxed{}$

$12+4 = \boxed{}$

$12+5 = \boxed{}$

Assessment   Portage & Main Press, 2006, Hands-On Mathematics, Level 2, ISBN: 978-1-55379-091-4

$12 + 6 = \boxed{}$

$13 + 0 = \boxed{}$

$13 + 1 = \boxed{}$

$13 + 2 = \boxed{}$

$13 + 3 = \boxed{}$

$13 + 4 = \boxed{}$

Assessment

$13 + 5 = \boxed{}$

$14 + 0 = \boxed{}$

$14 + 1 = \boxed{}$

$14 + 2 = \boxed{}$

$14 + 3 = \boxed{}$

$14 + 4 = \boxed{}$

Assessment

$15+0 = \boxed{}$

$15+1 = \boxed{}$

$15+2 = \boxed{}$

$15+3 = \boxed{}$

$16+0 = \boxed{}$

$16+1 = \boxed{}$

566 – 6.2.7

Portage & Main Press, 2006, Hands-On Mathematics, Level 2, ISBN: 978-1-55379-091-4

Assessment

$$16 + 2 = \boxed{}$$

$$17 + 0 = \boxed{}$$

$$17 + 1 = \boxed{}$$

$$18 + 0 = \boxed{}$$

Assessment Portage & Main Press, 2006, Hands-On Mathematics, Level 2, ISBN: 978-1-55379-091-4

3 Missing Addends

Background Information for Teachers

The concept of missing addends is not new to students, as they were informally introduced to it in grade one. This lesson builds on their previous experience by having students apply the concept in game-like situations. Exposure to these situations over an extended period of time can promote students' use of the think-addition strategy when solving subtraction problems.

Questions involving missing sums, such as the example below, are easier for students to solve than questions involving missing addends:

a + b = _____
    missing sum

Questions involving missing addends can be of two types:

Type 1: a + _____ = c   Type 2: _____ + b = c
         missing addend   missing addend

Note: The missing addend questions represented in type 2 are generally the most difficult for students to solve.

It is important to pre-assess students' abilities to solve questions involving missing sums before proceeding to questions involving missing addends. Students will experience more success solving problems with missing addends if they already have the ability to "count-on" from one number to another.

Materials

- counters
- ten frames (included in unit 5, lesson 4) (5.4.4)
- chart paper
- markers
- ten frames – dot mats (0-10) (included in the introduction to *Hands-On Mathematics Grade 2*, part 1, pages 53 to 55. Cut out each ten frame, 0 to 10, and mount onto sturdy tagboard.)

Activity: Part One

Distribute counters and ten frames to students. Write the number 4 on a piece of chart paper. Ask students:

- What number, when added to 4, do you think will make 10?

On chart paper, record an addition fact by writing "4 +" and the number students predict (4 + _____ = 10).

Now, have students use their counters and ten frames to determine whether or not their prediction is correct. Repeat the activity by asking students:

- What number, when added to 6, will make 10?
- What number, when added to 3, will make 5?
- What number, when added to 4, will make 9?
- What number, when added to 2, will make 8?

Have students use their counters and ten frames to check each prediction. Use different numbers to continue the activity.

Distribute copies of Activity Sheet A (6.3.1), and have students complete each number story and draw pictures to show how they determined what each missing addend is.

Activity Sheet A

Directions to students:

Complete each number story. Draw a picture to show how you figured out what each missing addend is (6.3.1).

3

Activity: Part Two

Hold up one of the ten frames with dots (0 to 10). Ask students:

- How many more dots do we need to fill the ten frame?

Repeat using various ten frames with dots.

Next Step

Introduce addition with missing addends to 18.

Problem Solving

- Alexis has 7 nickels. She finds more nickels under a chair. Now, she has 9 nickels. How many nickels did Alexis find?

- Thomas has a baseball card collection. He buys 5 more cards for his collection. Now, he has 18 cards in his collection. How many cards did Thomas have to begin with?

- Jack is hungry. He eats 8 almonds. He is still hungry, so he eats some walnuts. Altogether, he eats 16 nuts. How many walnuts did Jack eat?

Note: A reproducible master for these problems can be found on page 730.

Activity Centres

Note: For the following activity centre you will need four sets of 0-8 numeral cards (provided with part 1, unit 1, lesson 12: 1.12.1) for each working group of students. Photocopy, and cut out the cards ahead of time, and create a deck of thirty-six cards for each group.

- Divide the class into working groups of students, and have them play "Make 8." Provide each group with a deck of thirty-six 0-8 numeral cards, and have one player from each group divide all the cards among the players in the group. Tell players to put their cards facedown in a pile in front of them.

Have Player A in each group turn over the top card in his/her pile and place it, face up, in the centre of the playing space. Have Player B turn over his/her top card. If this card and the card in the centre add up to 8, Player B takes both cards and places them in his/her "win" pile. If the two cards make more than 8, they are placed in the discard pile. If the two cards make less than 8, Player C tries to make 8 with the next card.

Play continues until all players have used up all of their cards. The player with the greatest number of cards at the end wins.

Note: Vary the game by having students make other sums.

- Divide the class into groups of three students, and have them play "What Am I?" Give each group a set of numeral cards from 1 to 9 (provided with unit 1, lesson 12: 1.12.1). Have the groups shuffle their cards and place them, facedown, in the centre of the playing space.

Tell Player A and Player B to each take a card from the pile and, without looking at it, place it against their foreheads, facing outward. Then, have Player C add the two cards together and announce the sum. Have Players A and B, who can see each other's cards, use this information to determine the unknown value of their own cards. Then, have players switch roles and play again.

Extensions

- Add the word *addend* to your classroom Math Word Wall.

- Distribute to each student a set of numeral cards from 1 to 9 (1.12.1). Hold up a numeral card, and state a sum. Have each student

▶

Unit 6 • **Number Operations**

569

3

hold up a card from his/her set that, together with your card, makes the required sum. For example, if you hold up a 7 and state the sum 10, each student should hold up a 3.

- Divide the class into groups of three students, and have them play "5s Go Fish." Distribute to each group four sets of 0-5 numeral cards (each group should have a total of twenty-four cards).

Have a dealer for each group distribute five cards to each player and place the remaining cards, facedown, in a pile in the centre of the playing area. Tell players to take turns asking any other player for a number (numeral card) they need to make 5. If the player asked does not have the card, the asking player takes a card from the pile ("go fish").

When players have two cards that make 5, have them place the pair face up beside them. The game continues until one player has used all his/her cards. The player with the most pairs of cards that make 5 is the winner.

Note: Vary the game by having students "fish" for other numbers. For example, students can use the ace through 9 cards from a standard deck of playing cards to play "10s Go Fish."

Hands-On Mathematics • Grade 2

Date: _____   Name: _____

What Is Missing?

5 + ____ = 7

8 + ____ = 9

____ + 3 = 6

4 + ____ = 10

____ + 2 = 5

____ + 7 = 9

____ + 8 = 8

3 + ____ = 7

3A

Portage & Main Press, 2006, Hands-On Mathematics, Level 2, ISBN: 978-1-55379-091-4   6.3.1 – 571

4 Think-Addition Strategy for Subtraction

Background Information for Teachers

The activities in this lesson focus on subtraction to 18. Although grade-two students are only expected to recall subtraction facts to 10, they are also expected to learn various strategies for determining differences beyond 10, to 100. These activities introduce several subtraction strategies.

Once students know the addition facts, they can master the corresponding subtraction facts by using the "think-addition" strategy presented in this lesson.

Students will be more successful with the following tasks if they can count-on and if they can count backward by 1s, 2s, 5s, and 10s.

Materials

- overhead projector
- bingo chips
- blank piece of paper
- chart paper
- marker
- paper bags (one for each pair of students)
- interlocking cubes
- writing paper
- pencils
- index cards

Activity: Part One

Place nine bingo chips on the overhead, and have students count them. Then, cover the counters with a piece of paper, as in the following diagram:

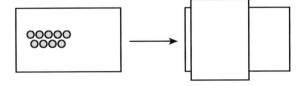

Now, remove five bingo chips from under the piece of paper, and place them on the overhead beside the covered chips, as in the following diagram:

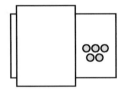

Ask students:

- How many chips are still covered?

Model the think-addition strategy for students. Say:

- Think. What number plus 5 makes 9?

Once students come up with the correct answer, say:

- Four. There are 4 bingo chips still covered, so 9 minus 5 is 4.

Uncover the four remaining bingo chips, as in the following diagram, and say:

- Four and 5 is 9, so 9 minus 5 is 4.

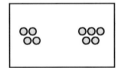

Model the strategy several more times for students. Then, record the following problems on a piece of chart paper, and have students explain how they would use the think-addition strategy to solve each one:

- 7 − 4 = ___
- 6 − 2 = ___
- 8 − 5 = ___
- 5 − 1 = ___

572 Hands-On Mathematics • Grade 2

4

Activity: Part Two

Note: Before beginning this activity, fill each of several paper bags with four to ten interlocking cubes (you will need one bag of cubes for each pair of students). Be sure the amount of cubes varies from bag to bag as much as possible. Use a marker to write the number of cubes on the outside of each bag.

Have students work in pairs, and give each pair some writing paper, a pencil, and a bag of interlocking cubes. Tell one student in each pair to remove a handful of cubes from the bag and show the cubes to the other student. Have the first student ask:

- How many cubes are still in the bag?

Have the second student in each pair use the think-addition strategy to determine the number of cubes left in the bag. Then, ask that student to record the appropriate subtraction fact as well as its corresponding addition fact. Tell students to check their answers by counting the number of cubes left in the bag. Then, ask partners to exchange roles. Have pairs repeat the activity until each student has used the cubes in the bag to practice the think-addition strategy five times.

Distribute Activity Sheet A (6.4.1), and have students use the think-addition strategy to help them find the missing number for each subtraction problem. Tell students to record the missing number for each problem as well as the addition fact they used. Finally, have students answer the question at the bottom of the activity sheet.

Activity Sheet A

Directions to students:

Use the think-addition strategy to help you find the missing number for each subtraction problem. Record the missing number. Also, record the addition fact that you used. Finally, answer the question at the bottom of the sheet (6.4.1).

Next Steps

- Repeat the previous activities using subtraction facts to 18.

- Repeat Activity: Part Two by having each pair of students exchange their paper bag with another pair of students.

- Distribute several blank index cards to each student. Select a group of addition facts (for example, all doubles facts to 18), and have students record the facts on their index cards, one fact per card, as in the following diagram:

$$8 + 8 = 16$$

On a piece of chart paper, record a subtraction fact that is related to one of the addition facts students have recorded on their index cards. Tell students to hold up the matching addition fact. Repeat several times.

- Distribute Activity Sheet B (6.4.2), and have students use the think-addition strategy to help them find the missing number for each subtraction problem (subtraction facts to 18). Tell students to record the missing number for each problem as well as the addition fact they used.

Activity Sheet B

Directions to students:

Use the think-addition strategy to help you find the missing number for each subtraction problem. Record the missing number. Also, record the addition fact that you used (6.4.2).

Unit 6 • **Number Operations**

573

4

Activity Centre

At an activity centre, have a set of twenty-four "Math-Fact Memory" cards (included) – twelve subtraction facts and twelve related addition facts. Have pairs of students play "Math-Fact Memory." Tell students to place all twenty-four cards facedown in six rows of four. Have players take turns turning over two cards. If players turn over a subtraction fact and its related addition fact – a match (as in the following diagram) – they keep the cards and take another turn:

$9 - 2 = \square$ $7 + 2 = \square$

If the cards do not match, the player turns the cards facedown again and the other player takes a turn. The player with the most matches when all cards are gone is the winner (6.4.3).

Assessment Suggestion

In one-on-one interviews, ask students to solve the following two facts in as many ways as they can:

- $7 + 8 = \underline{\hspace{1cm}}$
- $8 - 3 = \underline{\hspace{1cm}}$

Look for:

- correct answers
- use of near-doubles and think-addition strategies
- how students solve the problems (in their heads, on paper)

Use the Anecdotal Record sheet, found on page 22, to record results.

574   **Hands-On Mathematics • Grade 2**

Date: _____ **Name:** _____

Think Addition

Subtraction Fact	Addition Fact
9 – 4 = ____	____ + ____ = ____
7 – 6 = ____	____ + ____ = ____
4 – 1 = ____	____ + ____ = ____
6 – 3 = ____	____ + ____ = ____
8 – 4 = ____	____ + ____ = ____
9 – 3 = ____	____ + ____ = ____
10 – 5 = ____	____ + ____ = ____
8 – 6 = ____	____ + ____ = ____
5 – 1 = ____	____ + ____ = ____
7 – 2 = ____	____ + ____ = ____
6 – 4 = ____	____ + ____ = ____

How can you use addition to help you figure out subtraction problems?

_____

_____

_____

4A

Date: _____   **Name:** _____

More Think Addition

Subtraction Fact   **Addition Fact**

14 – 6 = _____   _____ + _____ = _____

16 – 9 = _____   _____ + _____ = _____

18 – 7 = _____   _____ + _____ = _____

12 – 8 = _____   _____ + _____ = _____

10 – 4 = _____   _____ + _____ = _____

13 – 6 = _____   _____ + _____ = _____

15 – 8 = _____   _____ + _____ = _____

17 – 8 = _____   _____ + _____ = _____

11 – 8 = _____   _____ + _____ = _____

17 – 9 = _____   _____ + _____ = _____

18 – 4 = _____   _____ + _____ = _____

16 – 7 = _____   _____ + _____ = _____

15 – 10 = _____   _____ + _____ = _____

14 – 9 = _____   _____ + _____ = _____

576 – 6.4.2   Portage & Main Press, 2006, Hands-On Mathematics, Level 2, ISBN: 978-1-55379-091-4   **4B**

Math-Fact Memory Cards

$3+6 = \boxed{}$

$8+2 = \boxed{}$

$2+6 = \boxed{}$

$3+3 = \boxed{}$

$4+5 = \boxed{}$

$0+7 = \boxed{}$

Activity Centre

Portage & Main Press, 2006, Hands-On Mathematics, Level 2, ISBN: 978-1-55379-091-4

6.4.3 – 577

$9 - 3 = \square$

$10 - 8 = \square$

$8 - 2 = \square$

$6 - 3 = \square$

$9 - 4 = \square$

$7 - 0 = \square$

578 – 6.4.3   Portage & Main Press, 2006, Hands-On Mathematics, Level 2, ISBN: 978-1-55379-091-4   **Activity Centre**

$1 + 8 = \boxed{}$

$5 + 3 = \boxed{}$

$6 + 4 = \boxed{}$

$7 + 2 = \boxed{}$

$4 + 4 = \boxed{}$

$2 + 2 = \boxed{}$

Activity Centre

Portage & Main Press, 2006, Hands-On Mathematics, Level 2, ISBN: 978-1-55379-091-4

6.4.3 – 579

$9 - 1 = \boxed{}$

$8 - 5 = \boxed{}$

$10 - 6 = \boxed{}$

$9 - 7 = \boxed{}$

$8 - 4 = \boxed{}$

$4 - 2 = \boxed{}$

580 – 6.4.3   Portage & Main Press, 2006, Hands-On Mathematics, Level 2, ISBN: 978-1-55379-091-4   **Activity Centre**

5 | Recalling Subtraction Facts

Materials
- chart paper
- markers

Activity

Divide the class into two teams. On chart paper, display the following series of numbers for each team:

Team A	Team B
9, 10, 18, 16	8, 10, 15, 17

Have one student from each team come up to the chart paper. When you give the signal to begin, have students subtract 4 from each number in the series. For example, the student from Team A would respond 5, 6, 14, 12 while the student from Team B would respond 4, 6, 11, 13. The student who finishes first and answers all the problems correctly scores a point for his/her team.

Repeat the activity with two new students from each team. Use the same series of numbers but have the two new students subtract a new number from each number in the series. Continue in this manner until each student has had a turn.

Distribute Activity Sheet A (6.5.1), and have students circle all of the subtraction combinations that equal the sum at the top of each box.

Then, distribute Activity Sheet B (6.5.2), and have students determine the secret number by crossing out each number in the box on the right that fits with one of the clues on the left.

Activity Sheet A

Directions to students:

Circle all the subtraction problems that equal the number at the top of each box (6.5.1).

Activity Sheet B

Directions to students:

Find the secret number. Cross out each number in the box on the right that fits with one of the clues on the left. The number you are left with is the secret number (6.5.2).

Problem Solving

- Name six subtraction facts that have a difference of 3.
- Are there other subtraction facts that have a difference of 3? What are they?
- Place the numbers 1, 2, 3, 4, 5, and 6 around the circle. The difference between any two numbers beside each other cannot be more than 2.

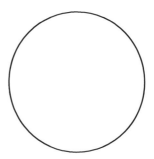

Note: A reproducible master for these problems can be found on pages 730 and 731.

Unit 6 • **Number Operations**   581

5

Activity Centre

Place "Subtraction-Fact Game" score sheets (included), pencils, and number cubes at an activity centre, and have students play the "Subtraction-Fact Game" in pairs. Have students take turns rolling two number cubes, subtracting the smaller number from the larger number, and recording the corresponding subtraction fact on their score sheets. After eight rounds, have each player add together the eight answers on his/her score sheet to determine a total score. The player with the *lower* score wins (6.5.3).

Extension

Note: Before beginning this activity, photocopy, and cut out a set of subtraction-fact cards (included) for each pair of students (6.5.4).

Divide the class into pairs of students, and have students play a variation of the game "Snap" (or "War"). Distribute a set of subtraction-fact cards to each pair, and have students divide their set evenly between each player. Tell players to put their cards in a pile, facedown, in front of them.

Have each player place one card, face up, in the centre of the playing space. Then, ask players to calculate the differences (answers) on their cards. The player with the larger difference gets both cards. If the answers are the same, students call, "Snap." Then, have each student place three more cards facedown and a fourth card face up. The player with the larger answer on the new face-up card gets all of the cards in play. Play continues until one player has no cards left.

Note: A set of subtraction-fact cards to 18 has also been included (6.5.5).

582   **Hands-On Mathematics • Grade 2**

Date: _____   **Name:** _____

Find the Facts

7
8 − 1 =
16 − 8 =
9 − 2 =
7 − 7 =
10 − 3 =
18 − 9 =

4
10 − 4 =
13 − 9 =
9 − 6 =
14 − 10 =
6 − 2 =
17 − 13 =

3
15 − 12 =
6 − 4 =
18 − 15 =
9 − 4 =
17 − 12 =
10 − 7 =

5
5 − 5 =
18 − 13 =
17 − 12 =
16 − 11 =
9 − 4 =
8 − 2 =

5A

Portage & Main Press, 2006, Hands-On Mathematics, Level 2, ISBN: 978-1-55379-091-4

6.5.1 − 583

Date: _____   **Name:** _____

What Is the Secret Number?

The secret number...

...is not 16 – 8.

...is not 5 – 5.

...is not 14 – 10.

...is not 4 – 3.

...is not 8 – 6.

...is not 18 – 9.

...is not 8 – 3.

...is not 15 – 8.

...is not 6 – 3.

...is not 12 – 6.

6 9 5 8 3 10 0 4 7 1 2

The secret number is: _____

584 – 6.5.2   Portage & Main Press, 2006, Hands-On Mathematics, Level 2, ISBN: 978-1-55379-091-4   **5B**

Subtraction-Fact Game Score Sheet

Player A

1. _____ – _____ = _____

2. _____ – _____ = _____

3. _____ – _____ = _____

4. _____ – _____ = _____

5. _____ – _____ = _____

6. _____ – _____ = _____

7. _____ – _____ = _____

8. _____ – _____ = _____

Total Score _____

Player B

1. _____ – _____ = _____

2. _____ – _____ = _____

3. _____ – _____ = _____

4. _____ – _____ = _____

5. _____ – _____ = _____

6. _____ – _____ = _____

7. _____ – _____ = _____

8. _____ – _____ = _____

Total Score _____

Activity Centre

Portage & Main Press, 2006, Hands-On Mathematics, Level 2, ISBN: 978-1-55379-091-4

Subtraction-Fact Cards to 10

$10 - 0 = \boxed{}$

$10 - 1 = \boxed{}$

$10 - 2 = \boxed{}$

$10 - 3 = \boxed{}$

$10 - 4 = \boxed{}$

$10 - 5 = \boxed{}$

586 – 6.5.4

Portage & Main Press, 2006, Hands-On Mathematics, Level 2, ISBN: 978-1-55379-091-4

Extension

$10 - 6 = \boxed{}$

$10 - 7 = \boxed{}$

$10 - 8 = \boxed{}$

$10 - 9 = \boxed{}$

$10 - 10 = \boxed{}$

$9 - 0 = \boxed{}$

Extension

$9 - 1 = \boxed{}$

$9 - 2 = \boxed{}$

$9 - 3 = \boxed{}$

$9 - 4 = \boxed{}$

$9 - 5 = \boxed{}$

$9 - 6 = \boxed{}$

Extension

$9 - 7 = \boxed{}$

$9 - 8 = \boxed{}$

$9 - 9 = \boxed{}$

$8 - 0 = \boxed{}$

$8 - 1 = \boxed{}$

$8 - 2 = \boxed{}$

Extension

Portage & Main Press, 2006, Hands-On Mathematics, Level 2, ISBN: 978-1-55379-091-4

6.5.4 – **589**

$8 - 3 = \boxed{}$

$8 - 4 = \boxed{}$

$8 - 5 = \boxed{}$

$8 - 6 = \boxed{}$

$8 - 7 = \boxed{}$

$8 - 8 = \boxed{}$

Extension

$7 - 0 = \boxed{}$

$7 - 1 = \boxed{}$

$7 - 2 = \boxed{}$

$7 - 3 = \boxed{}$

$7 - 4 = \boxed{}$

$7 - 5 = \boxed{}$

Extension

Portage & Main Press, 2006, Hands-On Mathematics, Level 2, ISBN: 978-1-55379-091-4

$7 - 6 = \boxed{}$

$7 - 7 = \boxed{}$

$6 - 0 = \boxed{}$

$6 - 1 = \boxed{}$

$6 - 2 = \boxed{}$

$6 - 3 = \boxed{}$

Extension

$6-4 = \boxed{}$

$6-5 = \boxed{}$

$6-6 = \boxed{}$

$5-0 = \boxed{}$

$5-1 = \boxed{}$

$5-2 = \boxed{}$

Extension

Portage & Main Press, 2006, Hands-On Mathematics, Level 2, ISBN: 978-1-55379-091-4

6.5.4 – 593

$$5 - 3 = \square$$

$$5 - 4 = \square$$

$$5 - 5 = \square$$

$$4 - 0 = \square$$

$$4 - 1 = \square$$

$$4 - 2 = \square$$

594 – 6.5.4

Portage & Main Press, 2006, Hands-On Mathematics, Level 2, ISBN: 978-1-55379-091-4

Extension

$$4 - 3 = \boxed{}$$

$$4 - 4 = \boxed{}$$

$$3 - 0 = \boxed{}$$

$$3 - 1 = \boxed{}$$

$$3 - 2 = \boxed{}$$

$$3 - 3 = \boxed{}$$

Extension

Portage & Main Press, 2006, Hands-On Mathematics, Level 2, ISBN: 978-1-55379-091-4

6.5.4 – 595

$$2 - 0 = \square$$

$$2 - 1 = \square$$

$$2 - 2 = \square$$

$$1 - 0 = \square$$

$$1 - 1 = \square$$

$$0 - 0 = \square$$

596 – 6.5.4

Portage & Main Press, 2006, Hands-On Mathematics, Level 2, ISBN: 978-1-55379-091-4

Extension

Subtraction-Fact Cards 11-18

$11 - 11 = \boxed{}$

$11 - 10 = \boxed{}$

$11 - 9 = \boxed{}$

$11 - 8 = \boxed{}$

$11 - 7 = \boxed{}$

$11 - 6 = \boxed{}$

Extension

Portage & Main Press, 2006, Hands-On Mathematics, Level 2, ISBN: 978-1-55379-091-4

6.5.5 – 597

$11 - 5 = \boxed{}$	$11 - 4 = \boxed{}$
$11 - 3 = \boxed{}$	$11 - 2 = \boxed{}$
$11 - 1 = \boxed{}$	$11 - 0 = \boxed{}$

598 – 6.5.5   Portage & Main Press, 2006, Hands-On Mathematics, Level 2, ISBN: 978-1-55379-091-4   **Extension**

$12 - 12 = \square$

$12 - 11 = \square$

$12 - 10 = \square$

$12 - 9 = \square$

$12 - 8 = \square$

$12 - 7 = \square$

Extension

Portage & Main Press, 2006, Hands-On Mathematics, Level 2, ISBN: 978-1-55379-091-4

6.5.5 – **599**

$12 - 6 = \boxed{}$

$12 - 5 = \boxed{}$

$12 - 4 = \boxed{}$

$12 - 3 = \boxed{}$

$12 - 2 = \boxed{}$

$12 - 1 = \boxed{}$

600 – 6.5.5

Portage & Main Press, 2006, Hands-On Mathematics, Level 2, ISBN: 978-1-55379-091-4

Extension

$12 - 0 = \boxed{}$

$13 - 13 = \boxed{}$

$13 - 12 = \boxed{}$

$13 - 11 = \boxed{}$

$13 - 10 = \boxed{}$

$13 - 9 = \boxed{}$

Extension

$13-8 = \boxed{}$

$13-7 = \boxed{}$

$13-6 = \boxed{}$

$13-5 = \boxed{}$

$13-4 = \boxed{}$

$13-3 = \boxed{}$

602 – 6.5.5

Portage & Main Press, 2006, Hands-On Mathematics, Level 2, ISBN: 978-1-55379-091-4

Extension

$$13-2 = \square$$

$$13-1 = \square$$

$$13-0 = \square$$

$$14-14 = \square$$

$$14-13 = \square$$

$$14-12 = \square$$

Extension

$14 - 11 = \boxed{}$

$14 - 10 = \boxed{}$

$14 - 9 = \boxed{}$

$14 - 8 = \boxed{}$

$14 - 7 = \boxed{}$

$14 - 6 = \boxed{}$

Extension

$$14-5 = \square$$

$$14-4 = \square$$

$$14-3 = \square$$

$$14-2 = \square$$

$$14-1 = \square$$

$$14-0 = \square$$

Extension

Portage & Main Press, 2006, Hands-On Mathematics, Level 2, ISBN: 978-1-55379-091-4

6.5.5 – **605**

$15 - 15 = \square$

$15 - 14 = \square$

$15 - 13 = \square$

$15 - 12 = \square$

$15 - 11 = \square$

$15 - 10 = \square$

606 – 6.5.5

Portage & Main Press, 2006, Hands-On Mathematics, Level 2, ISBN: 978-1-55379-091-4

Extension

$$15 - 9 = \boxed{}$$

$$15 - 8 = \boxed{}$$

$$15 - 7 = \boxed{}$$

$$15 - 6 = \boxed{}$$

$$15 - 5 = \boxed{}$$

$$15 - 4 = \boxed{}$$

Extension

Portage & Main Press, 2006, Hands-On Mathematics, Level 2, ISBN: 978-1-55379-091-4

6.5.5 – 607

$15 - 3 = \boxed{}$

$15 - 2 = \boxed{}$

$15 - 1 = \boxed{}$

$15 - 0 = \boxed{}$

$16 - 16 = \boxed{}$

$16 - 15 = \boxed{}$

608 – 6.5.5   Portage & Main Press, 2006, Hands-On Mathematics, Level 2, ISBN: 978-1-55379-091-4   **Extension**

$16 - 14 = \square$

$16 - 13 = \square$

$16 - 12 = \square$

$16 - 11 = \square$

$16 - 10 = \square$

$16 - 9 = \square$

Extension

Portage & Main Press, 2006, Hands-On Mathematics, Level 2, ISBN: 978-1-55379-091-4

16 – 8 = ☐

16 – 7 = ☐

16 – 6 = ☐

16 – 5 = ☐

16 – 4 = ☐

16 – 3 = ☐

610 – 6.5.5

Portage & Main Press, 2006, Hands-On Mathematics, Level 2, ISBN: 978-1-55379-091-4

Extension

$16 - 2 = \boxed{}$

$16 - 1 = \boxed{}$

$16 - 0 = \boxed{}$

$17 - 17 = \boxed{}$

$17 - 16 = \boxed{}$

$17 - 15 = \boxed{}$

Extension

Portage & Main Press, 2006, Hands-On Mathematics, Level 2, ISBN: 978-1-55379-091-4

6.5.5 – **611**

$17 - 14 = \boxed{}$

$17 - 13 = \boxed{}$

$17 - 12 = \boxed{}$

$17 - 11 = \boxed{}$

$17 - 10 = \boxed{}$

$17 - 9 = \boxed{}$

612 – 6.5.5

Portage & Main Press, 2006, Hands-On Mathematics, Level 2, ISBN: 978-1-55379-091-4

Extension

$17 - 8 = \square$

$17 - 7 = \square$

$17 - 6 = \square$

$17 - 5 = \square$

$17 - 4 = \square$

$17 - 3 = \square$

Extension

Portage & Main Press, 2006, Hands-On Mathematics, Level 2, ISBN: 978-1-55379-091-4

6.5.5 – 613

$17-2 = \boxed{}$

$17-1 = \boxed{}$

$17-0 = \boxed{}$

$18-18 = \boxed{}$

$18-17 = \boxed{}$

$18-16 = \boxed{}$

614 – 6.5.5

Portage & Main Press, 2006, Hands-On Mathematics, Level 2, ISBN: 978-1-55379-091-4

Extension

$18 - 15 = \square$

$18 - 14 = \square$

$18 - 13 = \square$

$18 - 12 = \square$

$18 - 11 = \square$

$18 - 10 = \square$

Extension

Portage & Main Press, 2006, Hands-On Mathematics, Level 2, ISBN: 978-1-55379-091-4

6.5.5 – **615**

18 – 9 = ☐

18 – 8 = ☐

18 – 7 = ☐

18 – 6 = ☐

18 – 5 = ☐

18 – 4 = ☐

616 – 6.5.5

Portage & Main Press, 2006, Hands-On Mathematics, Level 2, ISBN: 978-1-55379-091-4

Extension

$18 - 3 = \boxed{}$

$18 - 2 = \boxed{}$

$18 - 1 = \boxed{}$

$18 - 0 = \boxed{}$

Extension

Portage & Main Press, 2006, Hands-On Mathematics, Level 2, ISBN: 978-1-55379-091-4

6 The Identity Property of Addition – Zero Facts

Background Information for Teachers

The identity property of addition indicates the value of 0 in addition, such that:

$n + 0 = n$ or $n = 0 + n$

A *zero fact* for addition is any fact where at least one of the addends is a zero. For example:

$7 + 0 = 7$; $0 + 7 = 7$; $0 + 0 = 0$.

Materials

- counters
- part-part-whole boards (included. Make one photocopy for each student.) (6.6.1)
- chart paper
- markers
- dominos (one set for each working group)
- calculators (one for each student)

Activity: Part One

Introduce students to addition with 0. Distribute counters and part-part-whole boards to students. Ask students to use their counters and part-part-whole boards to solve the following story problems:

- Mark is playing a game of darts. He throws a dart and scores 6 points. He throws a second dart and scores 0 points. What is Mark's total score?

- Erika throws a dart and scores 0 points. On her next throw, Erika scores 9 points. What is Erika's total score?

- Eli went looking for rabbits twice on the weekend. On Saturday, she spotted 13 rabbits. On Sunday, she spotted 0 rabbits. How many rabbits did Eli spot altogether?

- Jared had a lemonade stand. He sold 0 glasses of lemonade in the morning. He sold 8 glasses in the afternoon. How many glasses of lemonade did Jared sell altogether?

Now, write an addition equation on chart paper for each problem. Have students describe how the problems are alike and how they are different.

Activity: Part Two

Divide the class into working groups of students, and provide each group with a set of dominos and copies of Activity Sheet A (6.6.2). Have students use the dominos to complete their activity sheets.

Note: Have small groups of students share one set of dominos but work individually on their own activity sheets.

Activity Sheet A

Directions to students:

Find all the dominos that show a zero fact for addition. Draw each of these dominos, and record the addition fact that goes with it (6.6.2).

Next Steps

- Write the following zero facts on chart paper:

  $0 + 12 =$ _____ $2 + 0 =$ _____

  $6 + 0 =$ _____ $0 + 16 =$ _____

  $14 + 0 =$ _____ $15 + 0 =$ _____

  $1 + 0 =$ _____ $9 + 0 =$ _____

  $0 + 17 =$ _____ $7 + 0 =$ _____

Have students use their counters and part-part-whole boards to solve each of the preceding problems. Then, discuss how the problems are alike.

▶

Hands-On Mathematics • Grade 2

6

- Have students predict the sum of each of the following problems and then use calculators to check their predictions:

  $95 + 0 = $ _____ $115 + 0 = $ _____

  $0 + 998 = $ _____ $214 + 0 = $ _____

  $0 + 753 = $ _____ $655 + 0 = $ _____

Note: Some students will not be aware that a property of an operation applies to numbers other than the ones with which they are working. This exercise helps students recognize that the 0 property for addition applies to any number, no matter how large or small.

Extension

Review, and present subtraction facts involving 0. For example:

$9 - 0 = 9$ and $9 - 9 = 0$

Assessment Suggestion

Have students complete Student Self-Assessment sheets, found on page 28, to reflect on what they learned about addition with 0.

Unit 6 • **Number Operations**

Part-Part-Whole Board

620 – 6.6.1

Portage & Main Press, 2006, Hands-On Mathematics, Level 2, ISBN: 978-1-55379-091-4

Date: _____   Name: _____

Zeros on Dominos

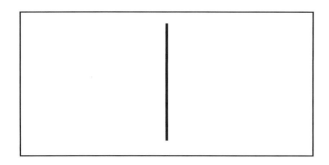

____ + ____ = ____

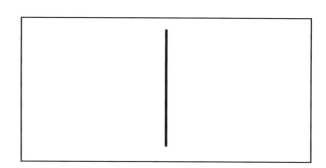

____ + ____ = ____

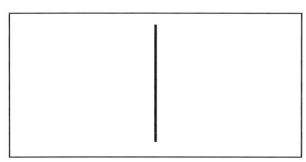

____ + ____ = ____

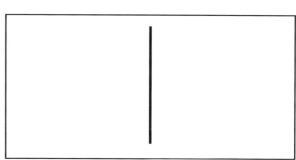

____ + ____ = ____

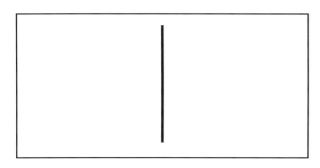

____ + ____ = ____

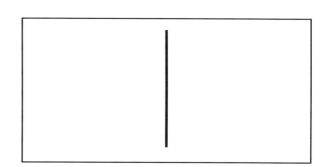

____ + ____ = ____

6A

7 Commutative Property of Addition

Background Information for Teachers

The commutative property of addition specifies that the order of addends is irrelevant so that

$a + b = b + a$.

Materials

- sets of dominos (one set for each small group of students)
- chart paper
- markers
- blue and green interlocking cubes (six blue cubes and eight green cubes for each student)
- blank paper
- pencils
- calculators (one for each student)

Activity: Part One

Show students a domino, and have them state the addition fact that describes it. Record the fact on chart paper. For example:

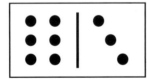

$6 + 3 = 9$

Rotate the domino 180 degrees, and ask students to state the addition fact that describes the domino now. Record this fact on chart paper.

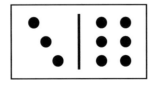

$3 + 6 = 9$

Ask students:

- How are the two addition facts alike?
- How are they different?

Repeat the activity with different dominos. Then, distribute sets of dominos and copies of Activity Sheet A (6.7.1), and have students use the dominos to complete their activity sheets.

Note: Have small groups of students share one set of dominos but work individually on their own activity sheets.

Distribute Activity Sheet B (6.7.2), and have students draw a line from each problem in column A to the matching answer in column B. Then, have students draw a line from each answer in column B to the turned-around problem in column C.

Activity Sheet A

Note: This is a two-page activity sheet.

Directions to students:

Find a domino to show each sum. Draw the domino, and record the addition fact. Then, draw the turned-around domino, and record the turned-around addition fact (6.7.1).

Activity Sheet B

Directions to students:

Draw a line from each problem in column A to the matching answer in column B. Then, draw a line from each answer in column B to the turned-around problem in column C.

Activity: Part Two

Distribute interlocking cubes, blank paper, and pencils to students. Have each student use blue interlocking cubes to make a six-car train and green interlocking cubes to make an eight-car train. Next, ask each student to attach the two

7

trains together to make a new, fourteen-car train. Have each student record an addition fact that matches the new train. Then, have each student turn the train around and record a corresponding turned-around addition fact.

Problem Solving

Tamar has 15 cents in her shirt pocket and 3 cents in her pants pocket. Her brother, Oren, has 3 cents in his shirt pocket and 15 cents in his pants pocket. Do Tamar and Oren have the same amount of money? Use pictures, numbers, and words to explain your answer.

Note: A reproducible master for this problem can be found on page 731.

Extensions

■ Have students use counters to determine whether or not subtraction problems can be turned around.

■ Distribute interlocking cubes, paper, and pencils to students. Ask each student to use seven interlocking cubes to make an interlocking-cube train. Then, ask each student to make a second seven-cube train. Now, tell students to break apart the second train into two pieces in as many different ways as possible. Have students record all the different combinations of broken trains. For example:

6 + 1; 1 + 6; 12 + 5; 5 + 12; 3 + 14; 14 + 3

Now, ask students to take the two pieces of their broken trains and line them up beside their unbroken trains. Have students examine the broken trains and then switch around the two parts (for example, 1 + 6 to 6 + 1). Ask:

■ When you switch around the two parts of your train, do you still have seven cubes?

Discuss the commutative property of addition with students. Use trains with different numbers of interlocking cubes to repeat the activity.

Next Step

Introduce the commutative property of addition as it applies beyond sums of 10. Ask students the following questions:

■ If 9 + 6 = 15, what is the sum of 6 + 9?
■ If 35 + 17 = 52, what is the sum of 17 + 35?
■ If 173 + 245 = 418, what is the sum of 245 + 173?
■ If 345 + 624 = 968, what else do you know?

Have students use calculators to check their answers.

Unit 6 • **Number Operations**

623

Turned-Around Dominos

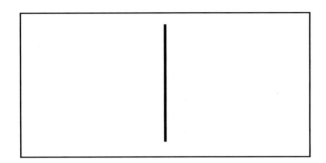

_____ + _____ = 5

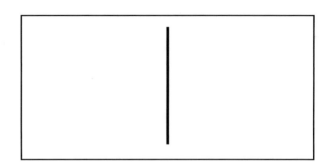

_____ + _____ = 5

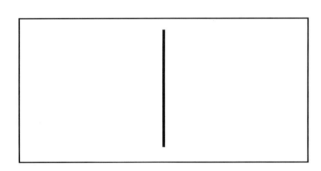

_____ + _____ = 7

_____ + _____ = 7

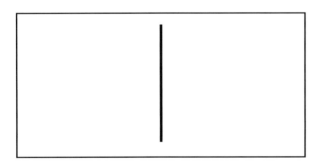

_____ + _____ = 10

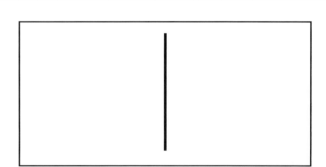

_____ + _____ = 10

Date: _____   Name: _____

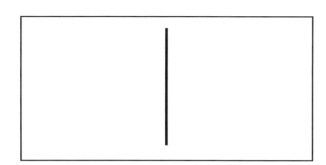

_____ + _____ = 9

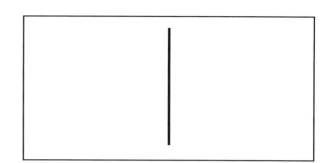

_____ + _____ = 9

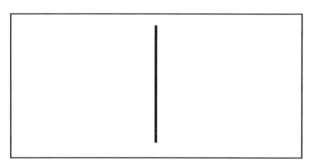

_____ + _____ = 12

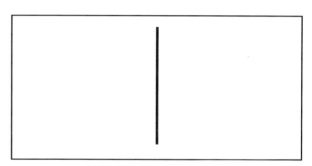

_____ + _____ = 12

Date: _____ **Name:** _____

Match Them Up

A	B	C
14+2	10	5+13
8+9	18	1+9
9+1	16	5+10
10+5	9	3+11
13+5	17	2+14
11+3	15	4+5
5+4	14	9+8

8 Addition of a One-Digit Number to a Two-Digit Number

Background Information for Teachers

This lesson focuses on addition of a one-digit number to a two-digit number. Encourage students to develop their own strategies for solving multi-digit addition (and subtraction) problems. Emphasizing self-discovered strategies rather than traditional algorithms strengthens students' understanding of place-value concepts and enhances their development of number sense.

Ensure that students learn to solve problems involving regrouping and problems not involving regrouping simultaneously. Focusing on only one or the other can lead to misconceptions about the operations.

Activity: Part One uses story problems to introduce students to higher-decade addition. Encourage students to look for more than one way to solve each problem and to share their strategies with each other. As students explain their methods, symbolize their strategies on an empty number line. For example, the sum of 16 + 8 can be found by adding 4 to 16 to get 20 and then adding 4 more to get 24. These solutions are shown on an empty number line like this:

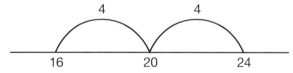

Note: Remember to use the horizontal format, not the vertical format, to present addition and subtraction algorithms to students. See the editorial note to teachers in the introduction to unit 6, found on page 521.

Materials

- beads with large holes (at least 100 beads for each student)
- 60-cm lengths of string (one for each student. Tie a knot at one end of each piece of string, and thread fifty beads onto it to create a fifty-bead string. Tie a knot at the other end. Be sure there is enough room on each piece of string to move the beads up and down freely.)
- 1-metre lengths of string (one for each student. Tie a knot at one end of each piece of string, and thread 100 beads onto it to create a 100-bead string. Tie a knot at the other end. Be sure there is enough room on each piece of string to move the beads up and down freely.)
- chart paper
- markers

Activity: Part One

Distribute fifty-bead strings, and have students use the bead strings to solve the following problems:

- Mr. Ramsey's class is selling wrapping paper to raise money for a camping trip. The students sold 7 rolls of wrapping paper the first week and 26 rolls the second week. How many rolls of wrapping paper did Mr. Ramsey's class sell in total?

- There are 41 computers in the school's computer lab and 8 more computers in the library. How many computers are there altogether?

- There are 6 cows and 12 horses on Mrs. Green's farm. How many animals does Mrs. Green have?

- Andrea has 37 stamps in her collection. Her friend gives her 9 more stamps. How many stamps does Andrea have now?

Note: Upon completion of the activity, save the fifty-bead strings for future activities.

▶

Unit 6 • **Number Operations**

8

Next Step

Distribute 100-bead strings to students. Have students use the bead strings to solve various addition problems involving one-digit addends added to numbers greater than 50.

Encourage students to use empty number lines (on chart paper) to show their thinking and solutions. For example, the sum of 55 + 9 can be shown in this way:

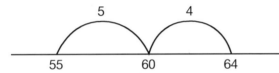

Show students how to use symbols to record their solutions to problems. For example:

55 + 9 = 55 + 5 + 4   or   55 + 9 = 64

or 55 + 5 + 4 = 64

Note: Upon completion of the activity, save the 100-bead strings for future activities.

Activity: Part Two

Note: The following activity helps students develop mental computational skills with addition.

Ask students to complete the following problems:

3 + 4 = ____   33 + 4 = ____

13 + 4 = ____   43 + 4 = ____

23 + 4 = ____   53 + 4 = ____

Have students look for patterns in the preceding problems.

Repeat using other series of problems, such as:

7 + 3 = ____   37 + 3 = ____

17 + 3 = ____   47 + 3 = ____

27 + 3 = ____   57 + 3 = ____

Distribute Activity Sheet A (6.8.1), and have students circle the corresponding problem in the middle column to each answer in the first column. In the third column, have students use pictures, numbers, or words to explain how they know each problem they selected corresponds with the answer in that row.

Activity Sheet A

Directions to students:

For each answer in the first column, circle the correct number story in the middle column. In the third column, use pictures, numbers, or words to explain how you know you are right (6.8.1).

Activity Centre

Place number cubes, paper, and pencils at an activity centre, and have pairs of students play "Turn to 50." To begin, have players in each pair roll the number cube and record the number rolled. Then, have players take turns *turning* – not rolling – the number cube *once*, in any direction. Players then add the number turned (the new number on the top of the number cube) to the number previously recorded. The game continues until one player reaches 50. A player forfeits his/her turn if the number turned results in a sum greater than 50 when added to the number previously recorded. For example, if the last-recorded number is 48 and a player turns a number that is greater than 2, it is the other player's turn.

Vary the game by having students start at 50 and play "Turn to 100."

Extensions

- Distribute to each student a number cube and a copy of the extension activity sheet called "Repeated Addition" (included). To begin, have students roll their number cubes

▶

twice to determine their starting numbers. The first roll represents the tens digit and the second roll represents the ones digit. For example, if a student rolls a 6 and then a 4, his/her starting number is 64.

Now, have students roll their number cubes again – this time, only once. Ask students to repeatedly add the new number rolled to their starting numbers until they get as close to 100 as possible. For example, if the same student's new roll produces a 5, he/she begins at 64 and adds 5 over and over, getting as close to 100 as possible. This student's completed activity sheet would appear as follows:

Tens	Ones	Add
6	4	5
6	9	5
7	4	5
7	9	5
8	4	5
8	9	5
9	4	5
9	9	5

Once students have completed their activity sheets, challenge them to look for patterns (6.8.2).

■ Distribute calculators and "On Target" score sheets (included), and have pairs of students play "On Target." Tell each pair to select a target number between 25 and 100 (modify this range to meet individual student needs) and record it in the blank box on their recording sheet.

Have Player *A* from each pair enter a one-digit number (1-9) into the calculator and record the number in the "Input" column of the score sheet. Also, tell Player *A* to carry the number over to the "Sum" column.

Now, have Player *B* from each pair select a one-digit number to add to Player *A*'s number. Tell player *B* to press "+" and the number on the calculator, record a number sentence in the "Input" column on the score sheet, and then record the sum in the "Sum" column.

Have players take turns adding one-digit numbers and recording the results, as in the following example, until one player reaches the target number. If a player exceeds the target number, the other player wins the round. Have students play several rounds (6.8.3).

Target Number: 56		
Player	**Input**	**Sum**
A	7	7
B	7 + 8	15
A	15 + 2	17
B	17 + 9	26
↓	↓	↓

Unit 6 • **Number Operations**

629

Name: _____

Date: _____

Match the Problem to the Answer

Answer	Problem		How Do You Know?
25	15 + 8	21 + 4	14 + 3	
29	38 + 9	34 + 6	25 + 4	
64	60 + 4	66 + 6	69 + 5	
32	45 + 8	37 + 4	24 + 8	
55	26 + 9	46 + 9	53 + 3	
49	46 + 2	42 + 7	44 + 4	

8A

630 – 6.8.1

Portage & Main Press, 2006, Hands-On Mathematics, Level 2, ISBN: 978-1-55379-091-4

Date: _____ **Name:** _____

Repeated Addition

Tens	Ones	Add

Extension A

Portage & Main Press, 2006, Hands-On Mathematics, Level 2, ISBN: 978-1-55379-091-4

6.8.2 – 631

Date: _____   **Name:** _____

On Target Score Sheet

Target Number:		
Player	**Input**	**Sum**

632 – 6.8.3   Portage & Main Press, 2006, Hands-On Mathematics, Level 2, ISBN: 978-1-55379-091-4   **Extension B**

9 Addition and Subtraction of Tens

Materials

- *One Watermelon Seed*, a book by Celia Barker Lottridge
- 100-bead strings (from lesson 8)
- materials that can be grouped into tens (coffee stirrers, straws, or wooden craft sticks)
- elastic bands
- hundred charts (included with part 1, unit 1, lesson 10. Make one photocopy for each student.) (1.10.1)
- drawing paper
- + or − tens cards (included. Photocopy one set for each pair of students.) (6.9.1)

Activity

Read the book *One Watermelon Seed* with students. Now, present students with the following problems:

- In the fall, Max and Josephine picked 20 pumpkins and 50 tomatoes. Altogether, how many pumpkins and tomatoes did Max and Josephine pick?

- Max and Josephine picked 90 potatoes and 30 eggplants. How many more potatoes than eggplants did Max and Josephine pick?

- Max and Josephine picked 60 blueberries and 40 peppers. Altogether, how many blueberries and peppers did they pick?

- Max and Josephine picked 100 ears of corn and 70 strawberries. Did they pick more corn or more strawberries? How much more?

After students solve each problem, have them give their solutions and explain why their solutions are reasonable.

Note: Students may find it helpful to use manipulatives such as bead strings, stir sticks and elastics, empty number lines, hundred charts, or their own drawings to give their explanations. Encourage students to use whichever supports best help them explain how they reached their solutions.

As students share their solutions, demonstrate how each problem can be solved using a variety of supports such as manipulatives, empty number lines, hundred charts, or drawings. Encourage students to use a variety of strategies to solve the problems.

Distribute Activity Sheet A (6.9.2), and have students use pictures, numbers, and words to solve each problem. Also, have students describe the strategy they used to solve each problem.

Activity Sheet A

Note: This is a two-page activity sheet.

Directions to students:

Use pictures, numbers, and words to solve each problem. Describe the strategy you used to solve each problem (6.9.2).

Problem Solving

- How many seeds did Max and Josephine plant altogether?

- How many fruits and vegetables did Max and Josephine pick altogether?

Next Steps

- Have students make up their own problems about the fruits and vegetables Max and Josephine picked.

Unit 6 • **Number Operations**

- Distribute to each pair of students a set of + or − tens cards (6.9.1), and have students play "Concentration" ("Memory").

Note: Each set of + or − tens cards should include twenty cards: ten cards with problems involving addition or subtraction of 10 and ten cards with the problems' related sums or differences.

Have each pair place their cards, facedown, in five rows of four cards. Tell players to take turns turning over two cards. If a player turns over a problem and its related sum or difference (a match), as in the following diagram, he/she keeps the cards and takes another turn:

If the cards do not match, the player turns the cards over again and his/her partner takes a turn. When all cards are gone, the player with the most matches wins.

- Have students use their 100-bead strings or hundred charts to add multiples of 10 to non-multiples of 10. For example: 20 + 42.

- Have students use their 100-bead strings or hundred charts to subtract multiples of 10 from non-multiples of 10. For example: 57 − 30.

Extension

Distribute hundred chart variations (included), and have students use them to further explore addition and subtraction of tens (6.9.3).

+ or – Tens Cards

$10 + 30$	$20 + 30$
$40 + 40$	$40 + 50$
$30 + 30$	$30 + 40$

Portage & Main Press, 2006, Hands-On Mathematics, Level 2, ISBN: 978-1-55379-091-4   6.9.1 – 635

80 – 70	**50 – 30**
90 – 60	**40 – 40**
0	**10**

636 – 6.9.1

Portage & Main Press, 2006, Hands-On Mathematics, Level 2, ISBN: 978-1-55379-091-4

20	**30**
40	**50**
60	**70**

Portage & Main Press, 2006, Hands-On Mathematics, Level 2, ISBN: 978-1-55379-091-4   6.9.1 – **637**

80

90

638 – 6.9.1

Portage & Main Press, 2006, Hands-On Mathematics, Level 2, ISBN: 978-1-55379-091-4

Date: _____   **Name:** _____

Solving Problems

1. Meagan has a bag of 20 marbles. She buys 40 more marbles. How many marbles does Meagan have now?

My strategy: _____

_____

2. Jeremy collects hockey cards. He has 30 cards. He gets 0 more cards for his birthday. How many cards does Jeremy have now?

My strategy: _____

_____

Date: _____   **Name:** _____

3. Nathan has 80 sheets of paper. He uses 40 sheets to draw pictures of racecars. How many sheets of paper does Nathan have left?

My strategy: _____

_____

4. Kaylee has 70 shells in her collection. Her brother, Bennett, has 90 shells in his collection. How many more shells does Bennett have than Kaylee?

My strategy: _____

_____

640 – 6.9.2   Portage & Main Press, 2006, Hands-On Mathematics, Level 2, ISBN: 978-1-55379-091-4   **9A**

Hundred Chart Variation 1

0	1	2	3	4	5	6	7	8	9
10	11	12	13	14	15	16	17	18	19
20	21	22	23	24	25	26	27	28	29
30	31	32	33	34	35	36	37	38	39
40	41	42	43	44	45	46	47	48	49
50	51	52	53	54	55	56	57	58	59
60	61	62	63	64	65	66	67	68	69
70	71	72	73	74	75	76	77	78	79
80	81	82	83	84	85	86	87	88	89
90	91	92	93	94	95	96	97	98	99

Extension

Hundred Chart Variation 2

1	2	3	4	5	6	7	8	9	10
11	12	13	14	15	16	17	18	19	20
21	22	23	24	25	26	27	28	29	30
31	32	33	34	35	36	37	38	39	40
41	42	43	44	45	46	47	48	49	50
51	52	53	54	55	56	57	58	59	60
61	62	63	64	65	66	67	68	69	70
71	72	73	74	75	76	77	78	79	80
81	82	83	84	85	86	87	88	89	90
91	92	93	94	95	96	97	98	99	100

Extension

Hundred Chart Variation 3

10	20	30	40	50	60	70	80	90	100
9	19	29	39	49	59	69	79	89	99
8	18	28	38	48	58	68	78	88	98
7	17	27	37	47	57	67	77	87	97
6	16	26	36	46	56	66	76	86	96
5	15	25	35	45	55	65	75	85	95
4	14	24	34	44	54	64	74	84	94
3	13	23	33	43	53	63	73	83	93
2	12	22	32	42	52	62	72	82	92
1	11	21	31	41	51	61	71	81	91

Extension

Portage & Main Press, 2006, Hands-On Mathematics, Level 2, ISBN: 978-1-55379-091-4

6.9.3 – 643

Hundred Chart Variation 4

9	19	29	39	49	59	69	79	89	99
8	18	28	38	48	58	68	78	88	98
7	17	27	37	47	57	67	77	87	97
6	16	26	36	46	56	66	76	86	96
5	15	25	35	45	55	65	75	85	95
4	14	24	34	44	54	64	74	84	94
3	13	23	33	43	53	63	73	83	93
2	12	22	32	42	52	62	72	82	92
1	11	21	31	41	51	61	71	81	91
0	10	20	30	40	50	60	70	80	90

644 – 6.9.3

Portage & Main Press, 2006, Hands-On Mathematics, Level 2, ISBN: 978-1-55379-091-4

Extension

Hundred Chart Variation 5

1	2	3	4	5	6	7	8	9	10	11	12	13	14	15	16	17	18	19	20
21	22	23	24	25	26	27	28	29	30	31	32	33	34	35	36	37	38	39	40
41	42	43	44	45	46	47	48	49	50	51	52	53	54	55	56	57	58	59	60
61	62	63	64	65	66	67	68	69	70	71	72	73	74	75	76	77	78	79	80
81	82	83	84	85	86	87	88	89	90	91	92	93	94	95	96	97	98	99	100

Hundred Chart Variation 6

0	1	2	3	4	5	6	7	8	9	10	11	12	13	14	15	16	17	18	19
20	21	22	23	24	25	26	27	28	29	30	31	32	33	34	35	36	37	38	39
40	41	42	43	44	45	46	47	48	49	50	51	52	53	54	55	56	57	58	59
60	61	62	63	64	65	66	67	68	69	70	71	72	73	74	75	76	77	78	79
80	81	82	83	84	85	86	87	88	89	90	91	92	93	94	95	96	97	98	99

Extension

10 Addition of Two-Digit Numbers

Materials

- 100-bead strings (from lesson 8)
- chart paper
- markers
- hundred charts (included with part 1, unit 1, lesson 10. Make one photocopy for each student.) (1.10.1)
- counters
- pencil crayons

Activity

Have students use their bead strings to solve the following problems:

- The library is selling old books. Sixteen books are sold in the morning, and another 28 books are sold in the afternoon. Altogether, how many books are sold?

- Omar scored 24 goals in the first half of the soccer season. He scored 27 goals in the second half. How many goals did Omar score during the full soccer season?

- There are 19 dogs and 27 cats for sale at the pet store. How many pets are for sale?

- Kristy has 32 hockey cards. Her father gives her 36 more. How many hockey cards does Kristy have now?

For each of the preceding problems, ask several students to explain their thinking processes for finding the solution. Have those students offer their solutions and explain why their answers are reasonable.

On chart paper, show students how they can use empty number lines to symbolize how they found their solutions. For example, 14 + 38 can be shown on an empty number line like this:

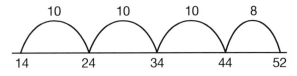

Or, it can be shown like this:

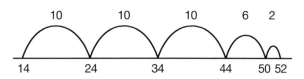

Distribute Activity Sheet A (6.10.1) and Activity Sheet B (6.10.2), and have students further explore addition of two-digit numbers.

Activity Sheet A

Directions to students:

Use the numbers in each box to complete the addition problems below the box (6.10.1).

Activity Sheet B

Directions to students:

Use a different coloured pencil crayon to circle each pair of numbers that adds up to 50 (6.10.2).

Next Steps

- Present students with more story problems, and have them use empty number lines to symbolize how they find their solutions.

- Show students how to use symbols to record problems and solutions. For example, 14 + 38 can be symbolized like this:

    14 + 38 = 14 + 30 + 8   or

    14 + 38 = 14 + 30 + 6 + 2   or

    14 + 38 = 52

646   Hands-On Mathematics • Grade 2

These solutions can also be represented on a tree diagram, as in the following example:

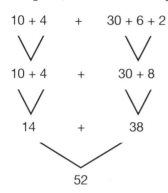

- Have students use hundred charts and counters to find sums of two numbers less than 100. For example, ask students to find the sum of 32 + 24 by placing a counter on the number 32, counting-on twenty to get to 52, and then adding four more to get to the sum, 56, as in the following diagram:

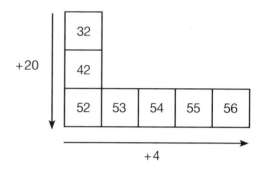

- Ask students to solve problems involving three or more addends.

Date: _____   **Name:** _____

Adding Two-Digit Numbers

20	18
19	16

_____ + _____ = 34   _____ + _____ = 39

_____ + _____ = 37   _____ + _____ = 36

22	45
40	24

_____ + _____ = 85   _____ + _____ = 69

_____ + _____ = 62   _____ + _____ = 46

37	20
36	15

_____ + _____ = 56   _____ + _____ = 35

_____ + _____ = 51   _____ + _____ = 57

648 – 6.10.1   Portage & Main Press, 2006, Hands-On Mathematics, Level 2, ISBN: 978-1-55379-091-4   **10A**

Date: _____ **Name:** _____

Making 50

6	8	17	7	43
44	23	14	12	29
27	15	32	16	21
25	33	18	41	9

10B

Portage & Main Press, 2006, Hands-On Mathematics, Level 2, ISBN: 978-1-55379-091-4

6.10.2 – **649**

11 Subtraction of One-Digit Numbers from Two-Digit Numbers

Materials

- calculators (one for each pair of students)
- 100-bead strings (from lesson 8) or other base-ten materials

Activity: Part One

Divide the class into pairs of students, distribute a calculator to each pair, and have students play "Target." Have one player in each pair enter the number 75 into the calculator. Then, tell players to take turns subtracting a number between 1 and 6 from the number (difference) on the display. The player who subtracts a number that results in 0 is the winner.

Have students play the game several times. Vary the game by using different starting numbers or by expanding the set of numbers students can subtract. For example, have students start with 85 and subtract any number from 1 through 8.

Activity: Part Two

Present students with the following problems:

- There are 46 trees in the park. Nine of the trees are maple trees and the rest are pine trees. How many pine trees are there?

- Julia's basketball team won 36 games and lost 8. How many more games did Julia's team win than lose?

- Quinn baked 75 cookies. Her dad ate 9 of them. How many cookies are left?

- Mr. Millar has 68 books in his classroom. Mr. Jones borrows 6 of Mr. Millar's books. How many books does Mr. Millar have now?

For each of the preceding problems, ask several students to explain their thinking processes for solving the problem. Have those students offer their solutions and explain why their answers are correct. For example, ask students to use 100-bead strings (or other base-ten materials)

or draw pictures to prove their solutions, or have therm use addition to check their answers.

Distribute Activity Sheet A (6.11.1), and have students circle the corresponding problem in the middle column for each answer in the first column. In the third column, have students use pictures, numbers, or words to explain how they know each problem they selected corresponds with the answer in that row.

Activity Sheet A

Directions to students:

For each answer in the first column, circle the correct problem in the middle column. In the third column, use pictures, numbers, or words to explain how you know you are right (6.11.1).

Next Steps

Note: The following activity will help students develop mental computational skills with subtraction.

Have students solve the following problems and then look for patterns:

8 – 4 = _____	38 – 4 = _____
18 – 4 = _____	48 – 4 = _____
28 – 4 = _____	58 – 4 = _____

Repeat the activity using other series of problems such as: 14 – 7, 24 – 7, 34 – 7, 44 – 7, 54 –7, 64 – 7.

Activity Centre

Place number cubes, paper, and pencils at an activity centre, and have pairs of students play "Race from 50." Have players in each pair record the number 50 on paper. Then, tell them to take turns *turning* – not rolling – the number cube *once*, in any direction. Players then subtract the number turned from the number previously recorded. The game continues until

▶

650   **Hands-On Mathematics • Grade 2**

11

one player reaches 0. A player forfeits his/her turn if the number turned results in a difference that is less than 0 when subtracted from the last-recorded number. For example, if the last-recorded number is a 3 and a player turns a number that is greater 3, it is the other player's turn.

Vary the game by having students start at 100 and race to 50.

Extensions

■ Distribute to each student a number cube and a copy of the extension activity sheet called "Repeated Subtraction" (included). To begin, have students roll their number cubes twice to determine their starting numbers. The first roll represents the tens digit and the second roll represents the ones digit. For example, if a student rolls a 3 and then a 4, his/her starting number is 34.

Now, have students roll their number cubes again – this time, only once. Ask students to repeatedly subtract the new number rolled from their starting numbers until they get as close to 0 as possible. For example, if a student's new roll produces a 5, he/she begins at 34 and subtracts 5 over and over until he/she can no longer subtract 5 (because the difference is less than 5).

This student's completed activity sheet would appear as follows:

Tens	Ones	Subtract
3	4	5
2	9	5
2	4	5
1	9	5
1	4	5
0	9	5
0	4	

Once students have completed their activity sheets, challenge them to look for patterns (6.11.2).

■ Distribute to students calculators and copies of the extension activity sheet called "Estimation Challenge" (included). Ask students to read each problem and circle the answer in the "Estimate" column they think is closest to the actual answer. Then, have students use calculators to check their answers (6.11.3).

When students have completed their activity sheets, discuss some of the strategies they used to make their estimates.

Unit 6 • **Number Operations**

Date: _____

Name: _____

Match the Problem to the Answer

Answer	Problem		How Do You Know?
15	27 – 8	14 – 3	
29	38 – 9	25 – 4	
64	66 – 6 69 – 5	72 – 7	
32	45 – 8 37 – 4	40 – 8	
12	27 – 8 21 – 6	14 – 2	
49	38 – 9 34 – 6	58 – 9	

652 – 6.11.1

11A

Portage & Main Press, 2006, Hands-On Mathematics, Level 2, ISBN: 978-1-55379-091-4

Date: _____   **Name:** _____

Repeated Subtraction

Tens	Ones	Subtract

Extension A

Portage & Main Press, 2006, Hands-On Mathematics, Level 2, ISBN: 978-1-55379-091-4

6.11.2 – 653

Date: _____   **Name:** _____

Estimation Challenge

Problem	Estimate				Answer
72 – 49	20	30	40	50	
93 – 61	20	30	40	50	
83 – 42	20	30	40	50	
61 – 18	20	30	40	50	
79 – 42	20	30	40	50	
57 – 38	20	30	40	50	
89 – 37	20	30	40	50	
43 – 18	20	30	40	50	
98 – 57	20	30	40	50	
69 – 38	20	30	40	50	

654 – 6.11.3   Portage & Main Press, 2006, Hands-On Mathematics, Level 2, ISBN: 978-1-55379-091-4   **Extension B**

12 Subtraction with Two-Digit Numbers

Materials

- *Mega-Funny Math Poems and Problems*, a book by Dan Greenberg
- fifty-bead strings (from lesson 8)
- chart paper
- marker

Activity

Read with students the poem "Bug City," found in the book *Mega-Funny Math Poems and Problems*. Ask students to use their bead strings to solve the following problems:

- Ruth and Max found 48 bugs and put them in a plastic bug box. Twelve of the bugs escaped from the box. How many bugs are left in the box?

- Oops – Ruth and Max lost another 12 bugs. How many bugs are left now?

- Fifteen of the bugs that are left have six legs. How many bugs do not have six legs?

- Some of the bugs that Ruth and Max found are crickets and the rest are beetles. If 29 of the 48 bugs they found are beetles, how many are crickets?

Discuss students' solutions for each problem, and ask several students to explain their thinking processes for solving the problem. On chart paper, show students how they can use an empty number line to symbolize the problem-solving strategies they use. For example, one strategy for solving the problem 44 – 17 is the think-addition strategy, as in the following two examples:

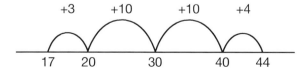

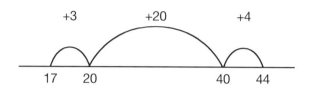

Another strategy for solving the same problem is the subtraction strategy: students begin at the far, right end of the number line and make backward jumps, as in the following example:

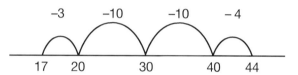

Distribute Activity Sheet A (6.12.1), and have students fill in the missing numbers by looking for patterns. Then, ask students to describe three patterns that they see.

Activity Sheet A

Directions to students:

Fill in the missing numbers for each problem by looking for patterns. Then, describe three patterns that you see (6.12.1).

Next Steps

- Have students make up their own bug problems for their classmates to solve.

- Have students solve subtraction problems involving two-digit numbers greater than 50.

- Have students use empty number lines to solve two-digit subtraction problems. For example, to solve the problem 64 – 37, a completed number line using the think-addition strategy might look like this:

12

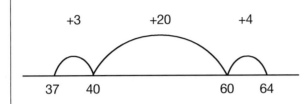

Or, using the subtraction strategy to solve the same problem, a completed number line might look like this:

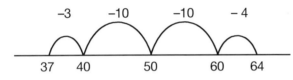

- Show students how to use symbols to record their solutions to subtraction problems. For example, the solution to 64 – 37 can be recorded like this:

$$64 \xrightarrow{-4} 60 \xrightarrow{-30} 30 \xrightarrow{-3} 27$$

- Have students use hundred charts and counters to find the difference between two numbers. For example, ask students to find the difference between 56 and 24 by placing a counter on the number 56, counting-back twenty to get to 36, and then counting-back four more to get to the difference, 32, as in the following diagram:

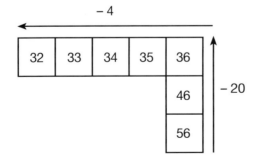

Encourage students to explore different ways of using the hundred chart to find the difference between two numbers, and have them discuss which method is the most efficient.

Note: To fully engage students in conceptualizing the different ways of solving the same problem, demonstrate the same problems using bead strings, empty number lines, and equations.

Distribute Activity Sheet B (6.12.2), and have students use hundred charts, 100-bead strings, and empty number lines to show how to solve each subtraction problem.

Activity Sheet B

Note: This is a two-page activity sheet.

Directions to students:

Use a hundred chart, a 100-bead string, and an empty number line to show how to solve each subtraction problem (6.12.2).

Extension

Distribute the extension activity sheet called "Solving More Subtraction Problems in Different Ways" (included), and have students continue to practice showing different ways of solving two-digit subtraction problems. Record problems on the activity sheet before photocopying it for students, or have students record their own problems to solve (6.12.3).

Note: You can also use this two-page extension activity sheet for continued practice of addition problems.

▶

656   Hands-On Mathematics • Grade 2

12

Assessment Suggestion

Have students solve the following problems:

- 44 + 18 = ____
- 53 − 27 = ____

For each problem, assess each student's ability to:

- determine the correct answer
- use a mathematically-correct algorithm to solve the problem
- use an algorithm to solve the problem efficiently (i.e., relatively quickly and without frustration)
- use the algorithm to solve other addition and subtraction problems

Record these criteria on the Rubric, found on page 25, and record your results.

Date: _____   **Name:** _____

Looking for Patterns

$$62 - 29 = 33$$

$$58 - 27 = 31$$

$$54 - 25 = 29$$

$$50 - 23 = \underline{}$$

$$46 - \underline{} = \underline{}$$

$$\underline{} - \underline{} = \underline{}$$

$$\underline{} - \underline{} = \underline{}$$

Three patterns that I see:

1. _____

_____

2. _____

_____

3. _____

_____

658 – 6.12.1   Portage & Main Press, 2006, Hands-On Mathematics, Level 2, ISBN: 978-1-55379-091-4   **12A**

Date: _____ Name: _____

Solving Subtraction Problems in Different Ways

| 77 − 28 = _____ |

Hundred Chart

0	1	2	3	4	5	6	7	8	9
10	11	12	13	14	15	16	17	18	19
20	21	22	23	24	25	26	27	28	29
30	31	32	33	34	35	36	37	38	39
40	41	42	43	44	45	46	47	48	49
50	51	52	53	54	55	56	57	58	59
60	61	62	63	64	65	66	67	68	69
70	71	72	73	74	75	76	77	78	79
80	81	82	83	84	85	86	87	88	89
90	91	92	93	94	95	96	97	98	99

Bead String:

Empty Number Line:

12B

Date: _____   Name: _____

44 − 19 = _____

Hundred Chart

0	1	2	3	4	5	6	7	8	9
10	11	12	13	14	15	16	17	18	19
20	21	22	23	24	25	26	27	28	29
30	31	32	33	34	35	36	37	38	39
40	41	42	43	44	45	46	47	48	49
50	51	52	53	54	55	56	57	58	59
60	61	62	63	64	65	66	67	68	69
70	71	72	73	74	75	76	77	78	79
80	81	82	83	84	85	86	87	88	89
90	91	92	93	94	95	96	97	98	99

Bead String:

Empty Number Line:

_____

Date: _____ Name: _____

Solving More Subtraction Problems in Different Ways

Problem: [　　　]

Hundred Chart

0	1	2	3	4	5	6	7	8	9
10	11	12	13	14	15	16	17	18	19
20	21	22	23	24	25	26	27	28	29
30	31	32	33	34	35	36	37	38	39
40	41	42	43	44	45	46	47	48	49
50	51	52	53	54	55	56	57	58	59
60	61	62	63	64	65	66	67	68	69
70	71	72	73	74	75	76	77	78	79
80	81	82	83	84	85	86	87	88	89
90	91	92	93	94	95	96	97	98	99

Bead String:

Empty Number Line:

Extension

Date: _____   Name: _____

Problem: [   ]

Hundred Chart

0	1	2	3	4	5	6	7	8	9
10	11	12	13	14	15	16	17	18	19
20	21	22	23	24	25	26	27	28	29
30	31	32	33	34	35	36	37	38	39
40	41	42	43	44	45	46	47	48	49
50	51	52	53	54	55	56	57	58	59
60	61	62	63	64	65	66	67	68	69
70	71	72	73	74	75	76	77	78	79
80	81	82	83	84	85	86	87	88	89
90	91	92	93	94	95	96	97	98	99

Bead String:

Empty Number Line:

662 – 6.12.3   Portage & Main Press, 2006, Hands-On Mathematics, Level 2, ISBN: 978-1-55379-091-4   **Extension**

13 | Identifying and Counting Coins

Background Information for Teachers

In addition to the commonly used coins, students should become familiar with the fifty-cent coin, which was reissued in 2003 as one of the 2003 Coronation commemorative coin products to celebrate the 50th anniversary of the Coronation of Queen Elizabeth II.

Materials

- Canadian coins and bills up to ten dollars (pennies, nickels, dimes, quarters, fifty-cent coins, one-dollar coins [loonies], two-dollar coins [toonies], five-dollar bills, ten-dollar bills. Use real coins, or make photocopies of the Canadian coins and the Canadian bills templates, included, and cut out.) (6.13.1, 6.13.2)
- Canadian coins templates (included. Make one or two copies of each sheet for each student.) (6.13.1)
- Canadian bills template (Make a photocopy of each bill for each student.) (6.13.2)
- plastic coins (optional)
- chart paper
- markers
- drawing paper
- *Alexander, Who Used to Be Rich Last Sunday*, a book by Judith Viorst
- large coins templates (included. Copy, cut out, mount on sturdy tagboard, and laminate.) (6.13.3)
- purchase price cards (included. Copy, cut out, mount on sturdy tagboard, and laminate.) (6.13.4)
- pocket chart
- envelopes, each with a random monetary amount (ten dollars or less) written on the front (You will need approximately twenty envelopes.)
- scissors

Activity: Part One: Identifying Canadian Coins and Bills

Divide the class into working groups, and provide each group with some pennies, nickels, dimes, quarters, fifty-cent coins, one-dollar coins, and two-dollar coins. Allow time for students to examine and discuss the coins. Have them put the coins in order by size and then challenge them to put the coins in order by value (from lowest to highest).

Next, have the groups sort their coins in a variety of ways (by colour, size, value, and so on), and have them share their sorting rules with the rest of the class.

Now, ask students to hold up the coin that is worth five cents. Ask:

- What do we call this coin?

Next, have students hold up the coin that is worth twenty-five cents. Ask:

- What do we call this coin?

Continue this activity for each coin. To reinforce the names and values of each of the coins, print the following sentences on chart paper.

A _____ is worth one cent or 1¢.

A _____ is worth five cents or 5¢.

A _____ is worth ten cents or 10¢.

A _____ is worth twenty-five cents or 25¢.

A _____ is worth fifty cents or 50¢.

A _____ is worth one dollar or $1.

A _____ is worth two dollars or $2.

Note: The correct way to draw the dollar sign is with one vertical line through it (not two). Be sure to model this when recording money values, and encourage students to do the same.

▶

Unit 6 • **Number Operations**

13

Now, give each student one set of coins, from a penny to a two-dollar coin. Have students sequence their coins in order of value (from lowest to highest). Circulate to monitor students' progress on this task. Ask:

- Which coin is worth more, a dime or a quarter?
- Which coin is smaller than a nickel but worth more?
- Which coin is worth more, a penny or a nickel?
- Which coin has two colours?
- Which coin is worth more, a toonie or a loonie?

Next, draw the cents symbol (¢) on chart paper. Ask:

- What does this symbol mean?
- Where do you see this symbol?

Explain that this symbol is always placed after the coin value. Now, provide each student with a sheet of drawing paper. Have students line up their coins on the paper in order of value, this time from highest to lowest value. Have students record the value underneath each coin. Remind students to use the cents symbol when recording these values.

Distribute to each student a paper five-dollar bill and a paper ten-dollar bill. Hold up a real five-dollar bill for students to see. Ask:

- What is this called?
- How do you know it is a five-dollar bill?
- What are five characteristics of a five dollar bill?

Record students' suggestions on chart paper.

Now, display a ten-dollar bill for students to see. Ask:

- What is this called?
- How do you know it is a ten-dollar bill?

- What are five characteristics of a ten-dollar bill?

Record students' suggestions on chart paper. Then, distribute Activity Sheet A (6.13.5) and have students record the name, value, and two interesting facts about each coin shown.

Activity Sheet A

Directions to students:

Record the name, value, and two interesting facts about each coin shown (6.13.5).

Activity: Part Two: Counting Coins

Read the book *Alexander, Who Used to Be Rich Last Sunday* with students. As a class, make a list on chart paper of how Alexander spent his money. Include how much each choice cost him.

Divide the class into pairs of students, and have the pairs calculate how much money Alexander spent in total. Distribute real, plastic, or paper coins to help students solve the problem. Have each pair share their strategies and solutions with the rest of the class. The final answer should be one dollar.

As a class, discuss different strategies for counting coins. For example:

- group similar coins together, then count
- count the coins in order of value (from the highest to the lowest)
- count the pennies by 1s, the nickels by 5s, the dimes by 10s, and so on
- put the coins in one-dollar piles (i.e., each pile is worth one dollar)
- "counting-on" (see note on following page)

13

Note: Counting on is a good strategy for students to use when making change. For example: April and Jared are playing "store." April wants to buy a pencil worth 37¢. She gives Jared 50¢. How much change should Jared give to April? Since it is often easier for students to count by 5s and 10s, Jared should start at 37, "count on," by 1s, to 40, and then count by 5s (nickels) or 10s (dimes) to get to fifty, and to the answer (13¢).

Display the large coins (6.13.3) in the top pockets of the pocket chart. Display the purchase price cards (6.13.4) in the lower pockets of the pocket chart. As a class, determine the combination of coins you need to make up the amount on each price tag. Encourage students to use some of the counting strategies discussed earlier.

Now, divide the class into pairs of students. Provide each pair with a handful of coins (real, plastic, or paper) and an envelope with a monetary amount written on the front. Have each pair examine the monetary figure, and then put the correct combination of coins inside. Then, have two pairs of students trade envelopes, and verify that the combination of coins inside the envelope equals the monetary amount written on the front. Have students repeat the activity several times, with different envelopes.

Distribute to students one or two copies of each sheet of Canadian coins (6.13.1), scissors, and a copy of Activity Sheet B (6.13.6). Have students cut out some of the coins and make two different coin combinations for each amount shown on the activity sheet. Ask students to glue the coin combinations onto each box, to show their answers.

Activity Sheet B

Directions to students:

Cut out some of your paper coins. Make two different coin combinations for each amount

shown. Glue the coin combinations onto each box, to show your answers (6.13.6).

Activity: Part Three: Estimating Coin Combinations

Use the large coins to display a coin combination in the pocket chart. Ask:

- Without actually adding up the coins, how many cents do you estimate are shown?

Record students' estimates on chart paper. Now, add the coins together with students. Ask:

- Was anyone correct with his/her estimate?
- Which estimates are too high?
- Which are too low?

Repeat this activity several times so that students are comfortable estimating, then adding, the coins.

Divide the class into pairs of students. Provide each student with Activity Sheet C (6.13.7) and a handful of coins (real, plastic, or paper). Have one student in each pair display a coin combination while the second student estimates the value of the coins and records this on the activity sheet. Then, have the second student add the value of the coins together and record the results on the sheet, along with the number of coins in the combination. Have students switch roles and repeat the task. Continue until the sheet is complete.

Activity Sheet C

Directions to students:

Estimate the value of the coins your partner shows you. Record your estimate in the first column of the chart. Add up the coins, and record their value in the second column. Count the number of coins in the combination, and record this in the third column. Switch roles. Repeat (6.13.7).

▶

Unit 6 • **Number Operations**

665

Problem Solving

- Make 43¢ in four different ways.

- I have three coins in my pocket. The coins add up to 40¢. Which coins do I have in my pocket?

- I have three coins in my pocket. Could the coins add up to 17¢? Why or why not?

Activity Centres

- Set up a pretend store in your classroom. Provide a variety of items, each one tagged with a different purchase price (less than one dollar). Have students select items to purchase and use plastic or paper coins to show the exact amount of change they need to purchase the items.

- Place a magnifying glass and a collection of coins on a table. Encourage students to use the magnifying glass to identify the similarities and differences of each coin.

Extensions

- Add the names for all the coins to your classroom Math Word Wall.

- Make overhead copies of each coin to use for flash math activities. Place several coins on the overhead, and turn it on for only a few seconds. Turn off the overhead, and challenge students to tell how much money they saw.

- Read the poem "Smart," found in the book *Where the Sidewalk Ends* by Shel Silverstein. Discuss the trading of the coins in the poem. Have students calculate the amount of money in each line of the poem and compare the values.

- Have students play this variation of "Simon Says," to help them remember the value of different coins:

> *Simon says: Turn around as many times as there are cents in a penny.*
> *Simon says: Jump up and down as many times as there are cents in a nickel.*

Once students get the hang of the game, your wording can change slightly, as follows:

> *Simon says: Do one dime's worth of toe touches.*
> *Simon says: Do one quarter's worth of jumping jacks.*

- Play a guessing game to identify coins. Give students one or two clues about a certain coin (for example, "I am worth the same amount as two nickels.") Have students listen to your clue and decide which coin you are describing.

- Plan a bake sale with students. Ask students to bring in baked goods to sell to other classes on the specific day. The sale will give them a real-life opportunity to practice counting and adding money, and providing change. Donate the money you raise to a local charity.

- Use your local transit system to take a field trip to a nearby store. Have students count out their own bus fare. Encourage students to also bring a small amount of money to purchase something at the store.

- Read *A Quarter from the Tooth Fairy*, a book by Caren Holtzman. Brainstorm a list of items students could buy for a quarter.

13

Assessment Suggestion

Meet with each student individually. Give the student a small collection of coins, and assess his/her ability to name each coin, identify its value, and count (add) the coins accurately. Record your results on the Individual Student Observations sheet, found on page 23.

Unit 6 • **Number Operations**

Canadian Coins Template

Canadian Coins Template

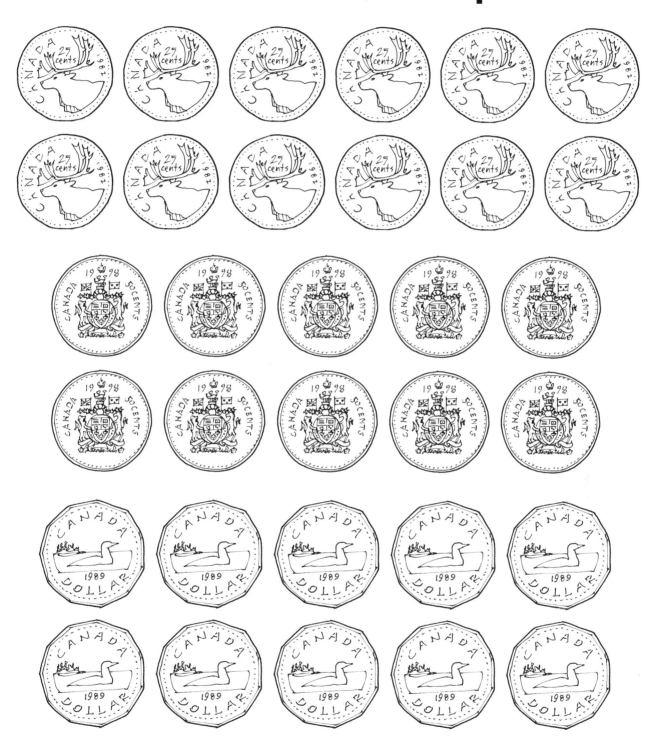

Coin designs © courtesy of the Royal Canadian Mint

Image des pieces © courtoisie de la Monnaie royale canadienne

Canadian Coins Template

Coin designs © courtesy of the Royal Canadian Mint

Image des pieces © courtoisie de la Monnaie royale canadienne

Canadian Bills Template

Large Coins Template

Large Coins Template

Large Coins Template

Purchase Price Cards

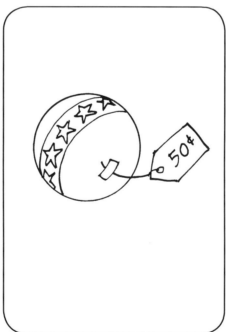

Purchase Price Cards

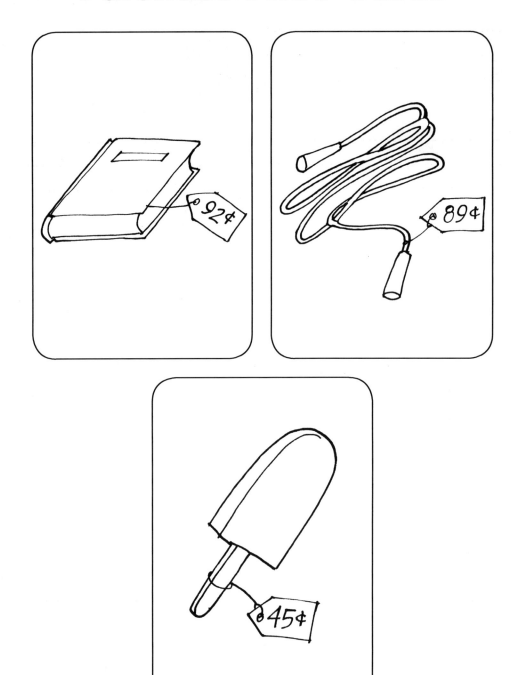

Date: _____   Name: _____

Identifying Canadian Coins

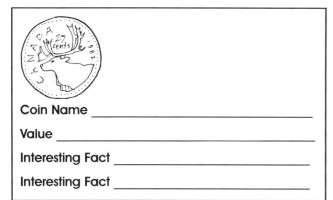

Coin Name _____
Value _____
Interesting Fact _____
Interesting Fact _____

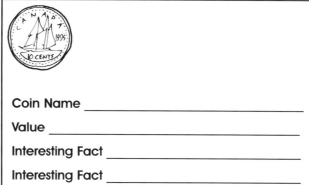

Coin Name _____
Value _____
Interesting Fact _____
Interesting Fact _____

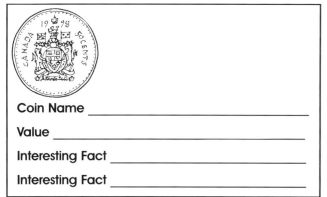

Coin Name _____
Value _____
Interesting Fact _____
Interesting Fact _____

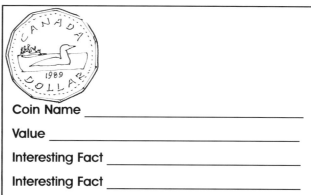

Coin Name _____
Value _____
Interesting Fact _____
Interesting Fact _____

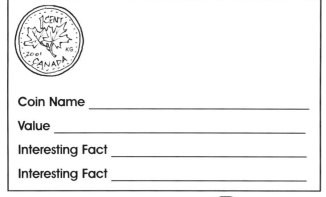

Coin Name _____
Value _____
Interesting Fact _____
Interesting Fact _____

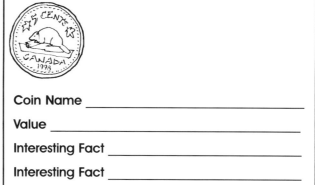

Coin Name _____
Value _____
Interesting Fact _____
Interesting Fact _____

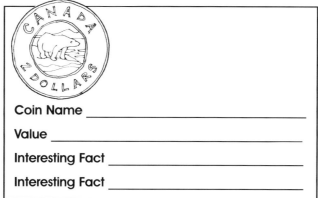

Coin Name _____
Value _____
Interesting Fact _____
Interesting Fact _____

13A

Coin designs © courtesy of the Royal Canadian Mint
Image des pieces © courtoisie de la Monnaie royale canadienne

Date: _____ Name: _____

Coin Combinations

18¢
or

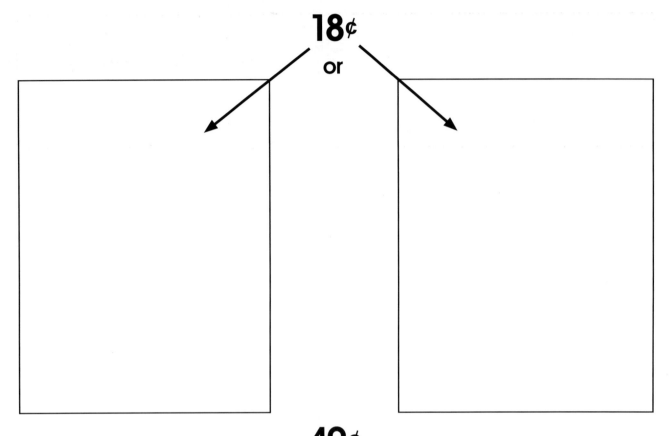

49¢
or

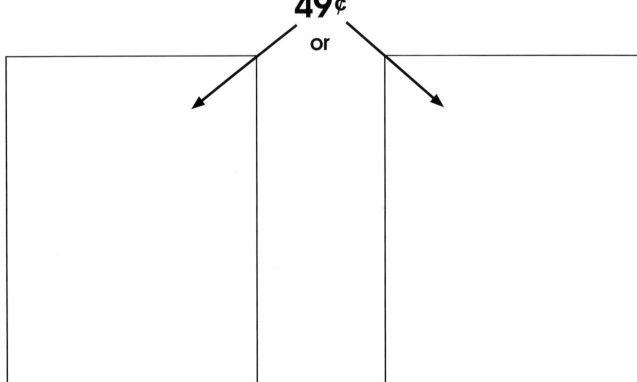

13B

Date: _____   **Name:** _____

Estimating and Counting Coins

Estimate	Value	Number of Coins

13C

14 Creating Equivalent Sets of Coins

Materials

- large coins templates (included with lesson 13. Photocopy, and cut out ten pennies, five nickels, five dimes, and four quarters.) (6.13.3)
- Bristol board or tagboard
- string
- scissors
- glue
- hole punch
- price tag cards (included. Photocopy, and cut out.) (6.14.1)
- chart paper
- markers
- paper coins (use Canadian coins templates included with lesson 13. Make two photocopies of each sheet for each pair of students.) (6.13.1)

Activity: Part One

Provide each student with one large coin (one of ten pennies, five nickels, five dimes, or four quarters), a piece of string, scissors, and glue, and have students make coin necklaces. Ask them to cut out their coins and trace them onto Bristol board or tagboard. Then, have students cut out their Bristol board circles and glue their paper coins onto the board. Next, have students punch single holes in the tops of the coins. Ask students to cut pieces of string long enough to make necklaces that will fit easily over their heads and thread their pieces of string through the coin holes.

Activity: Part Two

Have students sit in a large circle. Hand out one coin necklace to each student. Have each student identify the name and value of the coin on his/her necklace. Then, ask students:

- How do we count pennies? (by 1s)
- How do we count nickels? (by 5s)
- How do we count dimes? (by 10s)
- How do we count quarters? (by 25s)

Practice counting by 1s, 5s, 10s, and 25s with students.

Select three students to stand up. As a class, determine the value of these students' three coin necklaces. Ask:

- If we add together the value of each of these coins, how much money do we have?

Repeat this activity with five new students. Review the strategies for counting coins (see lesson 13).

Now, have ten new students stand up.

Note: Be sure the value of the coin necklaces on the students you select does not add up to more than one dollar.

Have the rest of the students suggest ways to physically rearrange the standing students to make it easier to add the coin values. For example, have all students with penny necklaces stand together, all students with nickel necklaces stand together, and so on.

Once the value of the ten coins has been determined, select ten new students to stand, and repeat the activity. Continue this procedure, counting the value of various coin combinations less than one dollar.

Now, display one of the price tag cards (6.14.1). Challenge students to name a set of coins (students wearing coin necklaces) that equals the amount shown on the price tag. Have the identified students stand in a line. Give students time to count the value of these coins to ensure they have selected the correct students/coins. Ask:

- How much money did I need?
- Did we collect the correct amount of money?
- How do you know?

680   Hands-On Mathematics • Grade 2

14

- Is there another way to make the same amount of money using a different combination of coins?

Have students discuss solutions and gather students/coins in different combinations. On chart paper, write out the various coin combinations students suggest to make the amount specified on the price tag. Discuss that there is usually more than one way to combine coins to make the amount shown.

Divide the class into pairs of students, and provide each pair with copies of Activity Sheet A (6.14.2), one price tag card (6.14.1), two copies of each sheet of paper coins (6.13.1), scissors, and glue. Have students work with their partners to find three different coin combinations to make the value on their price tag. Have students record their price tag amount in the space provided on their activity sheets. Students can then cut out the paper coins they need for each coin combination and glue them onto their sheets.

Activity Sheet A

Directions to students:

Record the amount of your price tag in the space provided on your activity sheet. Find three coin combinations to make the value on your price tag. Cut out the paper coins you need for each coin combination, and glue them onto the activity sheet (6.14.2).

Problem Solving

Present the following problem to students:

How many different ways can you make 25¢, using various coins?

Discuss different ways students can record their answers. For example, they can cut out and glue paper money onto a sheet of paper, draw the coins, or create a chart like the one below:

Quarters	Dimes	Nickels	Pennies

Extend this challenge to 50¢, and then to $1 (there are 293 different ways to make $1).

Extensions

- Play the game "How Much Money Is in the Piggybank?" Offer a clue to students, such as: "I have 5 coins in my piggybank. How much money could I have?" Have students brainstorm all the possible coin combinations and monetary amounts. Encourage students to come up with their own piggybank clues and offer them to a partner to solve.

- Build coin towers of different values up to $1 by stacking coins, one on top of the other. For example, create a tower of coins that equals 50¢.

Unit 6 • **Number Operations**

681

Price Tag Cards

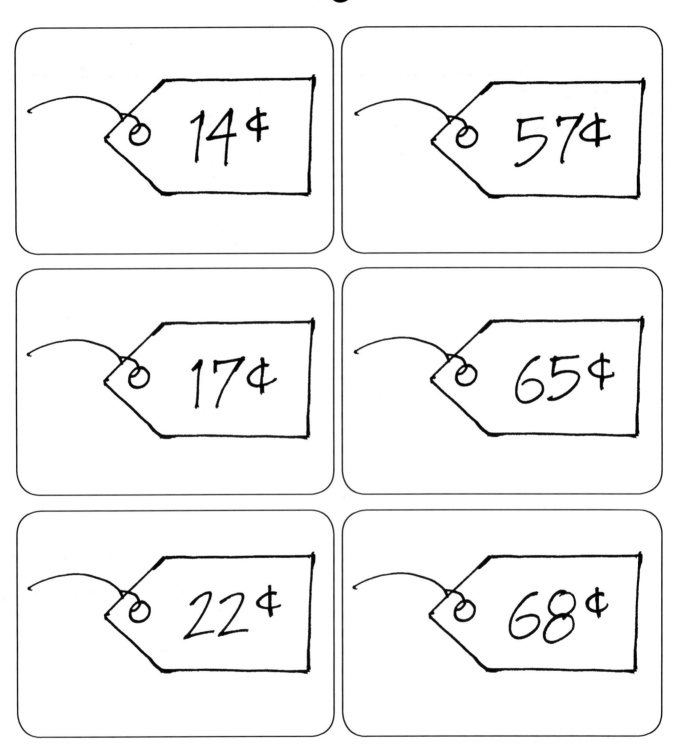

Price Tag Cards

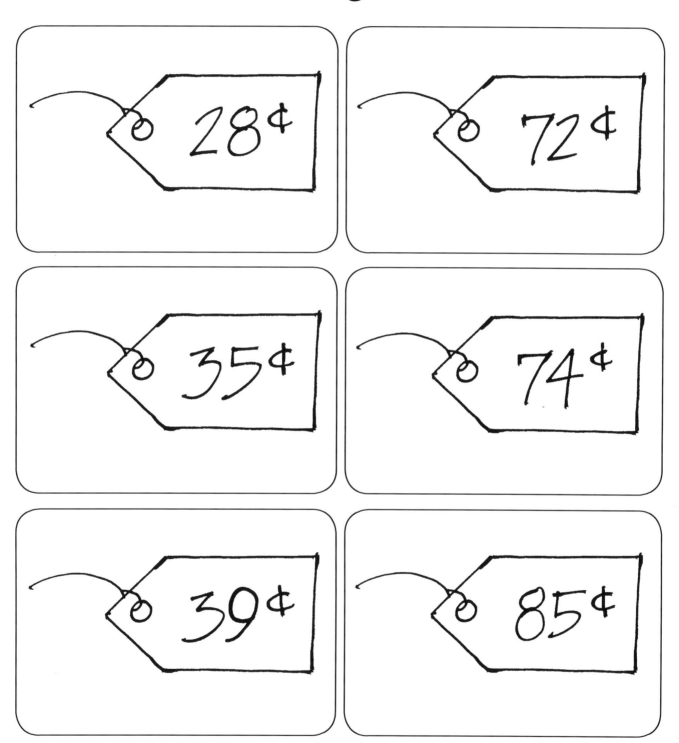

Price Tag Cards

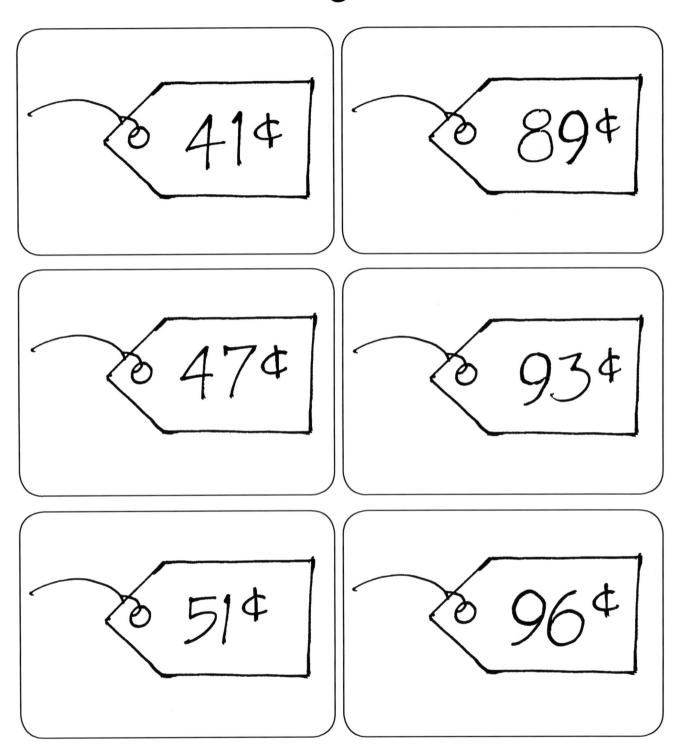

Date: _____ Name: _____

Coin Combinations

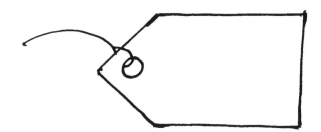

Coin Combination 1

Coin Combination 2

Coin Combination 3

15 Addition of Money

Background Information for Teachers

This lesson focuses on the addition of money to 100¢.

Materials

- store catalogues, store flyers, and magazines
- scissors
- glue
- markers
- large sheets of construction paper (one for each pair of students)
- paper
- pencils
- plastic or paper coins (use Canadian coins templates, included with lesson 13. For each student, photocopy two fifty-cent pieces, four quarters, several dimes, several nickels, and several pennies.) (6.13.1)

Activity: Part One

Show students various store catalogues. Discuss with students the catalogues' purpose as well as what is included in them. Tell students that they will be creating their own catalogues for make-believe businesses.

Divide the class into pairs of students to make catalogues. Distribute store catalogues, store flyers, and magazines to each pair, as well as scissors, glue, markers, and a large sheet of construction paper. Have each pair cut out pictures of six items they would like to include in their catalogue and glue the pictures onto the construction paper. Ask students to assign a price to each item in their catalogues. Prices should range from 10¢ to 100¢ ($1). Have students name their businesses and print the name at the top of the sheet.

Display students' catalogues throughout the classroom. Now, tell students they get to "go shopping." Each student has 100¢ ($1) to spend. Have students circulate the classroom and look at each catalogue before deciding which items to "buy." Then, distribute paper and pencils, and have students make lists of the items they would like to purchase. Remind students to include the cost of each item on their lists.

When students have finished shopping, distribute plastic or paper coins. Have students use the play money to check their lists and ensure they have not spent more than 100¢. Then, invite students to share what they "bought," how much money they spent, and how they decided on which items to buy.

Distribute Activity Sheet A (6.15.1), and have students solve each money problem. Encourage students to use their play money or to draw pictures to help them find the solutions.

Activity Sheet A

Directions to students:

Solve each problem, and print your answer in the space provided. Use play money, or draw pictures to help you find the answers (6.15.1).

Next Step

Divide students into groups of four. Have students combine their shopping lists from the previous activity and graph the results. Ask groups to write about their graphs and share their findings with each other.

Problem Solving

- In how many ways can you use different combinations of coins to make 100¢? Use pictures, numbers, and words to show your work.

Note: A reproducible master for this problem can be found on page 731.

15

- How can you use three coins to make 25¢? Use pictures, numbers, and words to show your work.

- Which three coins can you use to make 85¢? Use pictures, numbers, and words to show your work.

- Which eight coins can you use to make 100¢? Use pictures, numbers, and words to show your work.

- Make 95¢ using the fewest coins possible. Use pictures, numbers, and words to show your work.

- Make 95¢ using the most coins possible. Use pictures, numbers, and words to show your work.

Activity Centre

Photocopy, and cut out the "Coin Count" game money cards included with this lesson, and place the cards at an activity centre. Also, have plastic or paper nickels and dimes at the centre.

Have students play "Coin Count" in groups of four or five. Ask players to place the money cards facedown in a pile in the centre of the playing area. Tell each player to select either a nickel or a dime as his/her counting coin for the game.

Have Player *A* turn over the top card, place it face up in the centre of the playing area, and begin counting money by saying the amount his/her coin is worth (either five cents or ten cents). Have Player *B* count-on by the amount his/her coin is worth. The player who reaches the amount showing on the card on his/her turn keeps the card (if the player has a dime and must count five cents beyond the amount, he/she still keeps the card). For example, the card turned over says "30¢." Player *A*, who has a dime, says "ten cents." Player *B*, who also has a dime, says "twenty cents." Player *C*, who has

a nickel, says "twenty-five cents." Player *D*, who has a dime, says "thirty-five cents," and picks up the card.

Player *B* begins the second round by turning over the next card and initiating the money-counting procedure again. Once players have coin-counted all the cards, the player with the most cards is the winner (6.15.2).

Extensions

Note: The following activity helps students build their awareness of equivalent sets of coins.

- Distribute "Money Memory Game" cards (included. Photocopy, and cut out one set for each pair of students), and have pairs of students play the "Money Memory Game." Tell students to shuffle their cards and place them, facedown, in four rows of four in the centre of their playing space. Have the first player in each pair turn over two cards and determine if they display the same value (i.e., although the coins on each card are different, the sums of the coin values on each card are the same). If they do, the player has found a match. He/she keeps the cards and takes another turn. If the cards do not display the same value, the player turns the cards over again. The player with the most matches at the end of the game wins (6.15.3).

- Distribute the extension activity sheet called "How Much Is Your Name Worth?" Have students record their first names at the top of the sheet and then calculate the sum of the letters in their first names by adding together the coin values for each letter (6.15.4).

Unit 6 • **Number Operations**

687

Date: _____   **Name:** _____

Solving Money Problems

1. I have three coins. Together, the coins are worth more than 15¢ and less than 20¢. Which coins do I have?

_____

_____

2. Jay paid 45¢ for a cookie. He used four coins. Which coins did he use?

_____

_____

3. Monica has four dimes and one quarter. She needs one more coin to pay for a ball. How much could the ball cost?

_____

_____

688 – 6.15.1

Portage & Main Press, 2006, Hands-On Mathematics, Level 2, ISBN: 978-1-55379-091-4

15A

Coin Count Game Money Cards

20¢	25¢
30¢	35¢
40¢	45¢

Activity Centre

Portage & Main Press, 2006, Hands-On Mathematics, Level 2, ISBN: 978-1-55379-091-4

6.15.2 – 689

50¢	**55¢**
60¢	**65¢**
70¢	**75¢**

690 – 6.15.2 Portage & Main Press, 2006, Hands-On Mathematics, Level 2, ISBN: 978-1-55379-091-4

Activity Centre

80¢	**85¢**
90¢	**95¢**

Activity Centre

Portage & Main Press, 2006, Hands-On Mathematics, Level 2, ISBN: 978-1-55379-091-4

6.15.2 – 691

Money Memory Game Cards

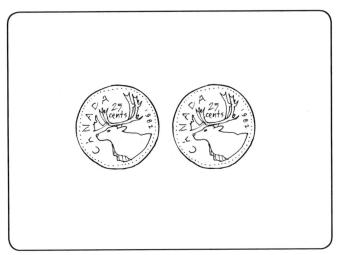

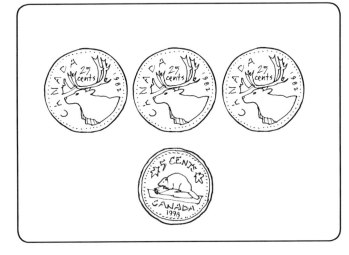

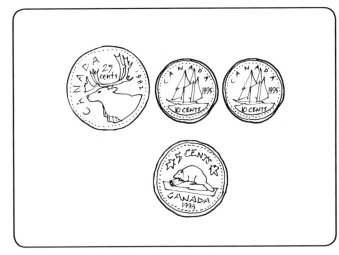
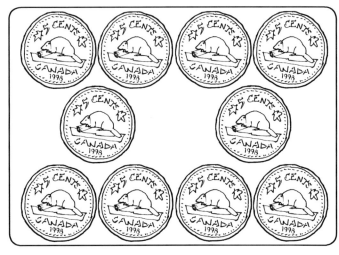

Coin designs © courtesy of the Royal Canadian Mint
Image des pieces © courtoisie de la Monnaie royale canadienne

Extension A

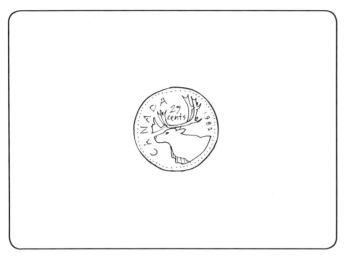
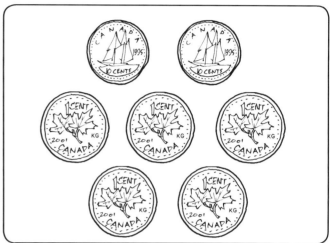
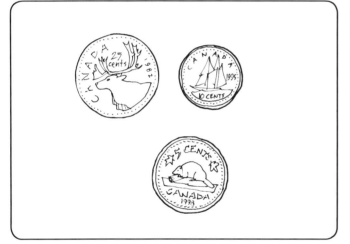

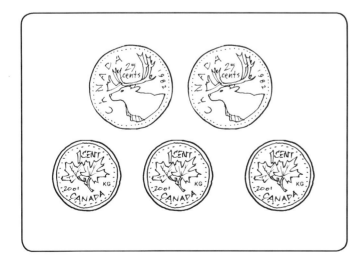
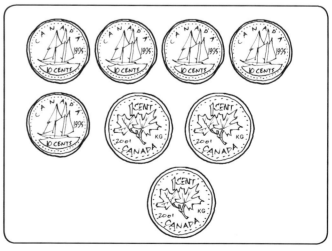

Extension A

Coin designs © courtesy of the Royal Canadian Mint
Image des pieces © courtoisie de la Monnaie royale canadienne

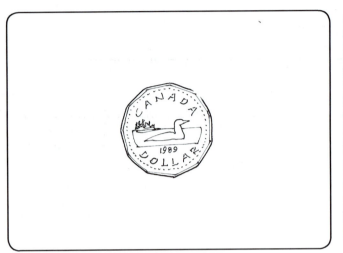

Coin designs © courtesy of the Royal Canadian Mint
Image des pieces © courtoisie de la Monnaie royale canadienne
Portage & Main Press, 2006, Hands-On Mathematics, Level 2, ISBN: 978-1-55379-091-4

Extension A

Date: _____   **Name:** _____

How Much Is Your First Name Worth?

My First Name, _____ **,...**

A	B	C	D	E	F	G

H	I	J	K	L	M	N

O	P	Q	R	S	T	U

V	W	X	Y	Z

...is worth: _____

Extension B

Coin designs © courtesy of the Royal Canadian Mint

Image des pieces © courtoisie de la Monnaie royale canadienne

Portage & Main Press, 2006, Hands-On Mathematics, Level 2, ISBN: 978 1 55379-091-4

6.15.4 – 695

16 Subtraction of Money

Background Information for Teachers

This lesson focuses on subtraction of money to 100¢.

Materials

- *Alexander, Who Used to Be Rich Last Sunday*, a book by Judith Viorst
- plastic or paper coins (see lesson 15)
- index cards
- markers
- pencils

Activity

Read the book *Alexander, Who Used to Be Rich Last Sunday* with students. Ask:

- How much money did Alexander's grandparents give to him?
- How many cents are there in one dollar?
- How can we check whether or not Alexander really did spend 100 cents?

Reread the book, and have students use plastic or paper coins to keep track of the amount of money Alexander spends and the amount of money he has left after each transaction.

Distribute Activity Sheet A (6.16.1) and have students find the solution to each money problem. Encourage students to draw pictures or use plastic or paper coins to help them find the answers to the problems.

Activity Sheet A

Directions to students:

Find the solution to each problem. You may draw pictures or use plastic or paper coins to help you solve the problems (6.16.1).

Next Steps

- Have students talk about their personal experiences with money.
- Ask students to write stories about how they might spend 100¢. Have them use plastic or paper coins to check that they spend no more than 100¢.
- Before beginning this activity, create for each pair of students a set of twenty index cards that display amounts of money between 5¢ and 85¢. Distribute the sets of cards as well as pencils and plastic or paper coins to pairs of students. Have the pairs place their cards facedown in a pile in the centre of their playing area.

Ask Player *A* in each pair to pick up the top card and subtract the amount of money on the card from 100¢. Have him/her record a corresponding number sentence on the back of the index card. Ask Player *B* to use play money to check Player *A*'s answer. Have players switch roles and continue the activity until they have gone through all the cards.

Activity Centre

Copy, and cut out a set of "What Is Your Change?" game cards (included). Mount each card onto heavy tagboard, and cut it apart along the dotted line. Place the card pieces at an activity centre.

Have students play "What Is Your Change?" in groups of two to four students. Tell students to place all the question-card pieces facedown in a pile in the centre of the playing space. Have students spread out the coin-card pieces, face up, also in the centre of the playing space. Tell Player *A* to pick up the top question-card piece,

16

read it aloud, and then choose a coin-card piece he/she thinks solves the problem. If the pieces fit together, Player *A* keeps the card (both pieces). Play continues with players taking turns drawing question-card pieces and looking for the matching coin-card pieces until all card pieces have been matched. The player with the most matches at the end of the game wins (6.16.2).

Extension

Read the poem, "Smart," found in the book *Where the Sidewalk Ends*, by Shel Silverstein. Discuss the poem with students, and have them determine whether or not the poem's narrator was truly smart about his money-trading decisions.

Unit 6 • **Number Operations**

Date: _____   **Name:** _____

Solving More Money Problems

1. Nicole has 95¢. She spends 45¢ on a Popsicle. How much money does Nicole have left?

   _____

   _____

2. Tyler earned 75¢ walking Mrs. Hoover's dog. He spent 28¢ on gum. How much money does Tyler have now?

   _____

   _____

3. You have four quarters. You spend 71¢ on a snack. How much change should you get back?

   _____

   _____

4. Phillip has five dimes and one nickel. He spends 25¢ on a gumball. How much does money does Phillip have left?

   _____

   _____

5. Gina has three quarters and one dime. Jenna has six dimes and one nickel. Who has more money? How much more money does she have?

   _____

   _____

698 – 6.16.1   Portage & Main Press, 2006, Hands-On Mathematics, Level 2, ISBN: 978-1-55379-091-4   **16A**

What Is Your Change? Game Cards

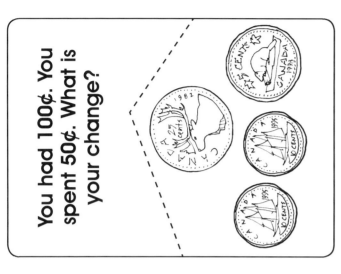

You had 100¢. You spent 50¢. What is your change?

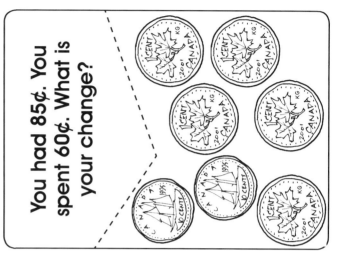

You had 85¢. You spent 60¢. What is your change?

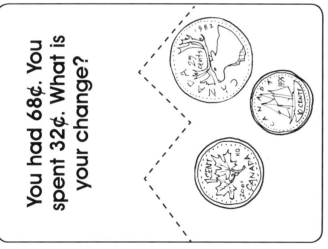

You had 68¢. You spent 32¢. What is your change?

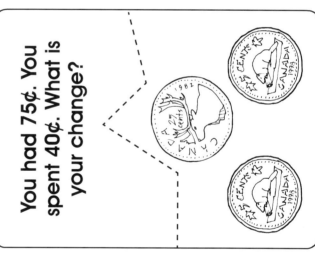

You had 75¢. You spent 40¢. What is your change?

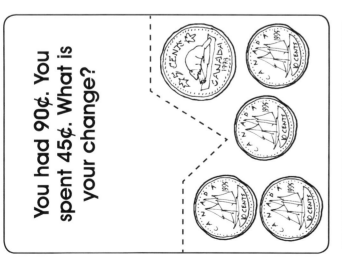

You had 90¢. You spent 45¢. What is your change?

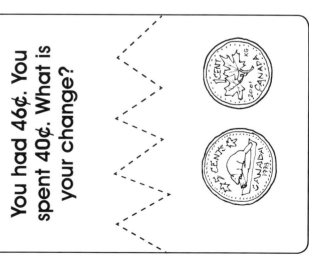

You had 46¢. You spent 40¢. What is your change?

Activity Centre

Coin designs © courtesy of the Royal Canadian Mint
Image des pieces © courtoisie de la Monnaie royale canadienne

Would you rather?

17 Exploring Multiplication – Part One

Background Information for Teachers

Students' understanding of addition must be fully entrenched before they are introduced to multiplication. When they are ready for it, students will begin making their own multiplication connections through exposure to skip-counting and repeated addition. Be sure to assess students' addition skills, including skip-counting and repeated addition, before formally teaching multiplication.

As they do with addition and subtraction, students acquire an understanding of multiplication and division operations by solving story problems. These problems provide students with a purpose for computing. They also offer a context that helps students grasp the meaning of an operation and when it is used.

In this lesson, students use manipulatives, diagrams, and symbols to illustrate the process of multiplication. The multiplication symbol is not introduced at this point.

Materials

- counters
- paper
- pencils
- chart paper
- markers

Activity: Part One

Divide the class into small, working groups of students, and distribute counters, paper, and pencils to the groups. Ask each group to discuss, and solve, the following problem:

- Coach McIntyre is making sandwiches for the baseball team. There are 12 boys on the team. He will make 1 sandwich for each player. How many pieces of bread will Coach McIntyre need?

Allow each group to determine the strategy they will use to solve the problem. Some groups may decide to use counters to help find a solution. Others may use a more abstract strategy such as drawing a picture or using symbols to add 2 + 2 + 2 and so on. Have the groups share their solutions and explain their strategies and reasoning.

Activity: Part Two

Ask students to name things that come in 2s (for example, two eyes, two wheels on a bicycle), and record their suggestions on chart paper. Then, distribute paper and pencils, and have students work with partners to make lists of things that naturally come in groups. Beside its name, have students record the number of items found in each group. For example:

- Legs on a table – 4
- Eggs in a carton – 12
- Wheels on a tricycle – 3
- Toes on one foot – 5

Have students share their lists, and record them on chart paper.

Activity: Part Three

Explain to students that *multiplication* is a way of determining how many items there are altogether when there are equally-sized groups of items.

Have students solve multiplication problems involving some of the items that come in groups, which they identified earlier. For example:

- We set up 3 tables for the party. Each table has 4 legs. How many table legs are there altogether?

- Max has 2 feet. He has 5 toes on each foot. How many toes does Max have?

▶

Unit 6 • Number Operations

17

Invite students to share their solutions to the problems and to explain their reasoning. Centre the discussion on questions such as:

- How many groups are there? (3 groups of table legs, 2 groups of toes)
- How many items are there in each group? (4 table legs, 5 toes)
- How many items are there altogether? How do you know?
- What is another way of finding out how many items there are altogether?
- How do you know your answer is right?

Problem Solving

Five owls go hunting at night. Each owl catches 3 mice. How many mice do the owls catch in total?

Note: A reproducible master for this problem can be found on page 731.

704   **Hands-On Mathematics • Grade 2**

18 Exploring Multiplication – Part Two

Background Information for Teachers

In this lesson, students use manipulatives, diagrams, and symbols to illustrate the process of multiplication. The multiplication symbol is still not introduced.

Materials

- counters (at least thirty-six for each pair of students)
- six-sided number cubes (one for each pair of students)
- paper cups (six for each pair of students)
- chart paper
- markers

Activity: Part One

Divide the class into pairs of students, and distribute counters, number cubes, and paper cups to each pair. Tell students they will be making groups of counters and putting each group into a paper cup. Ask the pairs to roll their number cubes twice. The first roll will determine how many groups (paper cups) of counters they should make. The second roll will determine how many counters they should put into each group. For example, if a pair of students rolls a 3 and then a 2, they should take 3 paper cups and put 2 counters into each cup.

Once students have made their groups of counters, have them determine the total number of counters they put into cups. Have each pair repeat the activity several times.

Activity: Part Two

Now, have students repeat the previous activity and record their results. Distribute Activity Sheet A (6.18.1), and demonstrate how to record the activity. Select a student to roll a number cube twice and report the numbers to the class. Draw sets on chart paper to match the numbers the student rolled. Write the corresponding number sentence below the sets, as in the following example:

3 groups of 2 equals 6

Now, have students work with the same partners as in the previous activity to complete their activity sheets.

Activity Sheet A

Directions to students:

Roll the number cube. Draw as many groups (large circles) as the number you rolled. Roll the number cube again. In each group (circle), draw as many dots, stars, or *Xs* as the second number you rolled. Record a number sentence under your drawing. Record the number of groups, the number of pictures (dots, stars, or *Xs*) in each group, and the total number of pictures. Repeat four more times (6.18.1).

Next Step

Introduce the concept of multiplication as repeated addition. Review Activity Sheet A (6.18.1) with students. Then, use one student's completed activity sheet to create repeated-addition number sentences on chart paper. For example:

3 groups of 2 equals 6   or

2 + 2 + 2 = 6

Date: _____ **Name:** _____

Partner: _____

Recording Sets of Counters

Sets	Number of Groups	Pictures in Each Group	Total
Example: ⊙ ⊙ ⊙ ___3___ groups of ___2___ equals ___6___	3	2	6

706 – 6.18.1

Portage & Main Press, 2006, Hands-On Mathematics, Level 2, ISBN: 978-1-55379-091-4

18A

19 Exploring Multiplication – Part Three

Background Information for Teachers

This lesson introduces students to the array model for multiplication. An *array* is an arrangement of objects into equal-sized rows. Real-life examples of arrays include muffin tins, sheets of stamps, and egg cartons.

Materials

- coloured tiles (twenty-four for each student)
- chart paper
- markers
- coloured pencils

Activity: Part One

Divide the class into pairs of students, and give each pair twenty tiles. Present students with the following scenario:

> Mrs. Diamond wants to rearrange the 8 desks in her classroom. She wants to put the desks in rows so that each row has the same number of desks.

Now, ask students to take eight tiles and arrange them into rows. Remind students that each row must have the same number of tiles.

Ask students to describe their arrangements. On chart paper, draw a picture of each arrangement, as in the following example:

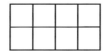

Explain to students that an array is an arrangement of objects into equal-sized rows. Tell students that this arrangement is a 2-by-4 array because there are 2 rows with 4 tiles in each row.

Activity: Part Two

Divide the class into pairs of students and give each pair at least twenty tiles. Have each pair use the tiles to make and describe:

- a 5-by-3 array
- a 2-by-9 array
- an array that has more rows than it has tiles in each row
- an array that has the same number of tiles in each row as the number of rows
- an array that has an even number of rows and an even number of tiles in each row
- an array that has an odd number of rows and an even number of tiles in each row

Activity: Part Three

Distribute to each student twenty-four tiles, coloured pencils, and a copy of Activity Sheet A (6.19.1). Have students use their tiles to make as many arrays as they can for each number. Have students use coloured pencils to record each array on the corresponding grid.

Activity Sheet A

Note: This is a two-page activity sheet.

Directions to students:

For each number, use tiles to make as many arrays as you can. Use coloured pencils to draw each array on the grid (6.19.1).

Extensions

- Add the term *array* to your classroom Math Word Wall.
- Have students use blank sheets of centimetre grid paper (included) to draw all the arrays possible for other numbers (6.19.2).

Unit 6 • Number Operations 707

19

- Challenge students to draw all the arrays possible for larger numbers. To provide space for larger arrays, have students tape together sheets of grid paper, or distribute sheets of graphed chart paper.

- Photocopy, and cut out a set of array/ product cards (included) for each pair of students. Have students play a version of "Concentration" ("Memory") in pairs. Tell students to sort their cards into array cards and product (number) cards. Then, have students place all their cards facedown in the centre of their playing space – the array cards on one side and the product cards on the other side.

Ask students to take turns turning over one array card and one product card. If the cards match, players keep the cards and take another turn. If they do not match, players turn the cards over again. The player with the most matches at the end of the game wins (6.19.3).

Date: _____ Name: _____

Making Arrays

12

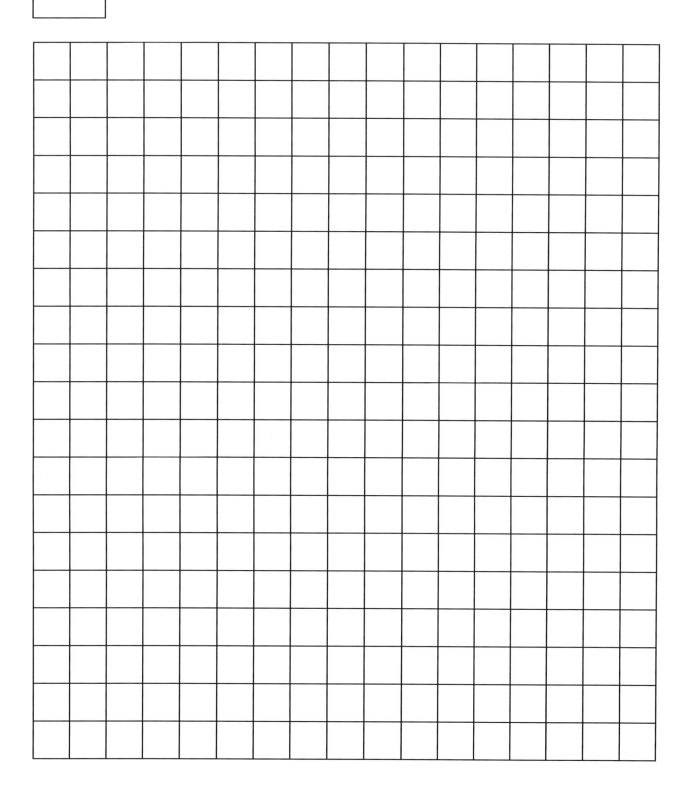

19A

Date: _____ Name: _____

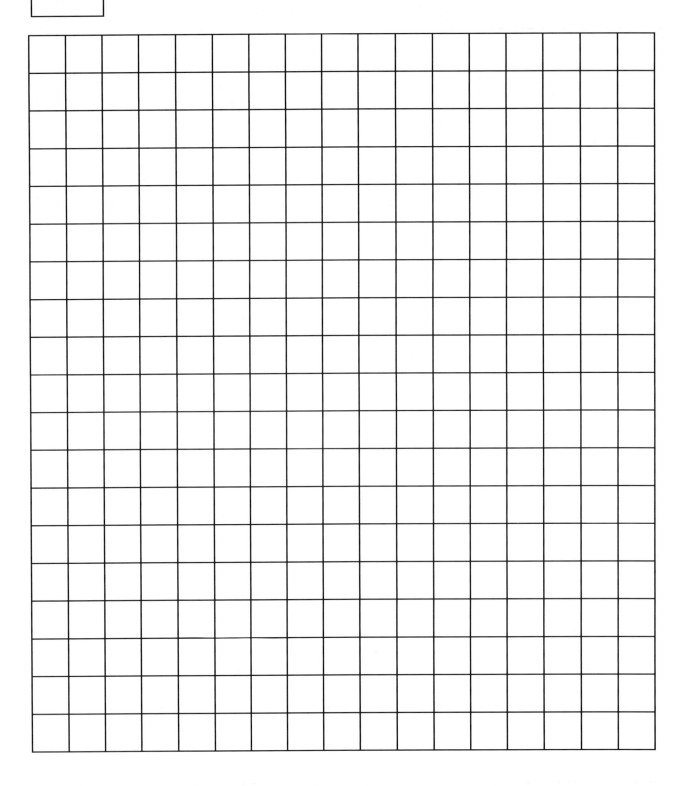

Centimetre Grid Paper

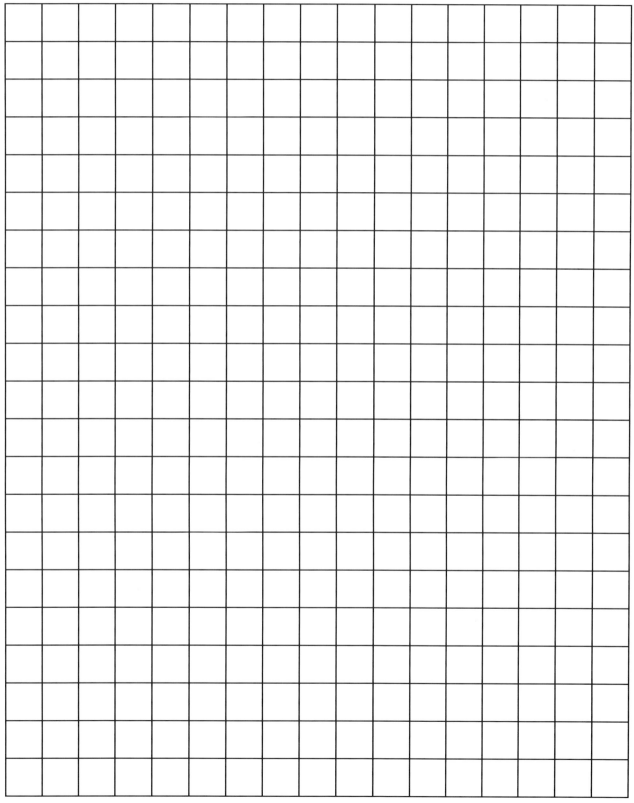

Extension A

Array/Product Cards

Array Cards

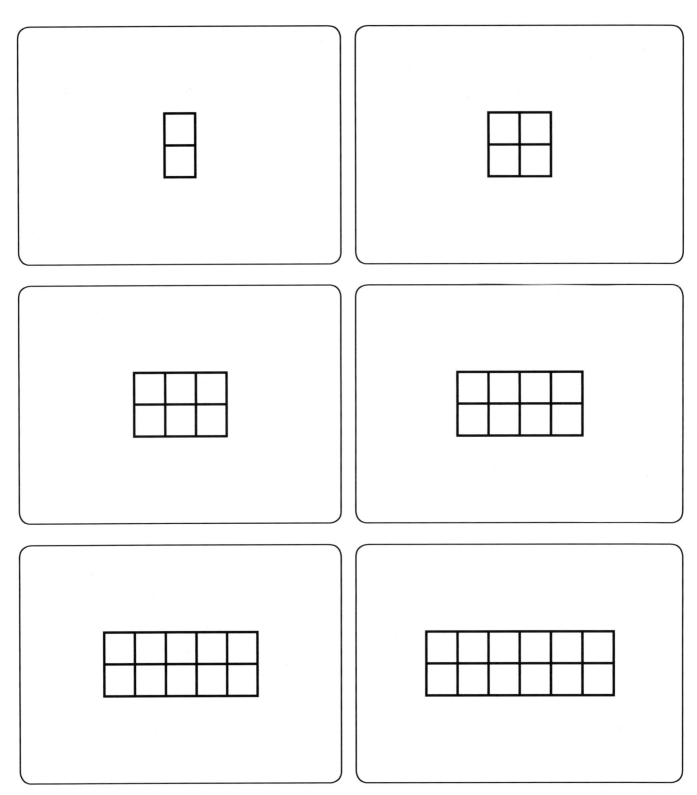

712 – 6.19.3

Extension B

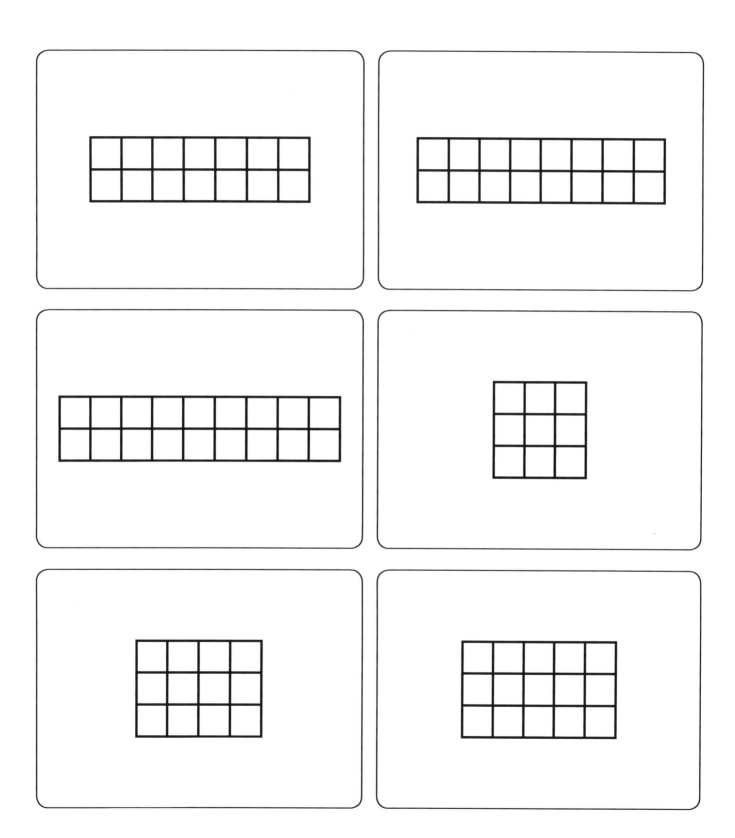

Extension B

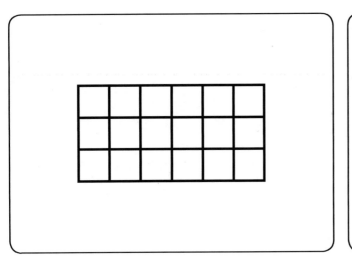
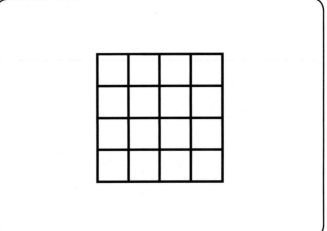

Product Cards

| 2 | 4 |
| 6 | 8 |

714 – 6.19.3

Extension B

Product Cards

10	**12**
14	**16**
18	**9**

Extension B

Portage & Main Press, 2006, Hands-On Mathematics, Level 2, ISBN: 978-1-55379-091-4

6.19.3 – **715**

12	**15**
18	**16**

716 – 6.19.3

Portage & Main Press, 2006, Hands-On Mathematics, Level 2, ISBN: 978-1-55379-091-4

Extension B

20 | Exploring Multiplication – Part Four

Background Information for Teachers

In this lesson, students are introduced to multiplication symbols and related number sentences.

Materials

- chart paper
- markers
- coloured tiles (several tiles for each small group of students)
- small paper bags
- centimetre grid paper (included with lesson 19) (6.19.2)
- coloured pencils

Activity: Part One

On chart paper, draw a 3-by-4 array, as in the diagram below, and ask students to describe it:

○ ○ ○ ○

○ ○ ○ ○

○ ○ ○ ○

Have students find the total number of objects in the array. Ask several students to explain how they calculated their answers.

Now, record the number sentence 3 x 4 = 12 below the array. Explain to students that this number sentence means "three rows of four" or "three groups of four."

Tell students that the x is called the *multiplication symbol*, and it means "groups of," "sets of," or "times." Explain that we can use multiplication to find the total number of objects in an array. Repeat the activity several times with students.

Activity: Part Two

Note: For this activity, you will need a small paper bag filled with tiles for each small group of students.

Divide the class into small groups of students, and give each group some centimetre grid paper, pencil crayons, and a small paper bag filled with tiles. Have students take turns removing a handful of tiles from the bag and making an array with some of the tiles.

Note: Students may have some leftover tiles from their handfuls, which do not fit into their arrays.

Ask each student to draw his/her array on the grid paper and write the corresponding multiplication sentence underneath.

Next Steps

- Ask students to use twelve tiles to make as many different arrays as they can. Have students use coloured pencils to draw each array they make on grid paper. Tell them to write the corresponding multiplication sentence underneath each array. Repeat the activity for other amounts of tiles such as thirteen, fifteen, and twenty-four tiles.

- Collect, and show students everyday examples of arrays such as a muffin tin, a sheet of stamps, and an egg carton. Have students create and then solve story problems that include these items.

▶

Unit 6 • **Number Operations**

717

20

Extensions

- Add the terms *multiplication, multiply*, and *times* to your classroom Math Word Wall.

- Read *What Comes in 2s, 3s, and 4s?* a book by Suzanne Aker. Use the concepts from the book to discuss the relationship and similarities between skip-counting, repeated addition, and multiplication. Use manipulatives, diagrams, and empty number lines to demonstrate this for students.

Assessment Suggestion

Have students complete Student Self-Assessment sheets, found on page 28, to reflect on what they have learned about multiplication.

21 | Exploring Division – Part One

Background Information for Teachers

There are two types of division problems: partition problems and measurement problems.

In *partition problems*, both the total number of objects and the number of groups are known, and the size of the groups must be determined. For example, Alison has 12 candies. If she gives candy to 3 friends, how many pieces of candy does each friend get?

Measurement problems involve finding the number of groups when both the total number of objects and the size of each group are known. For example, Alison has 12 candies. If she gives 3 candies to each friend, how many friends does she give candy to?

Be sure to provide students with opportunities to solve both types of problems.

In this lesson, students use manipulatives, diagrams, and symbols to illustrate the process of solving partition-division problems.

Materials

- *The Doorbell Rang*, a book by Pat Hutchins
- bingo chips (several for each pair of students)
- paper plates or cups (several for each pair of students)
- paper
- pencils
- counters (twenty to thirty for each pair of students)
- six-sided number cubes (one for each pair of students)
- small paper bags (one for each pair of students)

Activity: Part One

Read *The Doorbell Rang* with students. Have students describe situations when they shared things with their friends or family members. Ask students to tell how they made sure everyone got the same amount and what they did with any leftovers.

Now, divide the class into pairs of students, and distribute bingo chips and paper plates to each pair. Read the story again, and have students use their bingo chips and paper plates to represent each division situation that happens in the story. For example, if 12 cookies are shared between 2 people, tell students they must place an equal number of bingo chips onto each of 2 plates.

Next Steps

- Have students use bingo chips and paper plates again to represent each division situation in the story *The Doorbell Rang*, but this time, change the numbers from the story. For example:

  Problem: If you have 12 cookies to share among 5 people, how many cookies does each person get?

Note: The previous problem requires an explanation of the word *remainder* for students. Tell students that a "remainder" is the number left over when one number is divided by another number. In this case, 5 cannot be divided into 12 an equal number of times; there is a remainder of 2.

▶

Unit 6 • *Number Operations*   719

21

■ Divide the class into pairs of students, and distribute to each pair six paper plates, a six-sided number cube, paper, pencils, and a paper bag filled with twenty to thirty counters. The number of counters in each pair's bag represents the number of cookies they have.

Ask students to take turns rolling their number cubes to determine how many people get cookies. Then, have students use their counters and paper plates to help them determine the number of cookies each person gets.

22 | Exploring Division – Part Two

Background Information for Teachers

In this lesson, students use manipulatives, diagrams, and symbols to illustrate the process of solving measurement-division problems.

Materials

- bingo chips or counters
- paper plates or cups
- paper
- pencils

Activity

Divide the class into small groups of students; and distribute bingo chips, paper plates, paper, and a pencil to each group. Have groups discuss and solve each of the following problems. Allow each group to determine the strategy they will use to solve each problem. Some groups may choose to use bingo chips and paper plates, while others may choose a more abstract strategy such as drawing pictures or using symbols to repeatedly subtract a number.

Note: Two of the following measurement problems involve remainders. Tell students how they should deal with the remainders.

- Coach Saunders needs 18 tennis balls for the tournament. If tennis balls come in packages of 3, how many packages does Coach Saunders need to buy?

- Maria buys 12 eggs. If she needs 3 eggs to make 1 omelette, how many omelets can Marie make?

- Alex has 17 stickers. If he gives 3 stickers to each friend at his party, how many friends will he give stickers to?

- Thirty-six children sign up to play baseball. If there are 9 players on each team, how many teams will there be?

- Courtney and John picked 33 apples. If they put 8 apples into each bag, how many bags of apples will Courtney and John have?

Have students in each group share their solutions for each problem and explain their reasoning.

Unit 6 • **Number Operations**

23 Exploring Division – Part Three

Background Information for Teachers

In this lesson, students use manipulatives, diagrams, and symbols to solve division problems.

Materials

- "Sharing Game" number cards (included. Photocopy, and cut out one set of cards for each group of three students.) (6.23.1)
- small paper bags (one for each group of three students)
- bingo chips or counters
- "Sharing Game" score sheet (included. Make one photocopy for each student.) (6.23.2)
- counters (at least twenty-four for each pair of students)
- chart paper
- markers

Activity: Part One

Before beginning this activity, place a set of "Sharing Game" number cards into each paper bag. Divide the class into groups of three students, and provide each group with several bingo chips, a bag of cards, and copies of the "Sharing Game" score sheet (6.23.2). Have students play the "Sharing Game."

Tell Player A in each group to pull a card out of the bag, record this number in the "Number Drawn" column on the score sheet ("Round 1"), and take as many bingo chips as the number on the card. Then, ask this player to divide the bingo chips equally among all three players. Have this player record the number of chips each player receives in the "Score" column on the score sheet. Also have him/her record a diagram of the sharing process.

For example, if Player A draws the "15" card, he/she counts out 15 chips and gives each player 5 chips. He/she then records 15 in the "Number Drawn" column, "5" in the "Score" column, and draws a diagram of the sharing.

Ask Player A to return the card into the bag. Then, have Player B pull a card out of the bag and complete "Round 2" on the score sheet. After six rounds, have players add up their scores. The group with the highest total score wins the game.

Next Steps

- Vary the game by changing the numbers on the cards. For example, use multiples of 4.

- Have students associate division with arrays. For example, divide students into pairs, and give each pair twenty-four counters. Ask them to use all the counters to find the number of rows in an array that has 4 counters in each row. Have students describe the corresponding division problem. Vary the activity by asking students to determine how many counters are in each row of an array that has 4 rows.

Activity: Part Two

Present to students the following story problem:

- Jeremy has 8 strawberries. There are 4 plates on the table. How many strawberries will Jeremy put onto each plate?

Draw the four plates on chart paper. Explain that the strawberries must be divided evenly among the plates. Remind students that the term *divide* means to share *equally*. Draw one strawberry on each plate. Have students count aloud as you draw each strawberry. Now, draw a second strawberry on each plate. Have students continue counting aloud until you have drawn eight strawberries, as in the following diagram:

23

Discuss the diagram, explaining that 8 strawberries shared among 4 plates means there are 2 strawberries on each plate. On chart paper, record the number sentence for this story problem:

$8 \div 4 = 2$.

Explain to students that this number sentence means "Eight divided by four equals two." Repeat this procedure using similar problems involving both measurement and partition. Draw a diagram, and record a number sentence for each story problem.

Distribute Activity Sheet A (6.23.3), and have students draw sets to find the answer to each division problem. Then, tell students to record the answer in the space provided. Finally, have students write a story problem to go with one of the problems.

Activity Sheet A

Note: This is a two-page activity sheet.

Directions to students:

For each division problem, draw sets to find the answer. Then, write the answer in the space provided. Finally, write a story problem to go with one of the questions (6.23.3).

Extension

Add the terms *divide, division*, and *divided by* to your classroom Math Word Wall.

Assessment Suggestions

- Observe students as they work together to play the "Sharing Game." Focus on each student's ability to work in a group. Use the Cooperative Skills Teacher-Assessment sheet, found on page 27, to record your results.

- Have students complete copies of the Cooperative Skills Self-Assessment sheet, found on page 29, to reflect on their abilities to work together.

Unit 6 • **Number Operations**

Sharing Game Number Cards

3	6
9	12
15	18

21	24
27	30
33	36

Portage & Main Press, 2006, Hands-On Mathematics, Level 2, ISBN: 978-1-55379-091-4

Date: _____   **Names:** _____

_____

_____

Sharing Game Score Sheet

Round	Number Drawn	Score	Diagram of Sharing
1			
2			
3			
4			
5			
6			
	Total Score		

726 – 6.23.2

Portage & Main Press, 2006, Hands-On Mathematics, Level 2, ISBN: 978-1-55379-091-4

Date: _____   Name: _____

Solving Division Problems

Problem	Sets
1. 8÷4= __2__	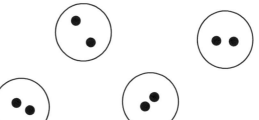
2. 9÷3= _____	
3. 8÷1= _____	
4. 16÷4= _____	

23A

Date: _____   **Name:** _____

5. $21 \div 7 =$ _____	
6. $5 \div 5 =$ _____	
7. $18 \div 9 =$ _____	
8. $10 \div 5 =$ _____	

Story Problem for Question Number _____ : _____

_____

_____

_____

23A

Problem-Solving Black Line Master: Number Operations

Copy the following three sheets onto overhead transparencies to present to students as daily problem-solving activities. Or, photocopy the pages, and cut them apart for students, problem by problem. Have students paste them into their math journals or agendas for completion independently.

✂ --

At snack time, each student gets 1 piece of cheese and 2 crackers. Make a chart to find out how many pieces of cheese and how many crackers are needed for 10 students. What about for 20 students? To help you, use the following sample chart for 4 students:

Students	Cheese	Crackers
1	1	2
2	2	4
3	3	6
4	4	8

From unit 6, lesson 1, page 523

✂ --

There are 5 trees in Jason's front yard. There are 4 trees in Jason's backyard. Altogether, how many trees are there in Jason's yard?

From unit 6, lesson 2, page 528

✂ --

Mandy has 8 pieces of candy. She buys 9 more pieces. How many pieces of candy does Mandy have now?

From unit 6, lesson 2, page 528

▶

Portage & Main Press, 2006, Hands-On Mathematics, Level 2, ISBN: 978-1-55379-091-4

729

Leila read 7 books in March and 8 books in April. How many books did Leila read altogether?

From unit 6, lesson 2, page 528

Alexis has 7 nickels. She finds more nickels under a chair. Now, she has 9 nickels. How many nickels did Alexis find?

From unit 6, lesson 3, page 569

Thomas has a baseball card collection. He buys 5 more cards for his collection. Now, he has 18 cards in his collection. How many cards did Thomas have to begin with?

From unit 6, lesson 3, page 569

Jack is hungry. He eats 8 almonds. He is still hungry, so he eats some walnuts. Altogether, he eats 16 nuts. How many walnuts did Jack eat?

From unit 6, lesson 3, page 569

Name six subtraction facts that have a difference of 3.

From unit 6, lesson 5, page 581

Are there other subtraction facts that have a difference of 3? What are they?

From unit 6, lesson 5, page 581

▶

730

Portage & Main Press, 2006, Hands-On Mathematics, Level 2, ISBN: 978-1-55379-091-4

Place the numbers 1, 2, 3, 4, 5, and 6 around the circle. The difference between any two numbers beside each other cannot be more than 2.

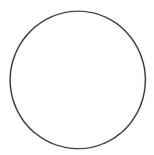

From unit 6, lesson 5, page 581

Tamar has 15 cents in her shirt pocket and 3 cents in her pants pocket. Her brother, Oren, has 3 cents in his shirt pocket and 15 cents in his pants pocket. Do Tamar and Oren have the same amount of money? Use pictures, numbers, and words to explain your answer.

From unit 6, lesson 7, page 623

In how many ways can you use different combinations of coins to make 100¢? Use pictures, numbers, and words to show your work.

From unit 6, lesson 15, page 686

Five owls go hunting at night. Each owl catches 3 mice. How many mice do the owls catch in total?

From unit 6, lesson 17, page 704

References for Teachers

Baratta-Lorton, Mary. *Mathematics Their Way.* Parsippany NJ: Dale Seymour Publications, 1995.

Burns, Marilyn, and Bonnie Tank. *A Collection of Math Lessons from Grades 1 through 3.* Sausalito, CA: Math Solution Publications, 1987.

Currah, Joanne, and Jane Felling. *Box Cars and One-Eyed Jacks.* Edmonton: Box Cars and One-Eyed Jacks Publications, 1996.

Fosnot, Catherine Twomey, and Maarten Dolk. *Young Mathematicians at Work: Constructing Number Sense, Addition, and Subtraction.* Portsmouth, NH: Heinemann, 2001.

Friederwitzer, Fredda, and Barbara Berman. *Mathematics Getting in Touch: Activities with Manipulatives.* Vernon Hills, IL: Cuisenaire, 1985.

Greenberg, Dan. *Mega-Funny Math Poems and Problems.* New York: Scholastic, 1999.

Reys, Barbara, and Robert Reys. *Number Sense: Simple Effective Number Sense Experiences, Grades 1-2.* Parsippany, NJ: Dale Seymour Publications, 1997.

Richardson, Kathy. *Developing Number Concepts: Place Value, Multiplication, and Division.* Parsippany, NJ: Dale Seymour Publications, 1998.

Wright, Robert J., et al. *Teaching Number: Advancing Children's Skills and Strategies.* Thousand Oaks, CA, 2002.